UG Manual for Psychiatry: CAP- ACE

[Cognition, Affective, Psychomotor - Attitude, Communication & Ethics]

Prof. Dr. Anusa A Mohandoss
Professor, & Head
Department of Psychiatry
Shri Sathya Sai Medical College & Research Institute
Affiliated to Shri Balaji Vidyapeeth (Deemed to be University),
SBV Chennai Campus, Ammapettai, Chengelpet, Tamil Nadu, India

Made with ❤ on the Notion Press Platform

www.notionpress.com

Dedicated

To all my ***Teachers*** *who mould me*

To all my ***patients*** *who teaches me everyday*

To all my ***students*** *who never ceases to amuse and make me think*

To my ***family and friends****, who believe, invests, supports and inspires me all days long*

&

To the transformative power of ***medical education****, fuelled by curiosity,*

empathy, and the a journey in pursuit of excellence

shared with teachers, patients, students,

and all who seek to understand

human mind

CONTRIBUTORS

Dr. Charanya Kaliamoorthy
Assistant Professor
Department of Psychiatry
Shri Sathya Sai Medical College & Research Institute
Affiliated to Shri Balaji Vidyapeeth (Deemed to be University)
SBV Chennai Campus, Ammapettai, Chengelpet, Tamil Nadu, India.

Dr. Mukhil Sakthi P,
Senior Resident
Department of Psychiatry
Shri Sathya Sai Medical College & Research Institute
Affiliated to Shri Balaji Vidyapeeth (Deemed to be University),
SBV Chennai Campus, Ammapettai, Chengelpet, Tamil Nadu, India.

Dr. Vaishali Katchi Kannan
Senior Resident
Department of Psychiatry
Shri Sathya Sai Medical College & Research Institute
Affiliated to Shri Balaji Vidyapeeth (Deemed to be University),
SBV Chennai Campus, Ammapettai, Chengelpet, Tamil Nadu, India.

Dr. Seytha Najva Naina Mohamed
Senior Resident
Department of Psychiatry
Shri Sathya Sai Medical College & Research Institute
Affiliated to Shri Balaji Vidyapeeth (Deemed to be University),
SBV Chennai Campus, Ammapettai, Chengelpet, Tamil Nadu, India.

Contents

Acknowledgments

I acknowledge the constant support, encouragement and guidance received from **Shri. M. K. Rajagopalan**, Founder and Chancellor, Chairperson, Shri Balaji Vidyapeeth and **Smt. Gowri Rajagoplan**, Chairperson of Shri Sathya Sai Medical College & Research Institute, the SBV Chennai campus.

I am thankful to **Prof. (Dr) Nihar Ranjan Biswas,** Vice Chancellor of Shri Balaji Vidyapeeth and **Prof. Dr. Joydeb Roychowdhury,** Dean of Shri Sathya Sai Medical College and Research Institute, SBV Chennai Campus, for their support and encouragement.

I am incredibly grateful to the all the past and present faculty of the **Department of Psychiatry, Madurai Medical College and Government Rajaji Hospital, Madurai**, who have played a pivotal role in shaping my understanding and passion for this field.

My deepest gratitude goes to my Professor and Guide, **Prof. Dr. T. Kumanan**, for his invaluable mentorship and guidance throughout my academic journey. His insights and support have been instrumental in my development as a psychiatrist and continues to do so.

I would also like to express my sincere thanks to the former Heads of Department, Madurai Medical College and Government Rajaji Hospital, Madurai **Prof. Dr. Ramanujam Venkatasamy** and **Prof. Dr. Ananda Krishnakumar**, for their leadership, dedication to academic excellence as well as for their roles during my study period.

I am indebted to **Prof. Dr. C. Ramasubramanian,** Founder cum Senior Consultant Psychiatrist, M.S. Chellamuthu Trust and Research Foundation, Ahana Hospital, Madurai; Former Head of Department, Department of Psychiatry, Madurai Medical College and Government Rajaji Hospital, Madurai and Former State Mental Health Nodal Officer for his continued mentoring and professional encouragement.

My thanks and appreciation extends to the current Head of Department, Department of Psychiatry, Madurai Medical College and Government Rajaji Hospital, Madurai **Prof. Dr. Geetanjali**, and **Dr. Kavitha**, Department of Psychiatry, Madurai Medical College and Government Rajaji Hospital, Madurai for their continued support and commitment to mental health education.

I am thankful to **Prof. Dr. John Xavier Sugadev** (Head of Department, Department of Psychiatry, Government Sivagangai Medical College and Hospital), **Prof. Dr. Amudha** (Department of Psychiatry, Madurai Medical College and Government Rajaji Hospital), and **Dr. Viswanathan (**Department of Psychiatry, Government Theni Medical College and Hospital) for their contributions to my learning experience.

I am immensely thankful **Prof. Dr. Karthikeyan** (Senior Consultant and Head, Department of Psychiatry, Madurai Meenakshi Mission Hospital) for teaching me and always helping me to naviagate the art of private practice of Psychiatry, at any time of the day.

I am immensely thankful to **Dr. Shahul Ameen,** Consultant Psychiatrist, St. Thomas Hospital Chethipuzha, Changanacherry, Kerala for moulding my research works and mentoring.

I am thankful to my former colleaguges – **Dr. R. Parthasarathy** (Department of Psychiatry, Pondicherry Institute of Medical Sciences, Pondicherry), Dr. **Rajesh Kannan** (Department of Psychiatry, Government Theni

Medical College and Hospital), **Dr. Kandeepan** (Consultant Psychiatrist, Chennai) and **Dr. Ramkumar** (Department of Psychiatry, Sri Lakshmi Narayana Institute of Medical Sciences, Pondicherry) for their support.

I am thankful to my fellow students during postgraduation for pushing me to my limits – **Dr. Ronald Roy** (Department of Psychiatry, Tirchy SRM Medical College and Hospital, Tirchy), **Dr. Geetha** (Department of Psychiatry, KAP Viswanathan Medical College and Hospital, Tirchy), **Dr. Kannan** (Department of Psychiatry, Government Medical College and Hospital, Coimbatore), **Dr. Bevin Sathya** (Institute of Mental Health, Kilpauk) **Dr. Lloyds E (**Department of Psychiatry, Government Sivagangai Medical College and Hospital, Sivagangai) and **Dr. Kirubakaran** (Department of Psychiatry, Madurai Medical College and Government Rajaji Hospital).

I am thankful to my Parents for their selflessness & kindness.

To my husband, without whose support this book would never have started at the first place and my son for being a constant pillar of emotional support and solace.

Prof. Dr. Anusa A Mohandoss
Professor, & Head
Department of Psychiatry
Shri Sathya Sai Medical College & Research Institute
Affiliated to Shri Balaji Vidyapeeth (Deemed to be University),
SBV Chennai Campus, Ammapettai, Chengelpet, Tamil Nadu, India

Introduction

Equipping Yourself to Provide Mental Healthcare

Welcome to this essential, **self-study guide** designed to complement your MBBS studies and equip you with the crucial skills needed for effective mental healthcare delivery. This book places a particular emphasis on the National Medical Commission's (NMC) AETCOM module, recognizing its significance in shaping future doctors who excel beyond medical knowledge.

For several years, the medical profession has been built on the foundation of clinical knowledge and skills. However, the landscape of medical education is changing. The focus is shifting towards a more holistic approach that includes not just cognition and psychomotor skills, but also affective aspects, attitudes, communication, and ethics. This manual aims to explore these often overlooked, yet crucial, aspects of undergraduate psychiatry, cognitive and behavioural sciences. To make it clear, the context in which these terms are used are listed below:

Cognition refers to the mental processes involved in gaining knowledge and comprehension, including attention, concentration, orientation, thinking, knowing, remembering, judging, and problem-solving. These are higher-level functions of the brain. In the context of medical education, cognitive learning involves the acquisition of new knowledge and information about diseases and patients themselves.

Affective learning, on the other hand, is concerned with the emotional sphere and has to do with feelings, values, appreciation, enthusiasms, motivations, and attitudes. In medical education, this might involve developing empathy for patients or learning to cope with the emotional challenges of the profession.

Psychomotor learning involves acquiring physical skills and the ability to perform physical tasks. This is a critical aspect of medical education, as healthcare professionals need to master various technical skills, from basic tasks like taking a patient's blood pressure, inspection, palpation, auscultation to complex surgical procedures.

Attitude in medical education refers to the development of professional behaviours and values. This includes understanding and adhering to ethical guidelines, demonstrating respect for patients and colleagues, and maintaining a commitment to lifelong learning.

Communication is a vital skill in medicine, as healthcare professionals must be able to effectively communicate with patients, families, and other healthcare providers. This involves not only verbal communication but also non-verbal communication, active listening, and the ability to explain complex medical information in a way that patients can understand.

Ethics in medical education involves understanding and applying ethical principles in the practice of medicine. This includes respecting patient autonomy, maintaining confidentiality, and striving for justice in healthcare.

Of these terms, attitude and affective have an overlap. But their distinctiveness needs to be set apart. This distinction is important because while **affective** components are more about **immediate emotional responses, attitudes** encompass a **broader range of elements** including these emotional responses (affective), thoughts and beliefs (cognitive), and actions (behavioural). Understanding both can help medical educator's tailor medical training to better address the needs and perspectives of students, ultimately improving their educational experience and patient care skills

These aspects have always been an innate part of the practice of medicine, they have often been considered **tacit knowledge** - something that is picked up along the way and with clinical practice, rather than explicitly taught and learned. This is changing, however, as medical educators recognize the importance of these skills and attitudes in providing high-quality patient care.

CAP- ACE is an acronym for **C**ognition, **A**ffective, **P**sychomotor - **A**ttitude, **C**ommunication & **E**thics. This manual aims to bring these aspects to the forefront of medical education, using a **case-based approach** to make the material engaging and relevant to real-world practice. Through this approach, it is hoped that medical students and professionals will gain a deeper understanding of the importance of cognition, affective learning, psychomotor skills, attitude, communication, and ethics in their profession, ultimately leading to better patient outcomes and a more fulfilling professional experience.

Why AETCOM Matters in Psychiatry

Mental health concerns are complex, often intertwined with social, emotional, and psychological factors. The AETCOM module equips you with the foundational skills to navigate these complexities. It fosters:

- **Effective Communication**: You'll learn to actively listen, empathize with patients, and build rapport – skills critical for understanding and addressing mental health issues.
- **Strong Ethical Framework:** You'll develop a robust understanding of ethical considerations in mental healthcare, including confidentiality, informed consent, and respecting patient autonomy.
- **Positive Attitude:** The AETCOM module tackles the stigma surrounding mental health, enabling you to approach patients with empathy and understanding.

The Growing Need for Mental Health Awareness

The prevalence of mental health conditions has assumed mammoth proportion. Rapid westernization, changing social values, technological complexities and economic uncertainties all contribute to this increase. This book equips you to recognize the signs and symptoms of common mental health issues, enabling earlier intervention and improved patient outcomes.

Treatment Seeking Behaviour: A Positive Shift and Destigmatization

Fortunately, awareness and openness regarding mental health are growing. People are increasingly seeking help, creating a greater demand for qualified healthcare professionals who can provide effective and compassionate support.

How to Use This Book

This book is designed to be a comprehensive resource throughout your AETCOM modules and beyond. This book ventures beyond the traditional textbook approach, aiming to equip you with the crucial human element often missing from purely theoretical learning. Here's how various elements within the book contribute to this goal:

- **Case Scenarios**: These real-world examples bring textbook concepts to life. By analyzing symptoms, communication patterns, and treatment decisions in each case, you'll develop a deeper understanding of how mental health conditions manifest in individuals. This fosters a more nuanced approach to diagnosis and treatment, recognizing the unique complexities of each patient.

- **Psychiatry Practice Pearls**: Pearls, or nuggets of wisdom gleaned from experienced professionals, offer practical insights honed through years of clinical practice. These pearls provide invaluable guidance for navigating real-world situations as well as human aspects of patient interaction.

- **Bloom's Taxonomy Questions:** This book incorporates questions across various domains of Bloom's Taxonomy – from recalling information (Remember) to applying knowledge in new situations (Apply) and evaluating different treatment options (Evaluate). By engaging with these questions, you'll not only solidify your knowledge base but also develop critical thinking and problem-solving skills essential for effective clinical decision-making.

- **Specific Points on Communication**: Effective communication is the cornerstone of building rapport and understanding a patient's experience. This book delves into specific communication techniques that foster trust and empathy. Learning to actively listen, validate concerns, and navigate sensitive topics like suicidal ideation will equip you to interact with patients in a way that promotes healing and positive outcomes.

- **Differential Diagnosis:** Mental health conditions often share overlapping symptoms. The book will guide you through the process of differential diagnosis, a crucial skill for accurately identifying the underlying cause of a patient's symptoms. This not only ensures tailored treatment plans but also avoids unnecessary procedures or medications

Each chapter builds upon the other, offering a practical and engaging approach to learning: Conversational **Competency and Decoding Patient Communication (Chapters 1 & 2)**: Hone your communication skills to effectively engage with patients and identify potential mental health concerns. Case scenarios provide real-world examples to enhance your understanding. **Psychomotor Skills and Decoding Mind and Behaviour (Chapters 3 & 5)**: Gain a solid understanding of the biological and psychological aspects of mental health, including laboratory tests, neurotransmitters, and the mind-body connection. **Ethical Considerations (Chapter 4):** Explore the ethical frameworks that guide patient interactions in mental health settings. **Clinical Cases and Lived Experiences (Chapters 6 & 7)**: Learn from real-life experiences shared by psychiatrists and individuals living with mental health challenges. **Tech Allies & E-Mental Health Tools (Chapter 8):** Discover the growing role of technology in mental healthcare delivery and explore relevant digital tools. **Practice Questions (Chapter 9):** Test your knowledge and solidify your understanding of key concepts through engaging practice questions.

Practice Questions: A Boon for Self-Directed Learning and Integration

The practice questions in this book serve a multifaceted purpose. They enable you to assess your understanding of key concepts, promoting active learning and knowledge retention. Furthermore, these questions can be used for self-directed study, allowing you to delve deeper into specific topics that pique your interest.

The questions are also designed to foster horizontal and vertical integration. Horizontal integration refers to connecting knowledge across different medical disciplines in the same year while vertical refers to integration between medical subjects in all or different year of study.

By considering the interplay between mental health conditions and physical illnesses in some case scenarios and practice questions, you'll gain a more holistic understanding of patient care. Vertical integration involves building knowledge upon existing foundations. The practice questions will challenge you to apply your understanding of AETCOM principles and psychiatric concepts to increasingly complex scenarios, solidifying your clinical reasoning skills.

Beyond Textbooks – Touching Human Lives

This book is not a traditional subject textbook designed for rote memorization. It aspires to be a clinical guide that prepares you to navigate the complexities of real-world mental healthcare. Here, the focus is on **touching and interacting with humans,** recognizing the emotional and social aspects of mental illness. By honing your communication skills, fostering empathy, and applying a holistic approach, you'll be well-equipped to not only diagnose and treat mental health conditions but also provide the compassionate and supportive care that is vital for patient well-being.

1. Conversational Competency

Points to Ponder while Communicating with Patients/Care-givers in Psychiatry Department

Initiating the Session - Establishing Rapport:

- Welcoming Gesture with a simple *vanakam* or *Namaste*, or a simple Hello
- Connect with patient:
    - Introduce yourself, stating your role
    - Ensure a comfortable and private environment for the conversation – Discourage **"Corridor Consultation"** or "**Consultation on the go**"
    - Seek consent if required, demonstrating respect for the patient's autonomy.
- Demonstrate Cultural Sensitivity:
    - Show respect for cultural norms and values.
    - Attend to the patient's physical comfort, considering cultural preferences.
- Reason(s) for the Consultation:
    - Ask an open ended question about the chief complaint. For example, "What brings you here today?"
- Attentive Listening:
    - Listen attentively to the patient's opening statement without interruption.
    - Allow the patient to express themselves freely.
- Confirmation and Further Inquiry:
    - Confirm the patient's concerns and inquire about additional issues.
    - Use culturally appropriate language to explore further, ensuring inclusivity.
- Negotiate Agenda Respectfully:
    - Negotiate the agenda collaboratively, considering both the patient's and physician's needs.
    - Be mindful of cultural nuances in negotiating the agenda.
- Consideration for Medical, Neurological, or Sensory Issues:
    - Be aware of potential communication barriers such as dysphasia, dysarthria, hypophonia, deafness, or visual impairment.
    - Adjust communication methods based on the individual's needs.
- Building Rapport:
    - Take extra care in developing rapport with individuals facing medical or sensory challenges.
    - When dealing with older patients, acknowledge the presence of caregivers and involve them in the communication process.

Screen:

- Prioritization and Screening of disabilities and disorders:
    - Recognize the importance of screening, especially with older patients who may have multiple problems or disabilities.
- Understanding Patient Priorities

    - Acknowledge that not all identified problems are current or require immediate attention.
    - Recognize that not all problems are on the patient's agenda, and prioritize based on their needs and concerns.
- Functional Assessment:
    - Understand that the presence of problems that does not always correlate with impaired function.
- Obtain or Seek a Backup (security), as soon as it appears that the patient is dangerous or threatening

Listen Attentively:

- Emotional State Awareness:
    - Gauge the patient's emotional state from the beginning and throughout the interaction.
    - Be attuned to subtle cues that may indicate violence so as to safe guard yourself.
- Active Listening:
    - Practice active listening by nodding, summarizing, and validating the patient's concerns.
    - Allow the patient to express themselves fully before responding.
- Non-Verbal Cues:
    - Pay attention to non-verbal cues, such as body language and facial expressions.
    - Note for any hallucinatory behaviour or abnormal movements
- Adapt Communication Style:
    - Adapt your communication style based on the emotional needs of the elderly patient.
    - Be patient and provide reassurance as needed, considering potential cognitive and emotional challenges.
- As for as possible, avoid all distractions during patient interaction

Gathering Information: Exploration of Patient's Problems

- Encouragement:
    - Encourage the patient to share their problem.
    - Use open questioning techniques, adapting to the patient's communication style.
    - Closed ended questioning not too early – Eg – Are you hearing voices?
    - Never frame a negative question. Eg: You don't hear voices. Do you?
- Cultural Sensitivity in Questioning:
    - Use open/closed questions that align with cultural norms.
    - Be aware of cultural variations in communication patterns.
- Attentive and Respectful Listening:
    - Listen attentively, respecting the patient's pace and allowing time for reflection.
    - Use culturally appropriate facilitation techniques, such as encouragement and silence.
- Ask Clarifying Questions:
    - Confrontation to call patient's attention to inconsistencies to response or body language.
    - Assess the time frame of the patient's narrative to understand the progression of their issues.
- Time Frame Clarification:
    - Explicitly request patients to explain the onset and progression of their problems over a specific time period, as describing significant stressors or life events
    - Emphasize the importance of understanding the temporal aspects of their experiences.
- Verbal and Non-Verbal Facilitation:
    - Facilitate patient responses using culturally sensitive verbal and non-verbal cues.
    - Be attuned to cultural expressions of emotion/aggression.

- Simplified Language Use:
    - Use concise, easily understood language, avoiding jargon.
    - Provide explanations for any medical terms using culturally familiar analogies.
- Awareness in Sequencing:
    - Establish dates and sequence of events, respecting cultural sensitivity.
    - Adapt your approach based on cultural variations in perceiving and expressing time.
- Cultural Exploration:
    - Actively explore the patient's cultural perspective, beliefs about the cause, worries, expectations, and how problems affect their life.
    - Encourage open expression of feelings within the cultural context.
    - Collateral information seeking is paramount – As symptoms are behavioural & patient may have varying amounts of insight.
- Cultural Sensitivity in Summarization:
    - Summarize at the end of each section, confirming understanding in culturally appropriate ways.
    - Acknowledge the patient's narrative with cultural sensitivity.
- Cultural Signposting:
    - Progress from one section to another using culturally sensitive signposting.
    - Provide a rationale for transitioning to the next section, considering cultural expectations.
- Logical Sequence:
    - Structure the interview logically, respecting cultural preferences.
    - Be mindful of the cultural significance of topics and their sequencing.
- Summarization Skills:
    - Develop skills in summarizing the information gathered during the conversation.
    - Summarize the patient's narrative to ensure clarity and accuracy.
- Pick Up Cues:
    - Encourage safe environment for all.
    - Be attentive to potential embarrassment or fear in older patients, especially regarding memory problems or stigmatized diagnoses.
    - Consider suicide or violence risk during clinical encounters.
- Addressing Reluctance:
    - Acknowledge potential reluctance due to fear of stigma or misconceptions about health and social services.
    - Enquiry towards domestic violence, unemployment, childhood abuse as these are psychosocial history risk factors.
    - Probe for social media presence and interaction.
    - Probe for sexual history – orientation, trauma without being judgemental
    - Create a safe and non-judgmental space to encourage open communication.
- Language Appropriateness:
    - Use clear and simple language, especially with patients who are confused, disoriented, upset, or have speech or hearing difficulties.
    - Check potential communication barriers, such as pain, medication side effects, or language comprehension issues
    - Consideration for Dysarthria or Deafness: Assess whether dysarthria or deafness is affecting communication; Check understanding and explore alternative communication methods, such as written communication, if needed.

  - Check for Hearing Aids: Inquire about the use of hearing aids and ensure they are in place and functioning properly; address any issues related to hearing aids that may hinder effective communication.

Discover the Patient's Perspective:

- Patient-Centred Approach and Personality risk factors.
  - Prioritize understanding the patient's perspective as it significantly influences treatment expectations and adherence.
  - Recognize that the impact of the condition on the patient's life is a key factor in predicting their needs and responses.
- Family Dynamics:
  - Consider the role of the patient's family in providing support and receiving assistance.
  - Explore the support system, expressed emotions etc.
  - Consider the generation Gap, parenting influence etc.,

Building and Maintaining the Therapeutic Relationship:

- Non-Verbal Communication:
  - Demonstrate appropriate non-verbal behaviour to convey openness and receptivity.
  - Use body language that reflects attentiveness and empathy.
  - Demonstrate culturally appropriate non-verbal behaviour, including eye contact, facial expressions, posture, and vocal cues.
  - Be attuned to cultural variations in non-verbal communication.
- Patience and Time:
  - Show patience and allocate sufficient time during interactions.
  - Adapt to the patient's pace, recognizing the importance of going at their speed for effective communication. For example – patient with delusional disorders by nature of disorder lack insight and tend to externalize rather than openly discuss the internal world.
  - Attend to timing, ensuring the interview stays on task.
  - Consider cultural norms regarding time management and pacing.
- Understanding Patient's Background:
  - Explore the patient's past life, current situation, and future plans or concerns.
  - Consider factors like the patient's upbringing or past experiences that may impact their current behaviour.
- Empathic and Respectful Responses:
  - Respond empathically and respectfully to issues that may initially seem awkward or unusual.
  - Provide practical help and support based on a deep understanding of the patient's predicament.
- Navigating Health and Social Care:
  - Assist patients and their families in navigating the complexities of health and social care agencies.
  - Provide guidance and support to ensure that they can access the appropriate resources.
- Respect for Diverse Views:
  - Accept the legitimacy of diverse cultural views and feelings, refraining from judgment.
  - Demonstrate openness to different cultural perspectives.
- Cultural Support and Acknowledgment:
  - Provide cultural-sensitive support, expressing concern, understanding, and willingness to help.

  - Acknowledge the patient's coping efforts and encourage appropriate self-care within their cultural framework.
- Cultural Sensitivity in Addressing Sensitive Topics:
  - Deal sensitively with embarrassing or disturbing topics, considering cultural taboos.
  - Approach physical pain with cultural sensitivity, especially during a physical examination.
- Shared Decision-Making with Cultural Considerations:
  - Share your thought process with the patient, encouraging their involvement in decision-making.
  - Explain the rationale for questions or examination parts with cultural sensitivity.
- Cultural Sensitivity in Physical Examination:
  - During the physical examination, explain the process, asking for permission with cultural respect.
  - Be mindful of cultural modesty and preferences.

Summarise and Signpost:

- Summarizing for Clarity:
  - Use summarization to distil complex narratives.
  - Assist patients in structuring their accounts, preventing them from becoming overwhelmed by their own stories.
- Clear Information Delivery:
  - Provide any preliminary information in a clear, culturally adapted manner.
  - Avoid or explain medical jargon using culturally familiar terms.
- Cultural Sensitivity in Summarization:
  - Briefly summarize the session, acknowledging cultural nuances.
  - Confirm key points in a culturally appropriate manner.
- Cultural Contracts for Next Steps:
  - Contract with the patient regarding the next steps for both the patient and the physician.
  - Respect cultural preferences in determining the plan for follow-up or further action.
- Aid Memory Recall:
  - Employ summarization to help elderly patients recall and organize their thoughts during the consultation.
  - Enhance the patient's ability to convey relevant information by providing concise summaries of their narrative.
- Structuring the Consultation:
  - Utilize summarizing and signposting to structure the consultation effectively.
  - This approach facilitates communication with both the patient and their caregivers, ensuring that important questions or plans are addressed.
- Involving Caregivers:
  - Check questions or plans with caregivers during the consultation, acknowledging the challenges faced by the patient. For example, verifying information with a caregiver about the patient's ability to perform certain tasks or live independently.
- Signposting for Clarification:
  - Use signposting to introduce a change in topic or seek additional information during the conversation.
  - Ensure clarity by signalling transitions, such as checking details with a family member or confirming the patient's residence.
- Memory Test Sensitivity:

    - Employ memory tests as assessment tools with elderly patients.
    - Signpost the use of memory tests carefully to avoid causing embarrassment or anger, emphasizing the assessment's importance in understanding their cognitive health.
- Preventing Embarrassment:
    - Be mindful of potential embarrassment or emotional reactions during memory assessments.
    - Use signposting to prepare the patient for any memory tests, ensuring a supportive and non-judgmental environment.
- Enhancing Communication Efficiency:
    - Combine summarization and signposting to enhance communication efficiency, especially in situations where cognitive challenges may affect the patient's ability to express themselves clearly.
    - Strive to make the consultation more structured and comprehensible for both the patient and the clinician.

Explanation and Planning:

- Chunk and Check:
    - Break down information into manageable chunks during explanations.
    - Regularly check for the patient's understanding to ensure clarity.
    - Use clear, jargon-free language to enhance comprehension.
- Use of Diagrams/schematics/ infographics:
    - Incorporate diagrams to visually represent information.
    - Particularly useful for those with memory loss, diagrams provide a visual aid for better understanding.
- Written Instructions:
    - Try to provide written instructions along with verbal explanations.
    - Offer written materials to reinforce important information, enhancing retention.
- Inquire About Helpful Information:
    - Ask patients what additional information would be helpful.
    - Consider discussing causes (aetiology) and potential outcomes (prognosis).
- Appropriate Timing for Explanation:
    - Provide explanations at suitable times.
    - Avoid giving advice, information, or reassurance prematurely.
- Organized Explanation:
    - Divide information into clear sections, developing a logical sequence.
    - Simplify complex details for easier comprehension. Example – anecdotes/story telling for explaining difficult concepts
- Use Explicit Categorization or Signposting:
    - Clearly categorize information using signposts.
    - For instance, "There are three important things to discuss. First..."
- Check Patient's Understanding:
    - Verify the patient's comprehension by asking them to restate information.
    - Clarify as necessary to ensure accurate understanding.
- Medication Guidance:
    - Utilize diagrams and written instructions, especially when discussing medication.

    - This helps patients and caregivers better comprehend dosage schedules, potential side effects, and any specific instructions related to medication management.
- Memory Loss Consideration:
    - Tailor explanations and planning to accommodate individuals with memory loss.
    - Recognize the challenges they may face and adjust communication strategies accordingly.
- Caregiver Involvement:
    - Involve caregivers in the explanation and planning process.
    - Share written materials and diagrams with caregivers to ensure consistent understanding and support for the patient.
- Repetition and Reinforcement:
    - Repeat key information and reinforce important points, as it builds trust.
    - Repetition aids in memory retention, particularly for individuals dealing with memory loss.
- Encourage Questions:
    - Create an open environment for questions and concerns.
    - Encourage patients and caregivers to seek clarification and ask questions for better understanding.
- Adapt to Individual Needs:
    - Recognize the unique needs of each patient and adjust the level of detail and explanation accordingly.
    - Be flexible in adapting the communication approach based on the individual's cognitive abilities and preferences.
- Relate Explanations to Patient’s Perspective:
    - Connect explanations to the patient's thoughts, concerns, and expectations.
    - Align information with the patient's cultural context.
- Encourage Patient Contribution:
    - Create opportunities for patients to ask questions and contribute.
    - Respond appropriately to their queries and concerns.
- Respond to Verbal and Non-Verbal Cues:
    - Be attentive to verbal and non-verbal cues indicating the need for patient contribution.
    - Address distress or information overload sensitively.
- Involve Patient Actively:
    - Offer suggestions and choices rather than directives.
    - Encourage patients to contribute their ideas and preferences.
- Explore Management Options:
    - Discuss various options for managing the illness/disorder.
    - Consider cultural preferences and traditional practices.
- Negotiate a Mutually Acceptable Plan:
    - Signpost your position on available options.
    - Determine the patient's preferences collaboratively.

****

Points to Ponder in Proper Communication in Psychiatry

- Clear explanation of the nature of disorder, its natural history, aetiology, predisposing factors etc., and the influence of systemic diseases.
- Explanation of the treatment plan, including the role of medications and cognitive rehabilitation therapy.
- Empathetic communication about the challenges of living with mental condition and other physical comorbidities.
- Encouragement of open communication about any concerns or questions the patient or caregiver may have.
- Involvement of family members in discussions, with the patient's consent, to ensure they understand the condition and how they can support the patient.
- Reassurance that with proper treatment, the prognosis is good.
- Encouragement of adherence to the medication regimen and follow-up appointments.
- Discussion of the potential side effects of medications and what to do if they occur.
- Respect for the patient's autonomy and preferences in decision-making about treatment.
- Documentation of all discussions and decisions in the medical record.
- Respect for confidentiality and privacy.
- Declaration of any potential conflicts of interest.
- Informed consent for any procedures or treatments, including a discussion of the risks and benefits.
- Acknowledgment of the patient's fears and anxieties, and reassurance that these are common and understandable reactions.
- Forewarning about the potential for recurrent episodes, if applicable, but reassurance that these can be managed with adjustments to the treatment plan.
- Discussion of the cost of treatment and diagnostic tests, and exploration of any financial concerns the patient may have.
- Acknowledgment of the stigma often associated with mental health conditions, and reassurance that these are legitimate medical conditions that deserve treatment.
- Encouragement of the patient to share his own feelings and experiences, and validation of these as an important part of the diagnostic and treatment process.
- Explanation of the importance of regular follow-up care, even during periods of remission.
- Reassurance that the healthcare team is available to provide ongoing support and assistance.
- Encouragement of the patient to contact the healthcare team with any questions or concerns, or if symptoms worsen.
- Explanation of the importance of early intervention and treatment to prevent complications and improve prognosis.
- Encouragement of the patient to take an active role in managing his condition, including learning about the condition, participating in treatment decisions, and adhering to the treatment plan.
- Explanation of the potential impact of the condition on daily life, including work, school, and relationships, and discussion of strategies to manage these challenges.
- Encouragement of the patient to express his feelings and to seek help if he is feeling overwhelmed.
- Explanation of the role of psychotherapy in helping the patient cope with the emotional impact of the condition.
- Encouragement of the patient to practice relaxation techniques, such as deep breathing, meditation, and yoga, to help manage stress and reduce symptoms.

- Explanation of the role of medication in managing symptoms and preventing episodes, and reassurance that the healthcare team will work with the patient to find the most effective and tolerable medication regimen.
- Explanation of the importance of monitoring for side effects of medication, and reassurance that the healthcare team is available to help manage any side effects that occur.
- Explanation of the importance of self-care including adequate sleep in managing symptoms and improving overall health, and encouragement of the patient to establish regular sleep habits, including a consistent sleep schedule and a relaxing bedtime routine.
- Explanation of the importance of avoiding triggers that can worsen symptoms, such as certain foods, alcohol, caffeine, and stress, and encouragement of the patient to keep a symptom diary to help identify personal triggers.
- Explanation of the importance of regular check-ups to monitor the condition and adjust the treatment plan as needed, and reassurance that the healthcare team is committed to providing the best possible care.
- Encouragement of the patient to seek support from others who understand what he is going through, such as support groups, online communities, and organizations that provide information and resources for people with his condition.
- Encouragement of the patient to be patient with himself and to recognize that managing a chronic condition is a journey, not a destination.
- Explanation of the importance of maintaining a positive attitude and focusing on strengths and abilities, rather than limitations, and reassurance that it's okay to ask for help when needed.
- Encouragement of the patient to take care of his physical health, in addition to his mental health, and reassurance that regular exercise will help, as sitting is the new smoking.

Develop Skills in the domains of

- **Establishing Expectations:** Clearly communicate the purpose and goals of the interaction to foster understanding.
- **Encouraging Patient Participation in communication and treatment:**
    - Actively encourage patients to ask questions and participate in the discussion.
    - Promote an open dialogue to enhance patient engagement and collaboration.
- **Sensitive Information Giving:**
    - Provide information in a sensitive and timely manner.
    - Be mindful of the patient's emotional state and deliver information with empathy.
- **Written Information Support:**
    - Offer 'take home' written information to reinforce verbal communication, example – When prescribing sedatives, clear warning to steer away from driving or handling machineries.
    - Provide written materials to aid memory and facilitate understanding, especially for those with cognitive impairment.
- **Relevance to Patient's Situation:**
    - Make discussions relevant to the patient's unique situation.
    - Tailor communication to address individual concerns and circumstances.
- **Demonstrating Empathy:**
    - Demonstrate a caring attitude by actively listening and showing empathy.
    - Acknowledge and validate the patient's emotions and concerns.

Special Mentions

- Communication with Cognitively Impaired Patients:
    - Develop communication skills specific to interacting with cognitively impaired patients.
    - Learn strategies for effective communication in triadic consultations involving both the patient and an informant.
- Assessment of Practical Ability and Risks:
    - Assess the current level of practical ability and risks in individuals with cognitive impairment.
    - Consider practical aspects and potential risks associated with the patient's condition.

Cognitive Function Assessments

- In most of cases, informal cognitive testing is adequate.
- Learn formal capacity assessment techniques for patients with cognitive challenges.
- Assess cognitive function in a sensitive manner.
- Stress Reduction:
    - Acknowledge that stress and anxiety can diminish cognitive performance.
    - Build rapport, help patients relax, and create a supportive environment, so it helps to improve cognitive performance.
- Flexibility in Timing:
    - Be flexible about the timing of cognitive assessments during the interview.
    - Consider early testing after forming a therapeutic alliance and timing assessments before discussing contentious issues.
- Clear and Concise Communication:
    - Use as few words as possible during cognitive assessments.
    - Add conversational phrases to make the patient feel more comfortable and repeat questions if not heard clearly.
- Monitoring Patient Engagement:
    - Watch for cues indicating loss of interest or irritation during assessments.
    - Be prepared to complete the examination at a later date if necessary.
    - Try to distinguish between true cognitive impairment and those with less motivation to take up the assessment.
- Sensitive Feedback:
    - Be sensitive about giving feedback on cognitive performance.
    - Use difficulties as an opportunity to start a discussion about the patient's cognitive challenges.

Mental Capacity Assessment

- Make every effort to help the patient perform their best
- Determine if there is an impairment or disturbance in functioning and evaluate if the person lacks the capacity to make a specific decision.
- Functional Test of Capacity:
    - Understand the components of the functional test of capacity.
    - Evaluate the patient's ability to understand, assess information, retain it, and communicate decisions.
- Optimizing Communication for Capacity Assessment:
    - Make efforts to optimize communication to ensure the patient understands relevant information.
    - Simplify terms and explanations for better comprehension.

- Ability to make decisions (capacity) can change depending on several factors:
    - Time: Patient's capacity can improve or worsen over time. For example, a confused patient might get better and be able to make decisions again. But someone with dementia, where things get worse over time, probably won't regain full decision-making ability.
    - The decision itself: What kind of decision needs to be made? A person with delusions might not trust a doctor and refuse medication, but they might still be able to handle their finances just fine.
    - How serious the outcome could be: The more serious the consequences of a decision, the more cautious we need to be about someone's ability to make it. For example, a homeless person with schizophrenia who wants to leave the hospital against medical advice (AMA) for dialysis treatment would be looked at more closely than someone with the same condition who just needs to finish one more day of antibiotics.
    - The situation: Who is around to help? An elderly man with dementia who lives alone would need to be more capable of taking care of himself before being discharged from the hospital than someone who lives with a healthy spouse.

- **Factors affecting Decision making capacity**

Step in Decision Making	How it can be Affected
Understanding Information	Attention problems, memory issues, difficulty grasping meaning
Appreciating the Situation	Not understanding the consequences of decisions
Making a Reasoned Decision	Difficulty with logic, comparing options, or making value-based choices
Communicating a Choice	Problems with thinking clearly or remembering information

Assessment of Capacity to Decide Where to Live/ Assisted Living

- Clinical Judgment Factors:
    - Recognize that judgment is based on clinical assessment for deciding where to live.
    - Consider factors such as the cause and severity of cognitive impairment, awareness of living circumstances, and the ability to manage risks.
- Key Considerations:
    - Assess the person's awareness of their problems, current living circumstances, and potential risks.
    - Consider the person's willingness to accept help or consider alternatives.
    - Evaluate the consistency and realism in their statements.
- Legal Criteria:
    - Acknowledge the absence of clear criteria or legal test cases for deciding where to live.
    - Base judgment on a comprehensive clinical assessment that considers multiple factors.

****

A step-by-step guide for talking about mental illness related misinformation and dispelling myths obtained from internet and or social media with focus on attitude, ethics, and communication with patients and caregivers:

Step 1: Identify the Misinformation:

- **Critical Thinking:** Don't blindly accept online information.
- **Analyse the source:** Is it a reputable organization or a random individual? Check for factual errors, logical fallacies, and emotional appeals.
- **Understand the Myth:** Research the specific mental illness the misinformation pertains to. Learn about its symptoms, causes, and treatment options from credible sources.

Step 2: Debunk the Myth:

- **Facts over Opinions:** Use scientifically backed evidence and statistics to contradict the misinformation. Share links to reliable resources that support your claims.
- **Address the Emotional Hook:** Often, misinformation plays on fear, stigma, or sensationalism. Acknowledge those emotions but offer a more balanced perspective based on facts.
- **Be Kind and Respectful:** Even when correcting others, maintain a respectful and empathetic tone. Avoid personal attacks or shaming, as this can backfire and further entrenched beliefs.

Step 3: Promote Understanding:

- **Focus on People, not Diagnoses:** Frame your message around people living with mental illness, emphasizing their humanity and experiences. Avoid dehumanizing language or relying solely on clinical terms.
- **Share Personal Stories:** If comfortable, share your own experiences or those of close ones to personalize the issue and break down stigma. Remember to protect anonymity and privacy.
- **Highlight Positive Examples:** Showcase successful stories of individuals managing mental illness, breaking stereotypes and fostering hope.

Step 4: Empower Others:

- **Encourage Critical Thinking:** Teach others how to evaluate online information and identify red flags. Share tips on verifying sources and finding reliable resources.
- **Promote Open Communication:** Encourage your community to talk openly about mental health, creating a safe space for sharing experiences and seeking help.
- **Advocate for Change:** Support initiatives that fight stigma and misinformation, like mental health awareness campaigns and social media movements.

Attitude to be exhibited in the process:

- **Cultivate Open-mindedness:** Approach the task with an open mind, acknowledging that individuals may have diverse beliefs and perspectives about mental health.
- **Empathy and Understanding:** Understand that myths and misinformation often stem from societal stigma. Adopt an empathetic attitude, recognizing the impact of such beliefs on individuals experiencing mental health conditions.

- **Cultural Sensitivity:** Consider cultural nuances and variations in beliefs. Be respectful of diverse cultural backgrounds prevalent in India, recognizing that misconceptions about mental health can vary across regions and communities.
- **Personal Reflection:** Reflect on your own biases and preconceptions. Ensure that your attitude towards dispelling myths is free from judgment and stigma. Examining personal biases and preconceived notions is crucial. One must challenge internalized stigma and cultivate empathy and understanding towards individuals with mental illness.
- **Education:** Going beyond the core curriculum by exploring resources so as to gain with in-depth knowledge about various mental illnesses.
- **Person-cantered approach:** Seeing individuals with mental illness as people first, not just their diagnoses, is imperative. Treating them with respect, dignity, and compassion fosters a positive therapeutic environment.
- **Advocacy:** Speaking up against discriminatory practices and promoting inclusive language encourages others to learn about mental health and challenge harmful stereotypes.

Ethics to be followed in this process:

- **Respect Patient Confidentiality:** Uphold the principles of medical ethics by respecting patient confidentiality. When discussing mental health conditions, ensure that patient privacy is maintained.
- **Informed Consent:** Before engaging in conversations about dispelling myths, obtain informed consent from the patient or caregiver. Clearly explain the purpose and potential outcomes of the discussion.
- **Cultural Competence:** Be ethically sensitive to cultural differences. Understand the cultural context of the patient or caregiver and tailor your communication accordingly.
- **Non-Discrimination:** Adhere to the principle of non-discrimination. Avoid making assumptions or perpetuating stereotypes based on mental health conditions.
- **Transparency:** Informing patients about limitations in knowledge and expertise demonstrates honesty. Directing them to relevant mental health professionals when needed ensures comprehensive care.

Communication with Patients and Caregivers in this process:

- **Establish Trust:** Build a trusting relationship with the patient and caregiver. This foundation is crucial for effective communication and dispelling myths.
- **Active Listening:** Practice active listening to understand the specific myths or misinformation that the patient or caregiver holds. Allow them to express their concerns without interruption.
- **Provide Accurate Information including sources:** Offer clear, concise, and evidence-based information to counter the myths. Use simple language and analogies to enhance understanding.
- **Clarify Misconceptions:** Address specific misconceptions by presenting facts and correcting inaccuracies. Ensure that your communication is patient-centred and tailored to the individual's needs.
- **Use Visual Aids:** Utilize visual aids, diagrams, or educational materials to enhance comprehension. Visual tools can simplify complex information and improve retention.
- **Encourage Questions:** Create an environment where questions are welcomed. Encourage the patient or caregiver to seek clarification and express their concerns openly.
- **Provide Resources:** Offer reliable sources of information, such as reputable websites, pamphlets, or contact details of mental health professionals. Empower patients and caregivers to access accurate information independently.

- **Offer Ongoing Support**: Reassure the patient and caregiver of your ongoing support. Let them know that they can reach out for further clarification or assistance at any time.
- **Collaborative Decision-Making:** Involve the patient and caregiver in decision-making processes related to treatment and management. Foster a collaborative approach that respects their autonomy.
- **Follow-Up Communication:** Schedule follow-up communications to assess the patient's understanding and address any lingering concerns. This ongoing dialogue reinforces the dispelling of myths.
- **Community Engagement:** Engage with community outreach programs to dispel myths at a broader level. Participate in awareness campaigns and mental health education initiatives.
- **Continued Learning:** Life long learning is essential. Be ready and open to learn new developments and details.

****

List of some patient concerns, specific reasons that causes the concerns and how the medical student- doctors need to take from the domains of knowledge, skill, communication and ethics to ensure that the patient is ensured that their concerns are addressed.

Concern	Specific reasons	Doctor Action (Knowledge, Skill, Communication, Ethics)
Anxiety about the effect of disease on	Social status Quality of life Ability to function – Economical productivity, financial independence, burden to family etc Lifespan	**Knowledge:** Understand the impact of the disease on these aspects of life. **Skill:** Assess patient's specific concerns through open-ended questions. **Communication:** Emphasize the importance of addressing these concerns. Discuss treatment options and potential impact on quality of life. **Ethics:** Treat patient with respect and avoid dismissive language.
Patients may hesitate to discuss certain health concerns (e.g., impotence, depression, fear of cancer) with their doctor due to	Embarrassment; avoid seeming ungrateful Distrust of doctors Communication difficulties Belief nothing can be done Reluctance to burden doctor Fear of confirmation	**Communication:** Create a safe and trusting environment. Use open-ended questions and active listening. Normalize these concerns and emphasize confidentiality. **Skill:** Elicit concerns through indirect questioning and addressing nonverbal cues. **Ethics:** Maintain patient confidentiality and avoid judgment.
Hesitation to accept recommended treatments owing to	Fear of side effects and embarrassment Financial limitations – Fear of being non-productive member of family. Lifestyle incompatibility Fear of dependence Disbelief in effectiveness	**Knowledge:** Educate patient about treatment options, including benefits, risks, and side effects. Explore alternative approaches if appropriate. **Skill:** Tailor treatment plans to individual circumstances and preferences. **Communication:** Discuss concerns openly and honestly. Address financial limitations and offer solutions. **Ethics:** Respect patient autonomy and involve them in decision-making.
Fear of asking for additional support	Information about disease Second opinion or higher centre referral Treatment from faith healers etc., Sick leave External support	**Knowledge:** Understand available resources and support systems. **Communication:** Offer information pamphlets or online resources. Encourage questions and provide clear explanations. **Skill:** Connect patient with relevant support services (social workers, therapists). **Ethics:** Respect patient's right to explore alternative therapies; understand potential risks and benefits.

Building Trust: Tips for Better Doctor-Patient Communication

When patient feels like doctor...	What the doctor can do to avoid such complaints and effective communication in that situation
Rushed	Explain why time might be limited, and work together to schedule a longer appointment if needed.
Ignored	Look at the patient while they talk and summarize what they've said to make sure you understand.
Didn't listen	Ask open-ended questions and give patients at least a minute to explain their concerns. Encourage shy patients to speak up, and gently guide those who talk a lot.
Didn't understand	Repeat back what you've heard from the patient to confirm understanding and clear up any confusion.
Didn't explain	Explain your diagnosis and treatment plan in simple terms. Ask if the patient has any questions or needs clarification.
Didn't meet expectations	Ask the patient about their expectations, concerns, and any ideas they might have about their illness or treatment.
Dismissive of Feelings	Ask the patient what worries them most about their condition. Show empathy and understanding.
Rude or Patronizing	Treat the patient with respect. Maintain eye contact, lean forward, and remove physical barriers like a desk. Speak calmly and use the patient's name correctly.

Understanding LGBTQ+ Identities and Experiences in India from AETCOM of Behavioural Sciences

Domain	Issues	Knowledge	Psychomotor Skills	Affective Skills
Knowledge	• Lack of understanding of LGBTQ+ identities and experiences in the Indian context. • Limited knowledge of specific mental health challenges faced by LGBTQ+ individuals in India (e.g., impact of Section 377, family pressure). • Unfamiliarity with LGBTQ+ terminology and resources available in India.	• Attend LGBTQ+ cultural competency training specific to the Indian context. • Stay updated on current research on LGBTQ+ mental health in India. • Utilize resources from Indian LGBTQ+ organizations.		• Develop a genuine interest in understanding LGBTQ+ experiences in India.
Additional Considerations		• Be aware of the legal landscape surrounding LGBTQ+ rights in India (Judgments on Section 377). • Understand the role of family and community in Indian society and their potential impact on LGBTQ+ mental health. • Research available mental health resources & support groups for LGBTQ+ individuals in India.	• Tailor communication and support strategies considering the unique needs of LGBTQ+ patients in India. • Explore referral options for patients seeking legal or social support.	• Demonstrate cultural sensitivity and respect for the complexities of LGBTQ+ life in India. • Advocate for creating a more inclusive and supportive environment for LGBTQ+ individuals.

Psychomotor Skills	• Difficulty taking a culturally sensitive history considering Indian context. • Challenges in using inclusive language while navigating complex family dynamics in India.	• Practice taking a sexual orientation and gender identity (SOGI) history considering Indian social norms. • Role-play using inclusive language while addressing potential concerns about family reactions. • Consult with colleagues experienced in LGBTQ+ care in India.		• Demonstrate respect for patients' self-identified names and pronouns, even if they differ from traditional naming practices. • Create a safe and welcoming environment for disclosure, acknowledging potential anxieties about family acceptance.
Affective Skills	• Unconscious bias towards heteronormativity compounded by societal norms in India. • Discomfort discussing LGBTQ+ issues due to personal beliefs or social stigma. • Difficulty in managing personal beliefs that may conflict with patient identity, and family pressures.	• Engage in self-reflection and identify personal biases specific to the Indian context. • Seek supervision and discuss challenges with colleagues experienced in LGBTQ+ care in India. • Recognize the importance of professional boundary & respect the family dynamics in India.	• Develop empathy and compassion for the unique experiences of LGBTQ+ individuals in India. • Challenge personal prejudices and commit to providing affirming care that considers both individual and family needs.	• How can you manage your own biases to provide unbiased care, considering the influence of family in Indian society?

How does the concept of "gender" differ in traditional Indian society compared to the Western understanding of gender identity?

Traditional Indian society often emphasizes assigned sex at birth and binary gender roles. However, LGBTQ+ identities acknowledge a spectrum of gender identities that may not strictly conform to male or female.

What are some of the challenges faced by LGBTQ+ individuals in India due to their sexual orientation or gender identity?

Challenges can include social stigma, discrimination (housing, employment), lack of family acceptance, and potential legal issues related to Section 377 (though partially repealed).

How can cultural factors in India impact the mental health of LGBTQ+ individuals?

The emphasis on family honour and societal expectations can lead to feelings of isolation, anxiety, and depression for LGBTQ+ individuals struggling with acceptance.

Mental Health Considerations

What are some specific mental health concerns that LGBTQ+ individuals in India might experience more than the general population?

Higher rates of depression, anxiety, substance abuse, and suicidal ideation are reported among LGBTQ+ individuals due to the aforementioned challenges.

How can a mental health professional take a culturally sensitive SOGI history in the Indian context?

Use open-ended questions, avoid assumptions about relationships, and acknowledge the potential role of family in the patient's life.

Resources and Support

How can a mental health professional stay updated on current research regarding LGBTQ+ mental health in India?

Subscribe to journals and publications focusing on LGBTQ+ issues in India, attend conferences or workshops on the topic, and connect with other professionals experienced in this area.

Self-Reflection and Professional Development

How can a mental health professional identify and address their own biases towards heteronormativity, especially considering the Indian social context?

Engage in self-reflection, participate in LGBTQ+ cultural competency training, and discuss challenges with colleagues experienced in LGBTQ+ care in India.

How can a mental health professional create a safe and welcoming environment for LGBTQ+ patients in their practice?

Utilize inclusive language, display educational materials about LGBTQ+ identities, and ensure confidentiality for all discussions.

How can a mental health professional advocate for a more inclusive and supportive environment for LGBTQ+ individuals in India?
Educate colleagues and the community about LGBTQ+ issues, speak out against discrimination, and support legal and social reforms that promote LGBTQ+ rights.

How Section 377 impacted the mental health of LGBTQ+ individuals in India (in the past)?
Section 377 criminalized homosexuality, leading to fear, stigma, and discrimination, impacting mental health. (Please note – it was decriminalized in 2018)

How can you take a culturally sensitive SOGI history considering the Indian context?
Use open-ended questions, avoid assumptions, and prioritize patient comfort while acknowledging the potential role of family.

****

Some Points for Indian Doctors in Deescalating Hospital Violence

Prevention through Communication:

- Establish clear communication channels with patients and their families, fostering an environment of trust and understanding.
- Provide comprehensive explanations about treatment plans, procedures, and potential outcomes to manage expectations and reduce misunderstandings.

Early Recognition of Warning Signs:

- Train hospital staff to recognize early indicators of escalating tension, such as raised voices, tendency to aggregate in groups, aggressive body language, or verbal threats.
- Encourage reporting of any concerning behaviour to designated personnel for prompt intervention **IMMEDIATELY**.
- Check for CCTV recordings. If you suspect escalation, meet in CCTV covered areas.
- **Trainees and Interns**: **Always work under supervision. Keep your chief or Duty Assistant Professor informed of every development.**

Respectful Engagement:

- Approach patients and their families with respect and empathy, acknowledging their concerns and emotions.
- Maintain a calm demeanour and avoid confrontational language or actions that may exacerbate the situation.

De-escalation Techniques:

- Use active listening skills to validate the feelings and concerns of patients and their families, demonstrating empathy and understanding.
- Remain non-confrontational and avoid escalating the situation further, seeking to diffuse tension through dialogue and negotiation.

Collaborative Problem-Solving:

- Involve patients and their families in decision-making processes regarding their care whenever possible, empowering them to participate in finding solutions.
- Offer alternative options or compromises to address grievances and alleviate tensions.

Utilization of Support Services:

- Access hospital resources such as social workers, counsellors, or patient advocates to provide additional support and mediation during challenging situations.
- Offer emotional support and counselling services to patients and their families to address underlying stressors or anxieties.

Training and Education:

- Provide ongoing training for hospital staff on conflict resolution techniques, cultural sensitivity, and communication skills.
- Conduct regular drills or simulations to practice responding to potential incidents of violence in a controlled environment.
- Make all stake holders aware of the prevention of violence against doctors, medical professionals and medical institutions bill.

- Doctors should not do procedures for which they are not trained.
- Doctors should be trained for effective communication and good interpersonal skills.
- Ensure that details of medical negligence as mentioned in the Section 106 of BNS that corresponds to erstwhile Section 304A of IPC are well known to medical professionals

Security Measures:

- Implement appropriate security protocols and measures to ensure the safety of patients, staff, and visitors in the event of a violent incident.
- Collaborate with law enforcement agencies or local authorities to develop emergency response plans and coordinate efforts in managing violent situations.
- A senior doctor not involved with the treatment should interact with the patient's relatives to de-escalate the situation.
- Establishments must have adequate security staff to protect the workers, and a security alarm system so security reaches the place of violence quickly. A drill for this should be done once a month to fine-tune the security system.
- Establishments should have CCTV cameras with 24-hour trained observers, panic buttons, and better control of the entry into the emergency department.
- Overcrowding at hospitals should be reduced by encouraging the patients to consult the family physician/general practitioner for mild ailments.

Documentation and Follow-Up:

- Document all incidents of violence or aggression in detail, including the individuals involved, actions taken, and outcomes.
- Conduct thorough reviews and debriefings following violent incidents to identify areas for improvement and implement corrective measures.

Community Engagement and Advocacy:

- Foster positive relationships with the local community through outreach programs, educational initiatives, and community partnerships.
- Advocate for policy changes and legislative measures to address systemic issues contributing to hospital violence and improve safety standards.

****

Volatile Crowd

In a rural hospital, at the room where Arjun, a bright-eyed 12-year-old boy, battles against advanced leukemia, that was diagnosed very late and parents could not accept the diagnosis. Instead they blamed medical negligence. Arjun's parents, humble villagers with scant medical understanding, cling to hope as they stand vigil by his bedside, their faces etched with worry and uncertainty. Despite the tireless efforts of the medical team, the devastating news shatters the fragile calmness—a whispered revelation that despite the relentless treatments, Arjun's condition has taken a turn for the worse. In the surrounding rural community, whispers of concern ripple through the tight-knit village, echoing the collective anguish felt by neighbours and friends who share in Arjun's plight. There is a strong rumour that due and appropriate treatment for the condition was not provided to Arjun. All villagers have converged in the evening seeking treatment for the poor child. The child's vitals go down and later succumbs. When the young duty doctor announces and confirms death, in a polite tone to parents, commotion break and entire village gheroes the duty doctor.

Psychiatric Practice Pearls:

- Be prepared for denial, anger, and bargaining in this situation. Patience and active listening are key.
- Encourage open dialogue between the medical team, Arjun, and his parents to address fears and concerns.
- Offer psychological support services tailored to parents as culturally appropriate resources for his parents.

Understanding the Patient's Perspective:

- What medical concepts should Arjun and his parents grasp?
- Do Arjun and his parents understand the implications of advanced leukemia?
- How can the doctor assess Arjun's parents understanding and address any misconceptions?
- What questions can the doctor ask Arjun and his parents to gauge their understanding?

Breaking the News:

Cognitive: How much medical detail should I share with the parents, considering their limited knowledge?

Use simple language. Focus on the current situation and avoid overwhelming them with complex medical jargon.

Affective:

How can the doctor demonstrate empathy and support to Arjun and his parents?

How can the doctor convey compassion while delivering difficult news?

How can I support the parents through this ordeal?

Actively listen and offer support resources like social workers or grief counselling.

Competence:

How can I ensure informed consent if the parents are emotionally distraught?

Break the news gradually. Offer breaks and allow them to ask questions. Respect their final decision, even if it differs from medical recommendations.

What information should the doctor provide about Arjun's prognosis and available support services?

What treatment options are available for Arjun at this stage?

Skills:

How can the doctor deliver the news in a sensitive and clear manner?

What language can the doctor use to convey the seriousness of Arjun's condition without causing unnecessary alarm?

How do I handle a volatile situation if the parents refuse to accept the news?

Maintain a calm and empathetic demeanour. Acknowledge their grief and validate their emotions.

Handling Caregivers and Society:

Cognition:

What are common reactions from Arjun's parents and the rural community?

How might Arjun's parents react to the news of his deteriorating condition?

Skills:
How can the doctor address any resistance or disbelief from Arjun's parents?
What strategies can the doctor use to reassure Arjun's parents and help them come to terms with the situation?

Affective:
How can the doctor help Arjun's parents cope with their emotions and provide adequate support?
What emotional support resources are available for Arjun's parents within the hospital and the community?

****

Misunderstood Diagnosis and Marital Discord (Urban Setting)

Setting: Private clinic in a bustling city

Patient: 38-year-old housewife, Meena, with suspected early-stage breast cancer

Caregiver: Controlling husband sceptical of the diagnosis

The News: A biopsy reveals breast cancer, requiring further investigation and treatment.

The Situation: Meena arrives at the clinic with her husband, who appears dismissive of her concerns. He questions the doctor's competence and insists on a second opinion. After the biopsy results confirm cancer, the husband becomes even more agitated, accusing Meena of neglecting her health and causing family stress.

Psychiatrist Practice Pearl: Anticipate potential marital discord and emotional strain on the patient. Encourage open communication and offer support systems.

Understanding the Patient's Perspective:
- **Cognitive:** How can the doctor explain the implications of breast cancer and available treatment options in a way that is clear and empowers Meena to make informed decisions?

Breaking the News:
- **Competence:** How can the doctor ensure informed consent for further investigations and treatment plans, considering the husband's resistance?
- **Affective:** How can the doctor address Meena's anxieties about the diagnosis and potential impact on her family life?

Handling Caregivers and Society:
- **Skills:** What communication strategies can the doctor use to de-escalate the husband's aggression and encourage him to be a supportive partner?
- **Affective:** How can the doctor address societal misconceptions about breast cancer and its impact on family dynamics?

****

Cultural Beliefs and Terminal Illness (Remote Village)

Setting: Makeshift clinic in a remote village

Patient: Elderly tribal leader, respected by the community, diagnosed with terminal lung cancer

Caregiver: Adult daughter, torn between modern medicine and traditional healing practices

The News: Despite some initial improvement, the cancer has progressed significantly, and there are limited treatment options left.

The Situation: The community leader has placed his faith in modern medicine but also seeks guidance from a local faith healer. When the doctor explains the limited treatment options, the daughter expresses her desire to return home and involve the faith healer in her father's care. The doctor anticipates resistance from the village if he pushes for aggressive medical interventions.

Psychiatrist Practice Pearl: Be respectful of cultural beliefs and acknowledge the importance of traditional healing practices for the community's emotional well-being.

Understanding the Patient's Perspective:

- **Cognitive:** How can the doctor discuss the limitations of modern medicine and explore the role of traditional healing practices in the patient's care plan, respecting his cultural beliefs?

Breaking the News:

- **Competence:** How can the doctor navigate the ethical dilemma of respecting patient autonomy while advocating for evidence-based treatment, especially when dealing with limited resources?

Handling Caregivers and Society:

- **Skills:** How can the doctor establish trust and collaborate with the local faith healer to ensure the patient receives holistic care that addresses both physical and spiritual needs?
- **Affective:** How can the doctor address the community's fear of death and anxieties surrounding the leader's illness?

****

AYUSH & Mental Health: What a Medical Professional Should Know

The Indian Complementary and Alternative Medicines healthcare system embraces a unique blend of traditional and modern medicine. AYUSH, an acronym for Ayurveda, Yoga & Naturopathy, Unani, Siddha and Homeopathy, represents a vast array of herbal remedies, supplements, and nutraceuticals that have found widespread use in the general public. While AYUSH offers a natural approach to healthcare, its increasing popularity in managing mental health conditions like anxiety, depression, and confusion necessitates a closer look at its potential risks and interactions. **The effectiveness of such systems is beyond the scope of this book and is not the primary intention too.** The **bottom-line fact is there is an increasing usage of the system of treatment.**

Some patients with mental health concerns may initially seek out AYUSH as a first-line treatment due to its natural approach. After a period of use, if without significant improvement, they might become disillusioned by the lack of instant relief and finally turn to a psychiatrist for conventional medical help. However, due to a perceived stigma or a desire for a more holistic approach, they may choose to conceal their AYUSH use from the psychiatrist, leading to the concerning possibility of taking both medications and supplements concurrently without proper oversight. The vice-versa is also a possibility.

In either of the above situation, one of the primary concerns surrounding the use of AYUSH in mental health is the possibility of drug-herb interactions. When a patient with a mental health condition seeks conventional psychiatric medication, they might unknowingly be consuming AYUSH remedies that could interfere with the prescribed drugs. This can lead to a number of complications, including reduced effectiveness of the medication, increased side effects, or even toxicity. For instance, St. John's Wort, a popular herbal supplement for depression, can interact with certain antidepressants, potentially leading to serotonin syndrome, a serious medical condition.

Furthermore, there is a risk of herb-herb interactions when multiple AYUSH remedies are consumed concurrently. Since these remedies are often complex mixtures of various herbs, their individual effects and interactions are not always fully understood. This lack of scientific rigor can lead to unpredictable and potentially harmful consequences.

Another significant concern is the potential for adverse reactions to AYUSH products. Just because something is natural doesn't necessarily mean it's safe. Certain herbs and drug formulations can cause allergic reactions, toxicity, or other unintended side effects. Additionally, the quality and standardization of AYUSH products can vary considerably, increasing the risk of consuming adulterated or contaminated remedies.

Given these potential risks, it is crucial for mental health professionals to take a comprehensive medication history from their patients. This history should not only include conventional pharmaceuticals but also encompass any complementary and alternative medicines (CAMs), supplements, and nutraceuticals the patient might be taking.

However, a thorough evaluation goes beyond just medication history. To ensure the safest and most effective course of treatment, mental health professionals should also conduct a **complete clinical examination of**

systems. This examination involves a detailed assessment of the patient's overall health, including their physical symptoms, medical history, and lifestyle habits. Additionally, **baseline parameter examinations, such as liver and renal function tests**, are crucial. These tests can reveal potential underlying health conditions that might influence medication choices or highlight red flags that warrant further investigation before starting any treatment, including AYUSH remedies or conventional medications.

Open communication is key to navigating the complexities of managing mental health with both traditional and modern approaches. With every visit, mental health professionals should reinforce the importance of disclosing all medications, including AYUSH remedies, supplements, and nutraceuticals. In some cases, it might be necessary to retake the medication history to ensure complete and up-to-date information.

While AYUSH offers a valuable addition to the healthcare landscape, its use in managing mental health conditions requires a measured and comprehensive approach. The potential for drug-herb interactions, herb-herb interactions, and adverse reactions necessitates a thorough clinical evaluation, including medication history, complete physical examination, and baseline parameter checks. Mental health professionals must emphasize the importance of disclosing all medications and supplements, and reinforce this with every patient interaction. By fostering open communication and prioritizing patient safety, one can hope to navigate the integration of traditional and modern medicine for optimal mental health outcomes.

Some common AYUSH herbal components that are used to treat mental illness

Herb Name (Latin)	**English Name**	***In Hindi***	***In Tamil***	**Conditions treated with**
Bacopa monniera	Brahmi, Waterhyssop, Indian Pennywort	*Brahmi*	*Vallarai*	Generalized anxiety disorder
Centella asiatica	Gotu Kola, Indian Pennywort	*Mandukparni*	*Vallarai*	• Generalized anxiety and stress, Generalized anxiety disorder
Citrus aurantium	Bitter Orange	*Khatta Narangi*	*Kathrikai Narthangai*	• Generalized anxiety disorder
Crocus sativus	Saffron	*Kesar*	*Kungumapoo*	• Major depressive disorder, Generalized anxiety disorder
Curcuma longa	Turmeric	*Haldi*	*Manjal*	• Major depressive disorder
Cuscuta spp.	Dodder	*Amarbel*	*Amudhavalli*	• Major depressive disorder
Hypericum perforatum	St. John's Wort	*Hansamanjari*		• Major depressive disorder, Social phobia, Obsessive-compulsive disorder, Attention deficit hyperactivity disorder, Dysthymia, Somatoform disorder, Seasonal affective

				disorder, Anxious depression
Galphimia glauca	Goldshower Bush	*Kanchan Phool*		• Generalized anxiety disorder
Ginkgo biloba	Ginkgo			• Generalized anxiety disorder, Seasonal affective disorder, Attention deficit hyperactivity disorder, Bipolar disorder
Lavandula spp.	Lavender			• Major depressive disorder
Matricaria recutita	Chamomile			• Generalized anxiety disorder
Melissa officinalis	Lemon Balm	*Nimbu Patti*	*Elumichchai*	• Generalized anxiety, stress, mood disturbance, Somatoform disorder
Nepeta spp.	Catnip			• Generalized anxiety disorder
Panax ginseng	Asian Ginseng			• Major depressive disorder, Generalized anxiety disorder
Panax quinquefolium	American Ginseng			• Schizophrenia, Attention deficit hyperactivity disorder
Passiflora incarnata	Passionflower	*Jangli Aam*		• Generalized anxiety disorder, Somatoform disorder
Petasites hybridus	Butterbur	*Banken*	*Adhathoda*	• Somatoform disorder
Pinus pinaster	Maritime Pine	*Samudri Saar*	*Kadal Cheppu*	• Attention deficit hyperactivity disorder
Piper methysticum	Kava			• Generalized anxiety disorder, Social phobia Anxious depression
Rhodiola rosea	Rhodiola	*Swarnabhanga*		• Major depressive disorder, Generalized anxiety disorder
Scutellaria lateriflora	Skullcap			• Generalized anxiety disorder
Silybum marianum	Milk Thistle	*Mariyathistul*		• Obsessive-compulsive disorder
Valeriana spp.	Valerian	*Tagar*		• Generalized anxiety disorder, Anxious depression, Somatoform disorder

Withania somnifera	Ashwagandha	*Ashwagandha*	*Ashwagandha*	• Schizophrenia, Bipolar disorder, Generalized anxiety disorder

Sarris, Jerome (2018). **Herbal medicines in the treatment of psychiatric disorders: 10-year updated review**. *Phytotherapy Research DOI*:10.1002/ptr.6055; Javed G, Anwar M, Siddiqui MA. **Perception of psychiatric disorders in the Unani system of medicine–a review**. European Journal of Integrative Medicine. 2009 Oct 1;1(3):149-54; Kumar N, Ashaq M. **Safety and Toxicity of Botanical Medicines: A critical Appraisal**. Int. J. All Res. Educ. Sci. Methods. 2021;9:2455-6211. Simkin DR, Arnold LE. **Complementary and Integrative Medicine/Functional Medicine in Child and Adolescent Psychiatric Disorders: Should It Be Taken Seriously?.** Child and Adolescent Psychiatric Clinics of North America. 2023 Apr 1;32(2):xiii-xiv; **For Toxicity refer to**: Philips CA, Ahamed R, Rajesh S, George T, Mohanan M, Augustine P. **Comprehensive review of hepatotoxicity associated with traditional Indian Ayurvedic herbs.** World J Hepatol. 2020 Sep 27;12(9):574-595. doi: 10.4254/wjh.v12.i9.574. PMID: 33033566; PMCID: PMC7522561.

****

2. Decoding Patient Communication with Case Scenarios

Heard. Seen. Healing.

During morning rounds on the female ward of a psychiatric hospital in Delhi, Dr. Sharma enters the room of Ms. Gupta, a 50-year-old patient with a history of schizophrenia. Ms. Gupta appears agitated and immediately launches into a complaint, "That new night nurse was so rude to me yesterday! She didn't listen to anything I said. Dr. Sharma replies "I apologize. I will speak to the nurse about what happened." **In your opinion, which communication aspect is Dr. Sharma MOST likely prioritizing in her initial response to Ms. Gupta?**

a) **Offering immediate discipline to the nurse**
b) **Dismissing Ms. Gupta's concerns**
c) **Validating Ms. Gupta's feelings**
d) **Providing justifications for the nurse's behaviour**
e) **Demanding specific details about the incident**

Explanation:

Choice A: This could damage staff morale and isn't the first step.
Choice B: Dismissing her concerns would be insensitive and unproductive.
Choice C (CORRECT): Validating her feelings shows empathy and encourages her to elaborate.
Choice D: Justifications wouldn't address Ms. Gupta's emotional state.
Choice E: While details might be important later, initial focus should be on her experience.

Specific Communication Aspects in Ward Rounds:

- **De-escalation:** Dr. Sharma avoids escalating the situation by maintaining a calm demeanour.
- **Active Listening:** Dr. Sharma pays attention to Ms. Gupta's verbal cues ("rude," "didn't listen") without interrupting.
- **Open Ended Questions:** A later question like, "Can you tell me more about what happened?" would encourage elaboration.

Pertinent Questions for OSCE Practice:

Cognition: How can symptoms of schizophrenia, such as paranoia or disorganization, affect a patient's perception of interactions with staff?

Symptoms like paranoia can lead patients to misinterpret neutral interactions as hostile or disrespectful.

Cognition: How can unresolved conflicts with staff contribute to a patient's overall mental health?

Unresolved conflicts can increase anxiety, feelings of isolation, and decrease trust in the treatment process.

Attitude: How can a healthcare professional demonstrate patience and understanding towards a patient who is frequently critical?

By acknowledging their frustrations, validating their feelings, and focusing on finding solutions to improve their experience.

Application: What are some strategies to improve communication between patients with schizophrenia and nursing staff?
Provide clear and concise instructions, avoid overly technical language, and allow ample time for questions and clarification.
Application: What are some ways to collaborate with the nursing staff to develop a communication plan to address a patient's history of complaints?
Work together to identify potential triggers for complaints, ensure clear communication practices, and offer opportunities for the patient to provide constructive feedback.

****

Chaos to Calm: How One Doctor Listens to Heal

During morning rounds on the adult male ward of a busy hospital in Chandigarh, Dr. Patel approaches a 30-year-old patient, Mr. Kapoor. Mr. Kapoor appears withdrawn and fidgety, clutching a worn notebook filled with detailed schedules. Dr. Patel greets him with a warm smile in Hindi, "Namaste, Mr. Kapoor. How are you doing this morning?" Mr. Kapoor hesitates before replying softly, "Namaste, doctor. I'm alright, but there's a lot going on here. It's difficult to follow my routine with all the activity and untidiness." Dr. Patel replies "“I am sorry. Please tell me what you experienced and let me know if you have any suggestions about how we can make it better.” **Which communication aspect is Dr. Patel primarily should be demonstrating in his response to Mr. Kapoor’s problem?**

- **a) Offering immediate solutions**
- **b) Sharing personal anecdotes**
- **c) Maintaining professional distance**
- **d) Validating his concerns**
- **e) Highlighting ward limitations**

Explanation:
Choice A: This might come later, but first understanding his needs is important.
Choice B: Sharing personal stories is not relevant here.
Choice C: Dr. Patel uses a warm greeting and avoids coldness.
Choice D: Validating his concerns about the busy, untidy environment shows empathy.[Correct]
Choice E: Highlighting limitations wouldn't address Mr. Kapoor's specific needs.

Specific Communication Aspects in Ward Rounds:

- **Cultural Sensitivity:** Dr. Patel uses the greeting "Namaste" acknowledging the cultural context.
- **Open Ended Questions:** "How are you doing?" invites Mr. Kapoor to elaborate on his experience later.
- **Active Listening:** Dr. Patel pays attention to Mr. Kapoor's nonverbal cues (fidgeting, hesitation) and verbal concerns ("difficult to follow my routine").

Pertinent Questions
Cognition: How can mental disorders manifest differently in patients from collectivistic cultures like India?
Patients from collectivistic cultures may express anxiety/depression more through somatic complaints or social withdrawal, rather than directly verbalizing their worries.

Cognition: How can a lack of routine contribute to anxiety symptoms?
Lack of routine can increase feelings of uncertainty and unpredictability in an OCD patient, which can worsen anxiety symptoms.

Attitude: How can a healthcare professional demonstrate respect for a patient's cultural beliefs and practices while also addressing mental health needs?
By actively listening to their concerns, exploring potential conflicts between cultural practices and treatment plans, and offering culturally sensitive treatment options.

Application: What are some strategies to create a more structured environment within a busy ward setting to benefit patients with anxiety disorders?
Develop predictable routines, provide designated quiet areas, offer relaxation techniques, and collaborate with staff to minimize unnecessary disruptions.
Application: What are some ways to collaborate with the nursing staff to create a therapeutic alliance with a patient who may be withdrawn or hesitant to communicate?
Approach the patient with patience and understanding, offer opportunities for communication (verbal and non-verbal), and involve them in decisions about their care plan as much as possible.

****

Blurred Lines: Doctor-Patient Dynamics

During morning rounds, Dr. Singh, a young female psychiatrist, is speaking with an 18-year-old male patient, Alex. As Dr. Singh reviews his chart, Alex leans in uncomfortably close and whispers, "You have really kind eyes, Dr. Singh." I**n your Opinion, Which of the following communication should Dr. Singh MOST likely prioritize in her response?**

a) **Offering compliments in return**
b) **Engaging in casual conversation**
c) **Maintaining professional boundaries**
d) **Humorously deflecting the comment**
e) **Demanding an explanation for his behaviour**

Explanation:
Choice A: Compliments would blur professional boundaries.
Choice B: Casual conversation wouldn't address the inappropriate behaviour.
Choice C (CORRECT): Maintaining boundaries is crucial to protect both patient and doctor.
Choice D: Humour might be misconstrued as flirting.
Choice E: While needing clarification later, the initial focus should be on boundaries.

Specific Communication Aspects in Ward Rounds:

- **Professional Boundaries:** Dr. Singh needs to address the comment directly to avoid any misinterpretations.
- **Clear Communication:** A firm but calm response is important to set clear expectations.
- **Redirection:** Dr. Singh can refocus the conversation on Alex's well-being.

Pertinent Questions for Ward Rounds:

Cognition: How can adolescents with mental health challenges struggle with understanding and maintaining appropriate boundaries?

Adolescents are still developing their sense of self and social cues. Mental health challenges can make it even harder to recognize and respect boundaries.

Cognition: How can romantic or sexual relationships between a healthcare professional and patient be harmful?

These relationships are a violation of trust, can exploit the patient's vulnerability, and jeopardize the patient's recovery.

Attitude: How can a healthcare professional remain respectful while firmly establishing professional boundaries with a patient who expresses romantic interest?

By acknowledging their feelings in a neutral way, clearly stating what is inappropriate behaviour, and remaining calm and professional. In addition, the illness behaviour should not be discounted in such situation – Conditions like mania can have these kind of symptomatology.

Application: What are some strategies to protect yourself and the patient from misunderstandings or accusations during patient interactions?

Maintain appropriate physical distance, conduct interviews in well-lit areas with the door open, and document all interactions thoroughly.

Application: What are some ways to address situations where a patient continues to make inappropriate comments or advances?

Inform them that the behaviour is unacceptable and will not be tolerated. If necessary, involve a supervisor or remove yourself from the situation and have a colleague interact with the patient.

****

Disagreements with another Physician in a Psychiatric Ward Round

During morning rounds in the adult female ward of a hospital in Mumbai, Dr. Krishnan approaches a 42-year-old patient, Mrs. Verma. Mrs. Verma has been admitted for treatment related to a recent cancer diagnosis. She has signs and symptoms of anxiety and depression, for which Dr. Krishnan, the Psychiatrist was called. Dr. Krishnan notices Mrs. Verma looks downcast and asks kindly, "How are you feeling today, Mrs. Verma?" Mrs. Verma sighs and replies, "Honestly, doctor, I'm feeling overwhelmed. On top of everything else, the oncologist I saw yesterday seemed very dismissive of my concerns." **In your opinion what should be Dr. Krishnan MOST likely replying in response to Mrs. Verma?**

- **a) Offering to directly confront the oncologist**
- **b) Minimizing the importance of Mrs. Verma's concerns**
- **c) Encouraging her to express her feelings**
- **d) Pressuring her to switch oncologists immediately**
- **e) Providing justifications for the oncologist's behaviour**

Explanation:

Choice A: Intervening directly might not be the best first step.

Choice B: Minimizing her concerns would be insensitive and unproductive.

Choice C (CORRECT): Encouraging her to express her feelings validates her experience.

Choice D: Pressuring a decision could be overwhelming.
Choice E: Justifications wouldn't address Mrs. Verma's emotional state.

Specific Communication Aspects in Ward Rounds:

- **Active Listening:** Dr. Krishnan pays attention to both Mrs. Verma's verbal cues ("overwhelmed," "dismissive") and nonverbal cues (sigh).
- **Empathy:** Dr. Krishnan acknowledges the burden Mrs. Verma is carrying by mentioning "everything else."
- **Open-Ended Questions:** "How are you feeling today?" invites Mrs. Verma to elaborate on her experience.

Pertinent Questions for OSCE Practice:

Cognition: How can anxiety and depression related to a cancer diagnosis affect a patient's communication with healthcare providers?

Anxiety and depression can make patients feel hesitant to speak up or assert themselves, potentially leading to misunderstandings or missed communication.

Cognition: How can unresolved conflicts with a physician contribute to a patient's stress and anxiety levels?

Unresolved conflicts can erode trust in the healthcare system, increase anxiety, and decrease treatment adherence.

Attitude: How can a healthcare professional demonstrate empathy and support towards a patient who is experiencing conflict with another physician?

By validating their feelings, actively listening to their concerns, and offering options for addressing the situation (e.g., mediation, communication tips).

Application: What are some strategies to improve communication and collaboration between different healthcares professionals involved in a patient's care?

Hold regular case conferences, encourage clear documentation and information sharing, and promote open communication among all team members.

Application: What are some ways to empower patients to advocate for themselves when they have concerns about their care?

Provide them with communication tips, encourage them to write down their questions beforehand, and offer to accompany them to appointments if needed.

****

When Tests Don't Tell All: A Doctor's Touch

Dr. Mehta enters a room in the ward to find Mr. Patel, a 40-year-old patient admitted for depression, pacing anxiously. Mr. Patel insists on having a CT scan, believing it will reveal a brain tumour causing his low mood. Dr. Mehta reviews the chart and sees no medical indication for the scan. He calmly approaches Mr. Patel. Dr. Mehta asks, "Tell me why you want the CT scan." **What is the primary communication aspect of this question?**

a) **Directing the conversation:** While this question guides the discussion, it's not the main focus.
b) **Challenging the patient's belief:** Dr. Mehta is not directly challenging Mr. Patel's belief yet.
c) **Building rapport:** By asking "why," Dr. Mehta shows interest in understanding Mr. Patel's perspective. (Correct)
d) **Providing medical information:** The focus is not on giving information here.

e) **Ending the conversation:** This question opens the conversation, not closes it.
Explanation: Dr. Mehta's question is a key example of **building rapport**. By asking "why," he shows Mr. Patel he's interested in understanding his concerns, fostering trust and a more productive conversation.

Additional Communication Aspects:

- **Non-verbal communication:** Dr. Mehta's calmness can de-escalate the situation.
- **Active listening:** Dr. Mehta will need to listen attentively to Mr. Patel's response.
- **Empathy:** Dr. Mehta should acknowledge Mr. Patel's anxiety and fear.
- **Shared decision-making:** Dr. Mehta can explain the risks and benefits of a CT scan and explore alternative solutions together.

Pertinent Questions:
Knowledge: What are some potential risks of unnecessary radiation exposure from CT scans?
Increased cancer risk, tissue damage

Attitude: How can a doctor balance patient autonomy with the ethical obligation to avoid unnecessary procedures?
Open communication, shared decision-making

Application: How might Dr. Mehta address Mr. Patel's fear of a brain tumour without resorting to an unnecessary CT scan?
Explain the low likelihood based on symptoms, offer a mental health assessment

Communication Skill: What is a good follow-up question after Dr. Mehta learns Mr. Patel's reasons for wanting the CT scan?
"What worries you most about a brain tumour?"

****

Unheard Fear

During morning rounds, Dr. Krishnan reviews the case of Mr. Sharma, a 35-year-old male who refuses a colonoscopy. Both his parents died of colon cancer before the age of 50. While the doctor explains the importance of screening, Mr. Sharma remains hesitant, stating he's heard the procedure is uncomfortable. Dr. Krishnan suspects a deeper concern. **Dr. Krishnan asks, "Tell me more about your concerns related to the procedure." What is the primary communication aspect of this question?**

a) **Minimizing the patient's fear:** Dr. Krishnan isn't trying to downplay her concerns.
b) **Discrediting outside information:** The focus isn't on the source of discomfort.
c) **Open-ended questioning:** This is the most effective way to explore Mr. Sharma's true feelings. (Correct)
d) **Providing reassurance:** While reassurance may come later, it's not the initial focus.
e) **Giving medical advice:** The goal here is to understand, not advice.

Explanation: Dr. Krishnan's question is an example of **open-ended questioning**. This technique encourages Mr. Sharma to elaborate on his fears and anxieties, allowing Dr. Krishnan to address the root cause of his refusal.

Additional Communication Aspects:

- **Non-verbal communication:** Dr. Krishnan should maintain eye contact and a warm demeanour.
- **Active listening:** Pay close attention to Mr. Sharma's verbal and nonverbal cues.

- **Empathy:** Acknowledge Mr. Sharma's family history and potential fear of cancer.
- **Shared decision-making:** Discuss the benefits of early detection and explore ways to manage discomfort during the procedure (e.g., sedation options).

Pertinent Questions:
Knowledge: What are the risk factors for colon cancer? (Age, family history, diet, lifestyle)

Attitude: How can doctors address patient anxiety related to medical procedures? (Open communication, education, offering choices)

Application: How might Dr. Krishnan address Mr. Sharma's fear of cancer in light of his family history? (Explain the benefits of early detection, offer genetic counselling)

Communication Skill: What is a good follow-up question after Dr. Krishnan hears Mr. Sharma's concerns? ("What would make you feel more comfortable about having a colonoscopy?")

Cultural Sensitivity: How might Dr. Krishnan adapt his communication if Mr. Sharma comes from a culture that emphasizes family decision-making? (Involve family members in the discussion, offer educational materials in their preferred language)

****

Balancing Religion and Medical Necessity

During ward rounds, Dr. Rao encounters Mrs. Gupta, a 68-year-old woman with a recently implanted pacemaker. Mrs. Gupta insists on having it removed, stating it interferes with her religious beliefs about purity. Dr. Rao understands the device is essential for her health. **Dr. Rao says, "Let's discuss ways that we can make the treatment more tolerable for you." What is the primary focus of Dr. Rao's communication here?**

a) **Dismissing religious beliefs:** Dr. Rao is not disregarding her beliefs.
b) **Pressuring for treatment:** The goal is to find a solution, not force compliance.
c) **Collaboration:** This response prioritizes working together to find a workable solution.
d) **Minimizing discomfort:** While comfort is important, it's not the sole focus.
e) **Explaining medical necessity:** Dr. Rao already understands this is necessary.

Explanation: Dr. Rao's statement reflects **collaboration**. He acknowledges Mrs. Gupta's discomfort while seeking a way to address it without compromising her health or religious beliefs.

Additional Communication Aspects:

- **Active listening:** Dr. Rao should listen attentively to understand Mrs. Gupta's specific concerns about the pacemaker and her religious beliefs.
- **Respect for beliefs:** Dr. Rao should validate Mrs. Gupta's religious perspective.
- **Empathy:** Acknowledge the emotional and physical discomfort Mrs. Gupta experiences.
- **Open-ended questioning:** Explore potential solutions with questions like, "Can you tell me more about what aspects of the pacemaker conflict with your beliefs?"

Pertinent Questions:
Knowledge: What are the ethical considerations when a patient's religious beliefs conflict with medical treatment? (Patient autonomy vs. beneficence, respecting beliefs while ensuring well-being)

Attitude: How can doctors balance patient autonomy with the ethical obligation to provide necessary care? (Open communication, collaboration, exploring alternatives)

Application: How might Dr. Rao involve a religious leader or chaplain in the discussion with Mrs. Gupta? (To facilitate understanding and explore religious accommodations)

Communication Skill: What is a good follow-up question after Dr. Rao hears Mrs. Gupta's concerns about the pacemaker? ("Is there anything we can adjust about the pacemaker placement or settings to make it less noticeable?")

Cultural Sensitivity: How might Dr. Rao adapt his communication style if Mrs. Gupta comes from a culture with a strong emphasis on family involvement in healthcare decisions? (Include family members and if feasible some religious person in the discussion, explain things in clear, concise terms)

****

Dietary Challenges in Diabetes Management

During ward rounds, Dr. Verma receives a report from a nurse about a 55-year-old diabetic patient, Mrs. Kapoor. The nurse observed Mrs. Kapoor adding sugar to her coffee despite dietary restrictions. Dr. Verma understands the importance of adherence but recognizes there might be underlying reasons for the behaviour. Dr. Verma politely asks Mrs. Kapoor, "Let's discuss your diet again." **What is Dr. Verma's primary focus in this communication?**

a) **Shaming the patient:** Dr. Verma avoids judgment and focuses on solutions.
b) **Simply repeating instructions:** This goes beyond basic instruction repetition.
c) **Collaborative problem-solving:** Dr. Verma aims to work with Mrs. Kapoor to find solutions.
d) **Providing a harsh reminder:** The approach is gentle and seeks understanding.
e) **Threatening consequences:** Dr. Verma avoids negativity and focuses on positive change.

Explanation: Dr. Verma's statement emphasizes **collaborative problem-solving**. He recognizes the need for further discussion to understand Mrs. Kapoor's challenges and explore ways to support her adherence.

Additional Communication Aspects:

- **Open-ended questioning:** Dr. Verma can ask, "Can you tell me why you felt the need to add sugar to your coffee?" to understand her cravings.
- **Empathy:** Acknowledge the difficulty of managing dietary restrictions, especially with a sweet tooth.
- **Motivational interviewing:** Encourage Mrs. Kapoor to identify her own goals and explore strategies for overcoming sugar cravings.
- **Education:** Discuss healthy alternatives to satisfy her sweet tooth and the long-term benefits of managing diabetes.

Pertinent Questions:

Knowledge: What are some common challenges patients with diabetes face in adhering to dietary restrictions? (Cravings, social pressures, emotional eating)

Attitude: How can healthcare professionals maintain a supportive and non-judgmental approach with non-compliant patients? (Empathy, motivational interviewing, focusing on collaboration)

Application: How might Dr. Verma explore alternative sweeteners or healthier snacks that Mrs. Kapoor might enjoy? (Discuss options, involve a dietician, and consider cultural preferences)

Communication Skill: What is a good follow-up question after Dr. Verma hears about Mrs. Kapoor's sugar cravings? ("What are some things you've tried in the past to manage your sweet tooth?")

Cultural Sensitivity: How might Dr. Verma adapt his communication if Mrs. Kapoor comes from a culture with strong family ties? (Involve family members in discussions, offer educational materials in their preferred language)

****

Addressing Misconceptions about Smoking

During ward rounds, Dr. Shah meets Mr. Patel, a patient with a nicotine dependence despite respiratory issues. Mr. Patel refuses to quit smoking many times in the past. Mr. Patel insists smoking calms him down and keeps him focused. Dr. Shah recognizes the need to address the health risks, but also the importance of understanding Mr. Patel's perspective. Dr. Shah asks, "Tell me more about how you feel about your cigarette smoking?" **What is the primary communication aspect of this question?**

a) **Giving medical advice:** Dr. Shah is prioritizing understanding, not immediate advice.
b) **Confronting the patient's belief:** The goal is to explore, not argue.
c) **Open-ended questioning:** This technique encourages Mr. Patel to elaborate on his beliefs.
d) **Expressing disapproval:** Dr. Shah avoids negativity and focuses on open communication.
e) **Minimizing the risks:** Dr. Shah will address the risks later, but first explores Mr. Patel's perspective.

Explanation: Dr. Shah's question is an example of **open-ended questioning**. This allows Mr. Patel to explain why he believes smoking benefits him, creating a foundation for Dr. Shah to address the misconception and explore alternative coping mechanisms.

Additional Communication Aspects:

- **Active listening:** Dr. Shah should pay close attention to Mr. Patel's verbal and nonverbal cues.
- **Empathy:** Acknowledge the stress Mr. Patel might be experiencing and the reasons he seeks relief in smoking.
- **Motivational interviewing:** Explore Mr. Patel's own motivations for potentially quitting smoking.
- **Education:** Once Mr. Patel is open to it, Dr. Shah can explain the health risks of smoking and offer smoking cessation resources.

Pertinent Questions:

Knowledge: What are the negative health consequences of smoking? (Increased risk of cancer, heart disease, lung disease)

Attitude: How can doctors address misconceptions patients may have about smoking and its supposed benefits? (Open communication, motivational interviewing, and providing accurate information)

Application: How might Dr. Shah suggest alternative stress management techniques to Mr. Patel? (Recommend relaxation exercises, deep breathing, and exploring support groups);

Application: How to measure nicotine dependence? (Fagerstrom test; Urinary cotine levels etc.,)

Application: What are the pharmacological treatment for nicotine cessation? (Bupropion, Vareniciline)

Communication Skill: What is a good follow-up question after Dr. Shah hears about Mr. Patel's belief that smoking calms him down? ("What situations typically make you feel stressed or overwhelmed?")

Cultural Sensitivity: How might Dr. Shah adapt his communication if Mr. Patel comes from a culture with a strong emphasis on social smoking? (Explore the social aspects of Mr. Patel's smoking habit, offer culturally appropriate cessation resources)

****

Addressing Body Image after Mastectomy

During ward rounds, Dr. Malhotra reviews the case of Ms. Mehta, a 28-year-old woman who recently underwent a mastectomy. Ms. Mehta expresses feelings of ugliness, particularly when undressing in front of her husband. Dr. Malhotra understands the potential impact on her intimacy but avoids immediate solutions. Dr. Malhotra asks, "Tell me about your relationship with your husband since the surgery." **What is the primary focus of Dr. Malhotra's question?**

a) **Blaming the husband:** Dr. Malhotra is not assigning blame, but exploring dynamics.
b) **Pressuring intimacy:** The focus is on understanding the emotional impact, not pressuring action.
c) **Exploring emotional impact:** This question delves into how Ms. Mehta's feelings affect her relationship.
d) **Providing medical information:** Dr. Malhotra will address this later, but first explores emotions.
e) **Minimizing her feelings:** Dr. Malhotra acknowledges her feelings and seeks to understand them.

Explanation: Dr. Malhotra's question focuses on **exploring the emotional impact**. By understanding how Ms. Mehta's feelings of ugliness affect her relationship, Dr. Malhotra can provide support and potentially explore solutions like couples therapy or support groups for mastectomy patients.

Additional Communication Aspects:

- **Non-verbal communication:** Dr. Malhotra should maintain eye contact and a warm demeanour. Preferably keep a female nurse of caregiver along during the discussion
- **Active listening:** Pay close attention to Ms. Mehta's verbal and nonverbal cues.
- **Empathy:** Acknowledge the emotional impact of the surgery and the challenges it may pose.
- **Validation:** Let Ms. Mehta know her feelings are common and valid.

Pertinent Questions:

Knowledge: What are the psychological challenges women may face after a mastectomy? (Body image issues, anxiety about intimacy, depression)

Attitude: How can healthcare professionals support patients facing body image changes after surgery? (Empathy, validation, offering resources like support groups)

Application: How might Dr. Malhotra explore ways to improve communication and intimacy between Ms. Mehta and her husband? (Suggest couples therapy, discuss resources for communication techniques)

Communication Skill: What is a good follow-up question after Dr. Malhotra hears about Ms. Mehta's relationship with her husband? ("Has there been any open communication with your husband about how you're feeling?")

Cultural Sensitivity: How might Dr. Malhotra adapt his communication if Ms. Mehta comes from a culture that avoids discussing intimacy openly? (Use respectful language, offer written resources on body image and intimacy after mastectomy)

Addressing Unvoiced Concerns in Hypertension Management

During ward rounds, Dr. Desai encounters Mr. Khan, a 54-year-old patient with hypertension. Mr. Khan repeatedly asks detailed questions about his condition and medications, but avoids mentioning any specific concerns. Dr. Desai suspects there might be more to the story and calls for a liaison psychiatrist. During the interaction, **t**he psychiatrist asks, "Tell me about the side affects you have been experiencing." **What is the primary focus of the psychiatrist's question?**

a) **Pressuring the patient for details:** The approach is gentle and open-ended.
b) **Making assumptions about the problem:** The goal is to understand, not assume.
c) **Creating a safe space for disclosure:** This question invites Mr. Khan to share his concerns openly.
d) **Providing reassurance:** While reassurance may come later, it's not the initial focus here.
e) **Minimizing the side effects:** The focus is on understanding the impact, not downplaying it.

Explanation: The psychiatrist's question aims to **create a safe space for disclosure**. By using open-ended language and focusing on side effects, the psychiatrist encourages Mr. Khan to share any concerns he might be hesitant to express directly, such as sexual dysfunction, a common side effect of some hypertension medications.

Additional Communication Aspects:

- **Non-verbal communication:** The psychiatrist should maintain eye contact and a warm, non-judgmental demeanor.
- **Active listening:** Pay close attention to Mr. Khan's verbal and nonverbal cues, even silences.
- **Empathy:** Acknowledge the challenges of managing a chronic illness and potential anxieties about side effects.
- **Normalization:** Let Mr. Khan know that side effects are common and there might be solutions.

Pertinent Questions:

Knowledge: What are some common, potentially embarrassing side effects of medications used to treat hypertension? (Sexual dysfunction, fatigue, dizziness)

Attitude: How can doctors encourage patients to openly discuss potentially embarrassing side effects of medications? (Empathy, creating a safe space, using open-ended questions)

Application: How might the psychiatrist explore alternative medications for Mr. Khan with fewer side effects, if appropriate? (Discuss options with Mr. Khan and his cardiologist, consider potential benefits and drawbacks)

Communication Skill: What is a good follow-up question after the psychiatrist hears about Mr. Khan's side effects? ("How have these side effects impacted your daily life?")

Cultural Sensitivity: How might the psychiatrist adapt their communication if Mr. Khan comes from a culture that emphasizes modesty? (Use respectful language, offer written information about side effects, and involve a trusted family member in the discussion)

****

Coping with Appearance-Related Stigma

During ward rounds, the medical team presents Mrs. Vani, a 45-year-old woman with a recent illness that caused noticeable skin lesions. Mrs. Vani expresses significant anxiety about her appearance and how others might react. Dr. Shiva, the psychiatrist, recognizes the need to equip Mrs. Vani with coping mechanisms. Dr. Shiva says, "Let's come up with something you can say to a person who has a reaction that bothers you." **What is the primary focus of Dr. Shiva's approach?**

a) **Ignoring other people's reactions:** While self-confidence is important, some reactions may require response.
b) **Confronting negative reactions:** The goal is to empower Mrs. Vani with a measured response.
c) **Empowerment through preparation:** This approach equips Mrs. Vani with a strategy to manage difficult situations.
d) **Providing medical information:** Education for others is important, but here the focus is on Mrs. Vani's coping.
e) **Minimizing the visibility of the lesions:** This might not be possible, and the focus is on emotional management.

Explanation: Dr. Shiva's approach centres on **empowerment through preparation**. By working with Mrs. Vani to develop a response to negative reactions, Dr. Shiva equips her with a sense of control and reduces her anxiety in such situations.

Additional Communication Aspects:

- **Validation:** Acknowledge Mrs. Vani's concerns about her appearance and the potential for social awkwardness.
- **Normalization:** Let Mrs. Vani know that negative reactions, while hurtful, are not uncommon.
- **Self-compassion:** Encourage Mrs. Vani to practice self-acceptance and focus on her inner strength.
- **Role-playing:** Rehearse potential conversations with Dr. Shiva to help Mrs. Vani feel prepared.

Pertinent Questions:

Knowledge: What are some psychological effects of chronic skin conditions like psoriasis or eczema? (Anxiety, depression, social isolation)

Attitude: How can healthcare professionals support patients struggling with the emotional impact of visible skin conditions? (Validation, empowerment, providing coping mechanisms)

Application: What are some examples of responses Mrs. Vani could practice with Dr. Shiva? ("I'm managing a health condition that caused these marks," or "Thank you for your concern, but I'm comfortable with my appearance")

Communication Skill: What is a good follow-up question after Dr. Shiva hears about Mrs. Vani's anxieties about social interactions? ("Imagine someone stares at you. What would you feel comfortable saying, if anything?")

Cultural Sensitivity: How might Dr. Shiva adapt their communication if Mrs. Vani comes from a culture that avoids direct confrontation? (Suggest polite but firm responses, offer to role-play with a cultural mediator)

****

Hope on Hold

During ward rounds, a 34-year-old HIV patient confides to the psychiatrist that he plans to end his life once discharged. In response, the psychiatrist calmly addresses the situation by saying, **"I would like you to remain in**

the hospital for a few more days." This immediate and supportive verbal response acknowledges the gravity of the patient's statement and emphasizes the importance of extended care. The psychiatrist's response primarily demonstrates:

a) **Empathy and understanding**
b) **Authoritative control**
c) **Sympathy and reassurance**
d) **Avoidance and dismissal**
e) **Humor and distraction**

The correct Answer is: a) **Empathy and understanding**: The psychiatrist's response is focused on empathizing with the patient's distress and understanding the seriousness of the situation. It prioritizes the patient's well-being by suggesting extended hospitalization. Option b) Authoritative control might seem plausible, but the emphasis here is on empathy rather than exerting authority. Options c), d), and e) are not suitable as they deviate from the compassionate and professional approach required in handling suicidal thoughts.

Additional Communication Aspects:

- **Empathy and active listening**: The psychiatrist demonstrates empathy by acknowledging the patient's emotions and actively listening to the concerns.
- **Supportive language**: The choice of words is crucial in conveying understanding and support, fostering a therapeutic alliance.
- **Collaboration**: By suggesting extended hospitalization rather than imposing it, the psychiatrist encourages collaboration and mutual decision-making.

Pertinent Questions:

What is the significance of expressing empathy when dealing with suicidal thoughts? (Empathy helps build trust and rapport, making the patient more likely to engage in treatment)
Why is it essential to use supportive language when addressing patients with suicidal ideation? (Supportive language promotes a therapeutic alliance and helps in establishing a safe and trusting environment)

How does collaboration play a role in managing patients expressing suicidal thoughts? (Collaboration empowers patients to actively participate in their treatment plan, fostering a sense of control and autonomy)

Discuss the importance of active listening in psychiatric care during ward rounds. (Active listening enhances understanding, enables accurate assessment, and demonstrates genuine concern for the patient's well-being)

When addressing a patient with suicidal thoughts, why is it crucial to consider collaborative decision-making over authoritative control? (Collaborative decision-making respects the patient's autonomy and contributes to a more patient-centered approach, enhancing treatment adherence)

****

Balancing Parental Choice and Open Communication

During ward rounds, Dr. Krishnan meets with a 9-year-old boy diagnosed with leukemia. The boy seems confused and asks Dr. Krishnan what's wrong with him. The parents, however, informed the doctor they prefer to keep the diagnosis confidential. Dr. Krishnan understands their desire to protect their son, but also recognizes the importance of age-appropriate communication. Dr. Krishnan asks, "What have your parents told you about your illness?" **What do you think is the primary purpose of this question?**

a) **Discrediting the parents' decision:** Dr. Krishnan respects the parents' choice while exploring communication.
b) **Pressuring the parents to share the diagnosis:** The focus is on understanding the current situation, not pressuring a change.
c) **Gently opening a dialogue with the child:** This question creates an opportunity to assess the child's understanding.
d) **Providing a medical explanation:** This will come later, depending on the situation.
e) **Shaming the parents:** Dr. Krishnan avoids judgment and focuses on the child's well-being.

Explanation: Dr. Krishnan's question aims to **gently open a dialogue with the child**. By understanding what the child already knows, Dr. Krishnan can determine the best course of action. He can address any anxieties the child might have and explore options for communication with the parents' permission.

Additional Communication Aspects:

- **Non-verbal communication:** Dr. Krishnan should maintain eye contact and a warm, reassuring demeanour.
- **Active listening:** Pay close attention to the child's verbal and nonverbal cues.
- **Age-appropriate language:** If the parents agree to share the diagnosis, Dr. Krishnan should explain it in a way the child can understand.
- **Empathy:** Acknowledge the child's fear and confusion, and offer support.
- **Confidentiality:** The parents of ill children decide what to tell the child about the illness. With the parents' permission ONLY, the doctor may present the information to the child in the most supportive and nonthreatening way possible giving hope and reassurances.

Pertinent Questions:

Knowledge: What are the ethical considerations of withholding a diagnosis from a child with the capacity to understand? (Autonomy vs. beneficence, considering the child's emotional well-being and right to information)

Attitude: How can doctors navigate situations where parents prefer not to disclose a diagnosis to their child? (Open communication, exploring the parents' concerns, offering support for open and honest communication)

Application: How might Dr. Krishnan approach the parents and discuss the potential benefits of age-appropriate disclosure, while respecting their wishes? (Explain the importance of honesty, offer support in having the conversation, emphasize shared decision-making)

Communication Skill: What is a good follow-up question after Dr. Krishnan hears what the child knows about his illness? ("Can you tell me a little bit about how you've been feeling lately?")

Cultural Sensitivity: How might Dr. Krishnan adapt his communication if the family comes from a culture with a strong emphasis on family decision-making? (Involve the parents in the discussion, explain the importance of open communication with the child in a culturally sensitive way)

****

Preparing a Child for a Minor Procedure

During ward rounds, Dr. Patel meets a young girl, Priya, who needs a minor procedure that might cause some discomfort. Priya seems nervous and apprehensive. Dr. Patel understands the importance of preparing Priya for the procedure in an age-appropriate way. Dr. Patel says, "This will feel like a bug bite and it will stop hurting after we count to five together." **What is the primary communication aspect of Dr. Patel's statement?**

a) **Providing a false reassurance:** While empathy is important, some discomfort is unavoidable.
b) **Using age-appropriate language:** This explanation uses a relatable comparison for a young child. (Correct)
c) **Giving a specific timeframe:** Counting to five provides a sense of control and a short duration.
d) **Focusing on the discomfort:** The focus is on minimizing anxiety, not dwelling on pain.
e) **Minimizing the procedure:** While honesty is important, some explanation is necessary.

Explanation: Dr. Patel's statement focuses on **using age-appropriate language**. By comparing the sensation to a bug bite, a common experience for children, Dr. Patel helps Priya understand the discomfort in a way that reduces fear. Counting to five provides a sense of control and a timeframe for the brief pain.

Additional Communication Aspects:

- **Non-verbal communication:** Dr. Patel should maintain eye contact and a calm, reassuring demeanour, communicate only in presence of parents or reliable caregiver of Priya.
- **Active listening:** Allow Priya to express her fears and answer her questions honestly.
- **Empathy:** Acknowledge Priya's nervousness and validate her feelings.
- **Offering choices:** If possible, offer Priya small choices, eg.-which arm to use for procedure, to empower her.

Pertinent Questions:

Knowledge: What are some effective communication strategies for reducing anxiety in children undergoing medical procedures? (Age-appropriate explanations, using calming language, offering choices, distraction techniques)

Attitude: How can doctors approach children with empathy and respect while ensuring they understand necessary procedures? (Active listening, validation, using play or storytelling to explain procedures)

Application: How might Dr. Patel involve Priya's parents in preparing her for the procedure? (Encourage parents to talk to Priya beforehand, answer her questions honestly, offer support and comfort)

Communication Skill: What is a good follow-up question after Dr. Patel explains the procedure to Priya? ("Is there anything you'd like to bring with you for the procedure, like a stuffed animal?")

Cultural Sensitivity: How might Dr. Patel adapt their communication if Priya comes from a culture with specific beliefs about illness and treatment? (Involve a cultural mediator or translator, acknowledge cultural beliefs, and tailor explanations to be respectful)

****

Supporting a Teen Mom - Exploring Options

During ward rounds, Dr. Sharma meets a 19-year-old girl whose husband ditched her, recently gave birth. The parents are pressuring their daughter to consider adoption, while the girl expresses a desire to raise the child. Dr. Sharma recognizes the complexity of the situation and avoids taking sides. Dr. Sharma says, "If you decide to keep the child, these are the things you can expect the child will need as he grows up." **What is the primary focus of Dr. Sharma's statement?**

a) **Pressuring the girl to keep the child:** Dr. Sharma remains neutral and presents options.
b) **Judgments about the parents' wishes:** The focus is on the girl's well-being and the child's needs.

c) **Providing information for informed decision-making:** Dr. Sharma empowers the girl with knowledge. (Correct)
d) **Advocating for adoption:** While adoption is an option, Dr. Sharma presents a balanced view.
e) **Shaming the parents:** Dr. Sharma focuses on supporting both the girl and her parents.

Explanation: Dr. Sharma's statement emphasizes **providing information for informed decision-making**. By outlining the responsibilities and needs of raising a child, Dr. Sharma equips the girl to make a thoughtful choice, considering the challenges and realities of parenthood at a young age.

Additional Communication Aspects:

- **Non-verbal communication:** Dr. Sharma should maintain eye contact and a supportive demeanour.
- **Active listening:** Pay close attention to the girl's verbal and nonverbal cues.
- **Empathy:** Acknowledge the emotional weight of the situation for both the girl and her parents.
- **Offering support:** Provide the girl with resources like social workers or support groups for teen mothers.

Pertinent Questions:

- **Knowledge: What are the social and psychological challenges faced by teen mothers?** (Social stigma, isolation, financial difficulties, emotional stress)
- **Attitude: How can healthcare professionals maintain a neutral and supportive approach when a family presents with conflicting desires?** (Active listening, empathy, focusing on the well-being of both mother and child)
- **Application: How might Dr. Sharma explore the girl's support system and resources available to her if she decides to keep the child?** (Discuss family support, childcare options, educational and financial resources)
- **Communication Skill: What is a good follow-up question after Dr. Sharma explains the needs of a child?** ("Have you thought about how you might manage school and childcare?")
- **Cultural Sensitivity: How might Dr. Sharma adapt their communication if the family comes from a culture with strong family ties?** (Involve extended family members in the discussion, explore cultural expectations of parenthood)

****

Discussing Sterilization Options for Couples

During ward rounds, Dr. Rao meets a couple seeking information about sterilization for birth control. They are unsure whether a tubal ligation (female sterilization) or a vasectomy (male sterilization) would be a better option for them. Dr. Rao understands the importance of informed decision-making. Dr. Rao says, "Here are the pros and cons of each procedure; think about them and let me know what you decide." **What is the key aspect of Dr. Rao's communication?**

- **Pressuring a decision:** Dr. Rao empowers the couple to make an informed choice on their own.
- **Not favouring one procedure over the other:** Dr. Rao presents a neutral and objective overview. (Correct)
- **Choosing the procedure for patients:** Dr. Rao avoids making medical decisions for patients.
- **Dictating which partner gets sterilized:** The couple has autonomy to decide who undergoes the procedure.
- **Minimizing the risks of either procedure:** Dr. Rao will discuss risks but also provide benefits.

Explanation: Dr. Rao's approach focuses on **presenting a neutral and objective overview**. By outlining the pros and cons of both tubal ligation and vasectomy, Dr. Rao empowers the couple to weigh the options and make a well-informed decision based on their specific circumstances and preferences.

Additional Communication Aspects:
- **Active listening:** Encourage the couple to ask questions and address any concerns they might have.
- **Clarity and understanding:** Ensure the couple understands the medical terminology and procedures clearly.
- **Reversibility:** Discuss the (limited) reversibility options for both procedures.
- **Recovery time:** Explain the typical recovery times for each procedure.

Pertinent Questions:
Knowledge: What are the medical considerations for tubal ligation and vasectomy? (Success rates, risks, recovery times, reversibility)

Attitude: How can doctors ensure couples considering sterilization have all the information they need to make an informed decision? (Open communication, neutral presentation of options, addressing individual concerns)

Application: How might Dr. Rao explore the couple's reasons for choosing sterilization and their individual preferences? (Discuss family planning goals, recovery considerations, long-term effectiveness)

Communication Skill: What is a good follow-up question after Dr. Rao outlines the procedures? ("Do you have any questions about the risks or recovery process for either procedure?")

Cultural Sensitivity: How might Dr. Rao adapt their communication if the couple comes from a culture with specific family planning expectations? (Acknowledge cultural beliefs, explore their family planning goals within a respectful context)

****

Facilitating Difficult Family Discussion - Unplanned Pregnancy

During ward rounds, Dr. Mehta encounters a complex situation. A 19-year-old woman with intellectual disability is pregnant. Her parents, concerned about her ability to care for a child, wish to pursue termination. However, the young woman expresses a desire to keep the baby, who has been diagnosed with Down syndrome. Dr. Mehta recognizes the need for open communication and avoids taking sides. MCQ: Dr. Mehta says, "Let's all discuss the possible options." **What is the primary purpose of Dr. Mehta's statement?**

a) **Pressuring the parents to accept the pregnancy:** Dr. Mehta facilitates a discussion for all parties involved.
b) **Pressuring the woman to consider abortion:** The goal is to explore options while respecting patient autonomy.
c) **Facilitating open communication:** This approach allows everyone to voice their concerns. (Correct)
d) **Recommending adoption:** Adoption might be an option, but Dr. Mehta avoids dictating choices.
e) **Focusing on the Down syndrome diagnosis:** The focus is on the woman's pregnancy and family dynamics. The fact that the baby has Down syndrome is irrelevant.

Explanation: Dr. Mehta's statement aims to **facilitate open communication**. By creating a safe space for discussion, Dr. Mehta allows the woman and her parents to express their feelings and explore all options, including parenting support resources, adoption, or continuing the pregnancy.

Additional Communication Aspects:

- **Non-verbal communication:** Dr. Mehta should maintain eye contact with all parties and a neutral demeanour. The doctor should communicate in presence of at least one another person, preferably a female.
- **Active listening:** Pay close attention to everyone's verbal and nonverbal cues.
- **Empathy:** Acknowledge the emotional weight of the situation for all involved.
- **Advocacy:** Ensure the woman with the intellectual disability has appropriate support for informed decision-making.

Pertinent Questions:

Knowledge: What are some ethical considerations surrounding pregnancy termination for women with intellectual disabilities? (Autonomy, informed consent, ensuring access to support and information)

Attitude: How can healthcare professionals facilitate open communication within families facing a complex pregnancy decision? (Empathy, creating a safe space, ensuring all voices are heard)

Application: How might Dr. Mehta explore the woman's understanding of pregnancy and potential challenges of parenthood? (Use simple language, consider involving a social worker or disability advocate, and assess her support system)

Communication Skill: What is a good follow-up question after Dr. Mehta suggests a discussion? ("Would each of you like to share your thoughts and feelings about this situation?")

Cultural Sensitivity: How might Dr. Mehta adapt their communication if the family comes from a culture with strong family decision-making structures? (Involve a cultural mediator, respect cultural beliefs while advocating for the woman's right to participate in the decision)

****

Respecting Autonomy and Beliefs - Abortion Request

During ward rounds, Dr. Kapoor encounters a 25-year-old woman requesting a first-trimester abortion. Dr. Kapoor has strong religious and moral beliefs against abortion. However, he understands his ethical obligation to respect patient autonomy. Dr. Kapoor says, "I do not perform abortions, but I will refer you to a doctor who does." **What is the key aspect of Dr. Kapoor's communication?**

a) **Pressuring the patient to continue the pregnancy:** Dr. Kapoor respects the patient's right to choose.
b) **Imposing his personal beliefs:** He avoids judgment and focuses on providing options.
c) **Recommending a specific doctor:** While providing a referral is helpful, it's best to offer a list of options.
d) **Expressing disapproval of the patient's decision:** Dr. Kapoor maintains a neutral and respectful tone.
e) **Shaming the patient for her decision:** Dr. Kapoor avoids judgment and focuses on patient care.

Explanation: Choice C. Dr. Kapoor's response emphasizes **respecting patient autonomy**. He acknowledges his own beliefs but prioritizes the woman's right to make her own informed decision. By offering a referral, he fulfils his professional duty to provide access to healthcare, even when it conflicts with his personal beliefs.

Additional Communication Aspects:

- **Non-verbal communication:** Dr. Kapoor should maintain eye contact and a professional demeanour.
- **Empathy:** Briefly acknowledge the sensitivity of the situation without judgment.

- **Information provision:** Offer resources and information on abortion services, even if he doesn't perform them himself.

Pertinent Questions:
Knowledge: What are the ethical considerations for doctors who have personal beliefs against procedures like abortion, but also have a duty to provide patient care? (Balancing personal beliefs with professional obligations, respecting patient autonomy)

Attitude: How can doctors maintain a professional and respectful demeanour when a patient's request conflicts with their personal beliefs? (Empathy, non-judgmental communication, focusing on patient well-being)

Application: How might Dr. Kapoor explore the woman's reasons for seeking an abortion to ensure informed decision-making, without pressuring his own views? (Actively listen to her concerns, ask open-ended questions, and provide resources on all pregnancy options)

Communication Skill: What is a good follow-up question after Dr. Kapoor offers a referral? ("Is there anything else I can do to help you with this decision?")

Cultural Sensitivity: How might Dr. Kapoor adapt his communication if the patient comes from a culture with strong religious or social views on abortion? (Acknowledge cultural beliefs, avoid imposing his own views, offer culturally sensitive resources and support)

****

Hard Choices and Foods laced with Anti-psychotic medication

In a Psychiatry outpatient department, the consultant psychiatrist encounters a family grappling with the challenge of managing medication for their son, who is diagnosed with schizophrenia. The patient vehemently refuses to acknowledge his illness, leaving the family in a quandary. Faced with limited mental health resources and the stigma associated with psychiatric hospitalization, the family resorts to covert medication, mixing anti-psychotic medication into the patient's food without his knowledge. In this scenario, answer the appropriate choice for the questions listed

1. **The ethical dilemma faced by the psychiatrist primarily involves:**
   a. Upholding patient autonomy versus ensuring prompt treatment
   b. Balancing familial concerns with legal and ethical obligations
   c. Ensuring patient safety versus respecting familial decisions
   d. Navigating cultural norms versus adhering to professional standards
   e. Addressing resource constraints versus prioritizing patient well-being
2. **The primary ethical concern raised by covert medication in this scenario is**:
   a. Violation of patient autonomy
   b. Lack of informed consent
   c. Compromising treatment efficacy
   d. Family's decision-making authority
   e. Resource allocation in mental healthcare

The psychiatrist's response to the father's inquiry about covert medication reflects:

a) Cultural sensitivity and understanding

b) Empathy and compassion towards the family's dilemma
c) Professional integrity and ethical standards
d) Advocacy for patient rights and safety
e) Collaborative decision-making with the family

3. **The father's decision to continue covert medication despite the psychiatrist's advice primarily demonstrates:**
    a) Lack of awareness about ethical implications
    b) Cultural norms influencing healthcare decisions
    c) Trust in the psychiatrist's expertise
    d) Familial desperation for effective treatment
    e) Disregard for patient autonomy
4. **The eventual breakdown of the family dynamic due to covert medication highlights the:**
    a) Impact of cultural stigma on mental illness
    b) Importance of patient-centered care in psychiatry
    c) Ethical complexities in mental healthcare delivery
    d) Need for legislative reforms in mental health policy
    e) Role of communication barriers in treatment outcomes
5. **The psychiatrist's role in addressing covert medication practices encompasses:**
    a) Balancing ethical principles with practical constraints
    b) Collaborating with families to explore alternative treatments
    c) Navigating legal ambiguities in mental health care
    d) Promoting community awareness on mental health issues
    e) Advocating for patient rights and autonomy
6. **According to the Mental Health Care Act, involuntary admission to a psychiatric hospital is permitted if:**
    a) The patient refuses to comply with treatment recommendations
    b) The patient's family requests admission due to the severity of symptoms
    c) The patient demonstrates impaired decision-making capacity
    d) The patient's condition poses a risk to their own health and safety
7. **In cases of covert medication, mental health professionals are ethically obligated to:**
    a) Respect the family's decision and support their chosen course of action
    b) Ensure the patient is informed of the medication administration method
    c) Document the covert medication practice in the patient's medical records
    d) Seek informed consent from the patient prior to covert medication
    e) Notify relevant authorities about the covert medication practice
8. **Which of the following principles of the Mental Health Care Act is directly relevant to the use of covert medication?**
    a) Right to access mental healthcare without discrimination
    b) Right to confidentiality and privacy of mental health information
    c) Right to appropriate medical treatment and healthcare
    d) Right to live in a community and be part of it
    e) Right to protection from cruel, inhuman, and degrading treatment
9. **Under the Mental Health Care Act, mental health professionals must prioritize:**
    a) Respecting patient autonomy and decision-making capacity
    b) Facilitating family involvement in treatment decisions

c) Implementing coercive measures to ensure treatment compliance
d) Protecting patients from harm through involuntary hospitalization
e) Minimizing the stigma associated with mental illness through covert treatment options

Answers:

1. The correct choice is A. Upholding patient autonomy versus ensuring prompt treatment. The core ethical issue revolves around the conflict between respecting the patient's autonomy and ensuring timely treatment for his mental illness. Covert medication raises concerns about breaching the patient's autonomy while potentially improving his quality of life by managing symptoms.
2. The correct choice is A. Violation of patient autonomy is correct answer. Explanation: Covert medication involves administering medication without the patient's knowledge or consent, thereby undermining the fundamental principle of patient autonomy.
3. The Correct Answer is D. But at the same time, should reflect the professional integrity and ethical standards. The psychiatrist should maintains professional integrity and emphasizing the importance of obtaining the patient's informed consent. In case, if there only is a vehement rejection of drug intake or poor insight of the patient, covert medication is the only choice ahead. The risk of the same would rest with the family/primary caregivers.
4. The Correct Answer is D) Familial desperation for effective treatment. The father's persistence in covert medication reflects the family's desperation to alleviate the patient's symptoms and improve his quality of life, despite ethical concerns.
5. The correct Answer is C. Ethical complexities in mental healthcare delivery. The family's reliance on covert medication leads to adverse consequences, underscoring the ethical dilemmas inherent in managing mental health conditions within familial and cultural contexts.
6. The Correct Answer is: e) advocating for patient rights and autonomy. The psychiatrist's ethical responsibility involves advocating for patient autonomy and ensuring that treatment decisions respect the patient's rights and preferences.
7. The correct Answer is: d) the patient's condition poses a risk to their own health and safety. The Mental Health Care Act permits involuntary admission to a psychiatric hospital when the patient's condition poses a risk to their own health and safety.
8. The Correct Answer is: b) in normal conditions, ensure the patient is informed of the medication administration method. In normal situations, mental health professionals must prioritize transparency and informed consent by ensuring that patients are informed of covert medication practices and their implications for treatment. But in extra-ordinary situation, vehement rejection of drug intake or poor insight of the patient, treatment procedure and ethics may change.
9. The Correct Answer is c) Right to appropriate medical treatment and healthcare. The principle of the right to appropriate medical treatment and healthcare encompasses ensuring that patients receive necessary treatment interventions, including covert medication if deemed clinically necessary and legally authorized
10. The correct Answer is a) Respecting patient autonomy and decision-making capacity. The Mental Health Care Act emphasizes the importance of respecting patient autonomy and decision-making capacity in all aspects of mental health treatment, including medication administration. **This is one grey zone in covert medication**.

Communication Aspects:

1. **Ethical sensitivity:** The psychiatrist demonstrates awareness of the ethical implications of covert medication and engages in ethical deliberation.
2. **Cultural competence:** Understanding cultural norms and familial dynamics is essential in addressing complex treatment decisions.

3. **Collaborative decision-making:** The case highlights the need for collaboration between the psychiatrist, patient, and family to navigate treatment options sensitively.

Pertinent Questions:

Discuss the ethical considerations involved in covert medication for patients with mental illness, particularly concerning patient autonomy and treatment adherence.

Covert medication poses challenges to patient autonomy while potentially improving treatment adherence. Ethical dilemmas arise in balancing these concerns to ensure the patient's well-being.

How might cultural factors influence the decision-making process regarding covert medication in families of patients with mental illness?

Cultural norms, familial dynamics, and societal perceptions of mental illness can significantly impact the acceptance and implementation of covert medication practices.

What are the potential risks and benefits of covert medication in managing mental illness, considering the implications for patient safety and treatment efficacy?

Covert medication may alleviate symptoms and prevent the need for involuntary hospitalization but raises concerns about medication safety, treatment monitoring, and patient autonomy.

How can psychiatrists navigate the tension between respecting patient autonomy and ensuring timely treatment in cases of covert medication?

Psychiatrists must engage in open dialogue with patients and families, respecting their perspectives while advocating for ethical and legal principles governing mental health care.

Discuss the role of mental health policies and regulations in addressing the challenges associated with covert medication and ensuring patient rights and safety.

Mental health policies should provide clear guidance on covert medication practices, balancing patient autonomy with the imperative of prompt and effective treatment, while safeguarding against potential misuse and harm.

Self-help Questions

- How can mental health professionals navigate the tension between promoting treatment adherence and respecting patient autonomy in cases of covert medication?
- What communication strategies can mental health professionals employ to engage families in open dialogue about treatment options while addressing concerns about covert medication?
- Discuss the potential consequences of covert medication on the therapeutic alliance between mental health professionals, patients, and families.
- How might cultural beliefs and norms influence attitudes towards covert medication, and how can mental health professionals address cultural factors sensitively in treatment decision-making?
- Reflect on the ethical implications of covert medication in terms of balancing beneficence, non-maleficence, autonomy, and justice. How can mental health professionals uphold ethical principles while providing compassionate care to patients and families facing complex treatment decisions?

****

Shy Bladder Syndrome

In a psychiatric OPD, a 28-year-old male patient presents with symptoms of paruresis, commonly known as Shy Bladder Syndrome (SBS). He describes significant distress and impairment in social and occupational functioning due to the inability to urinate in public restrooms or in the presence of others. The patient expresses feelings of embarrassment and shame associated with his condition.

Answer these questions

1. **The primary cognitive factor contributing to SBS is:**
   a) Attentional bias towards negative stimuli
   b) Deficits in executive functioning
   c) Cognitive distortions related to body image
   d) Impaired memory retrieval processes
   e) Heightened sensitivity to social cues
2. **The psychiatrist's attitude towards the patient's condition should prioritize:**
   a) Pathologizing the symptoms to justify medical intervention
   b) Normalizing the experience and reducing stigma
   c) Encouraging avoidance behaviours to alleviate discomfort
   d) Emphasizing the patient's responsibility to overcome the problem
   e) Minimizing the impact of social anxiety on daily functioning
3. **Effective communication strategies for addressing SBS include:**
   a) Encouraging exposure therapy to desensitize the patient to social situations
   b) Offering reassurance and validation of the patient's experiences
   c) Criticizing the patient for their avoidance behaviours
   d) Minimizing the significance of the symptoms to motivate behavioural change
   e) Ignoring the patient's concerns to avoid reinforcing avoidance behaviours

Answers

1. The Correct Answer is: e) Heightened sensitivity to social cues. Individuals with SBS often experience heightened sensitivity to social cues, leading to difficulty initiating urination in public settings where they perceive social scrutiny or judgment.
2. The Correct Answer is b) Normalizing the experience and reducing stigma. A non-judgmental and empathetic attitude towards the patient's condition can help reduce stigma and empower the individual to seek appropriate treatment and support.
3. The Correct Answer is: b) Offering reassurance and validation of the patient's experiences. Validation and empathy are essential communication strategies for building rapport and trust with patients experiencing Shy Bladder Syndrome, facilitating treatment engagement and progress.

What cognitive processes contribute to the development and maintenance of SBS, and how can cognitive-behavioural interventions address these factors?

Cognitive processes such as heightened social sensitivity, negative self-evaluation, and fear of evaluation by others contribute to the development and maintenance of SBS. Cognitive-behavioural interventions aim to address these factors through techniques such as cognitive restructuring, exposure therapy, and relaxation training. By challenging irrational beliefs and reducing anxiety-related cognitive biases, individuals can gradually overcome their avoidance behaviours and improve bladder control in social settings.

Discuss the impact of societal attitudes and cultural norms on individuals with SBS, and how mental health professionals can promote understanding and acceptance.

Societal attitudes and cultural norms that stigmatize discussions about bodily functions or impose unrealistic expectations regarding social behaviour can exacerbate the distress experienced by individuals with SBS. Mental health professionals play a crucial role in promoting understanding and acceptance by raising awareness, providing education, and advocating for destigmatization of the condition. By fostering empathy and creating supportive environments, professionals can help individuals feel validated and empowered to seek help.

How can mental health professionals effectively assess and diagnose SBS, considering the subjective nature of the symptoms and potential comorbidities?

Effective assessment and diagnosis of SBS require a comprehensive evaluation that considers both subjective symptoms and potential comorbidities such as social anxiety disorder or obsessive-compulsive disorder. Mental health professionals can use structured interviews, self-report measures, and behavioural observations to assess the severity and impact of symptoms on daily functioning. Collaborative assessment with urologists may also be necessary to rule out underlying medical conditions.

Reflect on the ethical considerations in providing treatment for SBS, particularly regarding patient confidentiality, autonomy, and informed consent.

Ethical considerations in treating SBS include respecting patient confidentiality, autonomy, and informed consent. Mental health professionals must ensure that patients' privacy is protected and that treatment decisions are made collaboratively, with full understanding and consent from the patient. Additionally, professionals should prioritize patient autonomy and respect their right to refuse or discontinue treatment at any time.

Describe the role of multidisciplinary collaboration in managing SBS, incorporating interventions from psychology, psychiatry, and urology to optimize patient outcomes.

Multidisciplinary collaboration is essential in managing SBS, as it allows for a comprehensive approach that addresses both psychological and physiological aspects of the condition. Psychiatrists and psychologists can provide psychopharmacological interventions and cognitive-behavioural therapy to address anxiety and avoidance behaviours, while urologists can offer medical interventions and bladder training techniques to improve urinary function. By working together, professionals can tailor treatment plans to individual patient needs and achieve optimal outcomes.

****

From Silence to Sensuality: A Woman's Journey

In a psychiatry clinic, a 25-year-old Indian woman presents with concerns about difficulties in consummating her marriage and establishing a healthy sexual relationship with her husband. She describes feelings of anxiety, shame, and inadequacy related to her conservative upbringing in a patriarchal family environment, where discussions about sexuality were taboo and female sexuality was often stigmatized.

1. **The primary cognitive factor contributing to the woman's difficulties with consummation is:**
    a) Negative self-schema related to body image
    b) Lack of knowledge about sexual anatomy and physiology
    c) Anxiety and fear of judgment or rejection

   d) Unrealistic expectations about sexual performance
   e) Cultural beliefs regarding female sexuality

2. **The psychiatrist's attitude towards the woman's concerns should prioritize:**
   a) Normalizing the experience and reducing stigma
   b) Promoting traditional gender roles and marital expectations
   c) Encouraging avoidance behaviours to alleviate discomfort
   d) Minimizing the significance of sexual intimacy in marriage
   e) Criticizing the woman for her conservative upbringing
3. **Effective communication strategies for addressing the woman's difficulties with consummation include:**
   a) Encouraging avoidance of sexual activities until she feels more comfortable
   b) Offering reassurance and validation of her feelings and experiences
   c) Criticizing the woman for her lack of sexual knowledge or experience
   d) Minimizing the importance of sexual intimacy in marital relationships
   e) Ignoring the woman's concerns to avoid reinforcing anxiety

Answers:

1. The Correct Answer is: c) Anxiety and fear of judgment or rejection. The woman's difficulties with consummation likely stem from anxiety and fear related to societal expectations, cultural beliefs, and the anticipation of judgment or rejection from her husband.
2. The Correct Answer: a) Normalizing the experience and reducing stigma. A supportive and non-judgmental attitude towards the woman's concerns can help reduce stigma and empower her to explore healthy communication and intimacy within her marriage.
3. The Correct Answer is b) Offering reassurance and validation of her feelings and experiences. Reassurance and validation are essential communication strategies for building trust and rapport with the woman, facilitating open dialogue about her concerns and experiences.

Additional Questions:

What cultural beliefs and societal attitudes may contribute to the woman's difficulties with consummation, and how can mental health professionals address these factors sensitively?

Cultural beliefs and societal attitudes that stigmatize discussions about female sexuality or impose unrealistic expectations on women's sexual behaviour can exacerbate the woman's feelings of anxiety and shame. Mental health professionals can promote understanding and acceptance by providing psychoeducation, challenging harmful stereotypes, and creating safe spaces for open dialogue about sexuality.

How can mental health professionals assess and address the woman's anxiety and fear related to sexual intimacy within the context of her conservative upbringing?

Mental health professionals can conduct a thorough assessment of the woman's anxiety symptoms and explore the underlying factors contributing to her fear of sexual intimacy. Cognitive-behavioural interventions, relaxation techniques, and couple's therapy may be beneficial in addressing anxiety and enhancing communication and intimacy within the marriage.

Discuss the ethical considerations in providing treatment for the woman's difficulties with consummation.

Ethical considerations in treating the woman's difficulties with consummation include respecting patient confidentiality, autonomy, and informed consent. Mental health professionals must ensure that the woman feels safe and supported in discussing sensitive issues related to her sexual health and marital relationship, while also respecting her right to make informed decisions about her treatment.

Describe the role of cultural competence in mental health professionals' approach to addressing the woman's concerns about consummation and healthy married life.
Cultural competence is essential in understanding the woman's cultural background, values, and beliefs related to sexuality and marriage. Mental health professionals should approach the woman's concerns with sensitivity and respect for her cultural context, while also challenging harmful cultural norms that may perpetuate stigma or inhibit open communication about sexual health.

How can mental health professionals collaborate with other healthcare providers, such as gynaecologists or sex therapists, to provide comprehensive care for the woman's difficulties with consummation and marital intimacy?
Collaborative care involving mental health professionals, gynaecologists, and sex therapists can provide the woman with a holistic approach to addressing her concerns about consummation and marital intimacy. By working together, healthcare providers can tailor treatment plans to the woman's individual needs and promote her overall well-being and sexual health.

****

Spiritual Trance

Meena, a 35-year-old woman, is illiterate but active member of her small rural community. She is extremely devoted to her village deity, which is much revered by her tribe, a marginalized small community. The males in her family are alcohol addicts suffering from health issues and poverty. She too, has been diagnosed with depression and anxiety. She had medications when there was access to it by the devoted ASHA health care worker, who unfortunately was transferred. There was no replacement hence she did not bother to get consulted with District Mental Health Authority, who would provide treatment to her. The extended community gather annually to celebrate a festival dedicated to their presiding deity. During this festival, Meena immerses herself in organizing the spiritual rituals and ceremonies. In course of the ceremony, she goes into state of trance and spiritual ecstasy during which she criticizes and threatens over the wrongs done by her male family members of the community.

Answer the following from the choices.

1. **Which of the following best describes the cultural significance of dancing in trance during spiritual rituals in India?**
   a) A form of entertainment to pass time during festivals
   b) An expression of religious devotion and connection to the divine
   c) A means of socializing and bonding within the community
   d) A way to showcase traditional dance forms to outsiders

2. **What role does traditional dance play in facilitating spiritual experiences during the festival?**
   a) It provides entertainment for the villagers
   b) It promotes physical fitness and agility among participants
   c) It induces a state of trance and spiritual ecstasy

d) It serves as a competition between different communities

3. How might Meena's participation in the festival rituals impact her mental health?
a) It may exacerbate her depression and anxiety due to social pressures
b) It could provide her with a sense of belonging and spiritual fulfilment
c) It would have no effect on her mental health
d) It may lead to isolation and withdrawal from the community

Answers

1. Answer: b) An expression of religious devotion and connection to the divine
2. Answer: c) It induces a state of trance and spiritual ecstasy
3. Answer: b) It could provide her with a sense of belonging and spiritual fulfilment

Questions with Answers:

How does the cultural context of India influence the perception of spiritual trance and dance within communities?

In India, spiritual trance and dance are deeply ingrained in traditional belief systems and cultural practices. For marginalized communities, these rituals serve as a source of identity, community cohesion, and spiritual solace amidst socio-economic challenges. Participation in such rituals is often seen as a means of connecting with ancestral traditions and seeking divine blessings for prosperity and well-being.

What are some potential mental health benefits and risks associated with engaging in spiritual trance and dance?

Engaging in spiritual trance and dance can offer individuals a sense of belonging, purpose, and transcendence, thereby promoting psychological well-being and resilience. However, excessive or involuntary participation in these rituals may also contribute to stress, exhaustion, and emotional distress, particularly for individuals with pre-existing mental health conditions or those facing social pressures.

How can mental health professionals approach the integration of traditional spiritual practices into mental health interventions for marginalized communities?

Mental health professionals should approach the integration of traditional spiritual practices with cultural sensitivity, respect, and collaboration with community leaders and healers. This may involve incorporating culturally appropriate interventions, such as group therapy sessions combining elements of spiritual rituals, storytelling, and expressive arts, to address the holistic needs of individuals within marginalized communities.

In efforts to integrate spirituality with psychiatric treatments in India, initiatives such as the *Dhawa & Dhuva*, *Theerthams & Tablets, Prasadhams & Pills* schemes have been established in places like Erwadi dargah, Gunaseelam Prasanna Venkatachalapathy temple and St Anthony's Shrine in Tamil nadu as well as Hazrat Saiyed Ali Mira Datar dargah in Mehsana district in Gujarat. These schemes recognize the importance of traditional spiritual practices in promoting mental well-being and aim to incorporate them into psychiatric interventions. The *Dhawa (medicines) and Dhuva (prayers)* scheme focuses on providing community members with access to spiritual healers and counsellors who can offer guidance, support, and prayer-based interventions for individuals experiencing mental health challenges. Similarly, the *Theerthams (holy water- prayers)* scheme facilitates access to sacred water sources believed to possess healing properties, allowing individuals to participate in ritualistic bathing and purification ceremonies as part of their treatment regimen. Additionally, the *Tablets* scheme involves the distribution of psychiatric medications alongside blessings from religious leaders or spiritual elders, emphasizing the holistic approach to mental health care that integrates biomedical interventions with spiritual support.

By bridging the gap between traditional spiritual practices and psychiatric treatments, these schemes strive to address the multifaceted needs of individuals in rural communities, fostering a collaborative approach to mental health promotion and recovery.

What ethical considerations should mental health professionals consider when working with individuals participating in spiritual trance and dance?
Mental health professionals must uphold principles of autonomy, beneficence, and cultural competence when working with individuals engaged in spiritual trance and dance. This includes respecting participants' right to religious freedom and self-determination, ensuring informed consent and confidentiality, and addressing any potential conflicts between traditional beliefs and evidence-based practices in mental health care.

How can effective communication strategies be employed to promote mental health awareness and support within marginalized communities practicing spiritual trance and dance?
Effective communication strategies involve active listening, empathy, and cultural humility in understanding the beliefs, values, and experiences of individuals within marginalized communities. Mental health professionals should engage in open dialogue, collaborate with community leaders, and provide psychoeducation on mental health and well-being, while acknowledging the significance of traditional spiritual practices in promoting resilience and healing.

****

Possession by Spirit

Ms. Rani, a 25-year-old woman who experiences episodes of trance-like states and altered behaviour during such states, which her family interprets as possession by either a deity or spirit. Rani's symptoms include speaking in a different voice, exhibiting unusual body movements, and displaying knowledge of events beyond her normal awareness. Concerned about Rani's well-being, her family seeks help from a traditional healer, who performs rituals and ceremonies to exorcise the perceived spirit.

As an evidence based medical practitioner, answer the question below

1. **Which of the following best describes possession attack in the context of mental health?**
   a) A neurological disorder characterized by seizures and loss of consciousness
   b) A cultural belief that individuals are inhabited by spirits or supernatural entities
   c) A psychiatric condition marked by hallucinations and delusions of possession
   d) A religious phenomenon associated with divine inspiration and spiritual enlightenment
2. **What is the primary approach taken by traditional healers to address possession attack in many cultures?**
   a) Prescribing medication to treat underlying psychiatric symptoms
   b) Performing rituals and ceremonies to exorcise perceived spirits
   c) Referring individuals to psychiatric hospitals for further evaluation
   d) Educating the community about the scientific basis of mental illness

3. **How might possession attack be interpreted differently within cultural and religious contexts?**
   a) As a sign of spiritual enlightenment and divine favour
   b) As a manifestation of underlying psychiatric or neurological disorders
   c) As a form of social stigma and discrimination
   d) As a challenge to traditional religious beliefs and practices

ANSWERS

1. Choice B. A cultural belief that individuals are inhabited by spirits or supernatural entities
2. Choice B. Performing rituals and ceremonies to exorcise perceived spirits
3. Choice C. As a sign of spiritual enlightenment and divine favour

Questions with Answers:

What are some potential risks associated with the traditional treatment of dissociative identity disorder?

While traditional healing practices may offer comfort and support to individuals and communities, they can also pose risks, including delays in accessing appropriate medical care, impair quality of life/daily functioning, and perpetuation of stigma and discrimination against those experiencing symptoms. Additionally, reliance solely on traditional healing methods may overlook the need for holistic approaches that integrate biomedical and psychosocial interventions.

How can mental health professionals navigate the intersection of culture, spirituality, and mental health in addressing dissociative identity disorder?

Mental health professionals must approach possession syndrome with cultural humility, respect, and sensitivity to the beliefs and practices of the affected community. This may involve collaboration with religious leaders, and community members to develop culturally adapted interventions that honour spiritual beliefs while also addressing underlying mental health needs. Effective communication, empathy, and collaboration are essential in fostering trust and promoting holistic healing within diverse cultural contexts.

What ethical considerations should mental health professionals consider when working with individuals experiencing dissociative identity disorder?

Mental health professionals must uphold ethical principles of autonomy, beneficence, and cultural competence when working with individuals experiencing possession syndrome. This includes respecting individuals' rights to religious and cultural practices, obtaining informed consent for treatment, maintaining confidentiality, and avoiding actions that may perpetuate stigma or harm the individual's well-being. Additionally, mental health professionals should remain mindful of their own cultural biases and limitations, seeking ongoing education and supervision to provide culturally sensitive care.

How can community-based approaches be utilized to address dissociative identity disorder and promote mental health within cultural contexts?

Community-based approaches involve engaging with community members, leaders, and organizations to raise awareness, reduce stigma, and enhance access to culturally appropriate mental health services. This may include training local volunteers as mental health advocates, conducting outreach programs to dispel myths and misconceptions about possession syndrome, and integrating mental health education into existing cultural and religious practices. By fostering collaboration and empowerment within communities, these approaches can support resilience, healing, and social inclusion for individuals experiencing possession syndrome.

****

Supporting Independence - Addressing Falls in Elderly Patients

During ward rounds, Dr. Desai meets with an 82-year-old woman who recently had two falls at home. Her children, who are living abroad, are concerned and pushing for her to move to an assisted nursing home. However, the woman adamantly expresses her desire to remain independent and stay in her own home. Dr. Desai understands the importance of respecting patient autonomy while prioritizing safety. Dr. Desai says, "In that case, let's try to find out why you are falling." **What is the primary focus of Dr. Desai's approach?**

a) **Pressuring the woman to move to a nursing home:** Dr. Desai focuses on solutions for independent living.
b) **Ignoring the concerns of the children:** All parties involved need to be heard and addressed.
c) **Prioritizing patient autonomy and safety:** This approach explores solutions that respect her wishes.
d) **Making promises she may not be able to keep:** Dr. Desai focuses on realistic solutions & shared decision-making.
e) **Criticizing the children for wanting the best for their mother:** Dr. Desai avoids judgment and focuses on collaboration.

Explanation: Dr. Desai's approach emphasizes **prioritizing patient autonomy and safety**. By investigating the cause of the falls, Dr. Desai can explore solutions that allow the woman to stay at home safely. This might involve medication adjustments, physical therapy, or home modifications to reduce fall risks.

Additional Communication Aspects:

- **Active listening:** Pay close attention to the woman's concerns and reasons for wanting to stay home.
- **Shared decision-making:** Involve the woman and her children in the discussion and decision-making process.
- **Empathy:** Acknowledge the concerns of both the woman and her children.
- **Respectful communication:** Maintain a calm and respectful tone throughout the conversation.

Pertinent Questions:

Knowledge: What are some common medical conditions or medications that can increase fall in elderly patients? (Visual problems, Neurological disorders, Vestibular and ENT issues, certain medications)

Attitude: How can doctors balance patient autonomy with the safety concerns of family members when addressing fall risks in elderly patients? (Shared decision-making, exploring solutions that promote independence, open communication)

Application: How might Dr. Desai conduct a home evaluation to identify potential fall hazards in the woman's living environment? (Assess lighting, flooring, furniture placement, bathroom safety features, use of Internet of Things devices etc.,)

Communication Skill: What is a good follow-up question after Dr. Desai suggests investigating the falls? ("Can you tell me a little bit more about where and how the falls happened?")

Cultural Sensitivity: How might Dr. Desai adapt their communication if the family comes from a culture with strong emphasis on filial piety (respect for elders)? (Acknowledge cultural values, involve children in discussions while respecting the woman's autonomy, and explore culturally appropriate in-home support options)

****

Facing Mortality with Honesty and Empathy

During ward rounds, Dr. Singh meets with a 60-year-old terminally ill patient who directly asks, "Doctor, how much longer do I have?" Dr. Singh understands the importance of honest communication while remaining sensitive. Dr. Singh says, "While there have been exceptions, most people at this stage of the illness live about three months." **What is the key aspect of Dr. Singh's communication?**

a) **Providing absolute certainty about lifespan:** Prognosis can be uncertain, so Dr. Singh uses cautious language.
b) **Giving false hope:** Honesty is important, even when delivering difficult news.
c) **Avoiding the question altogether:** Open communication is necessary for end-of-life discussions.
d) **Focusing on treatment options:** While treatment might be ongoing, the patient's question deserves a direct answer.
e) **Offering religious platitudes:** Dr. Singh respects the patient's right to their own beliefs.

Explanation: A. Dr. Singh's statement prioritizes **providing absolute certainty about lifespan - honest and cautious information**. By acknowledging the variability in prognoses while offering a general timeframe, Dr. Singh allows the patient to make informed decisions and prepare for the end of life.

Additional Communication Aspects:

- **Non-verbal communication:** Maintain eye contact and a compassionate demeanour.
- **Active listening:** Allow the patient to express their emotions and concerns freely.
- **Empathy:** Acknowledge the difficulty of the situation and validate the patient's feelings.
- **Open-ended questions:** Invite the patient to share their thoughts and wishes for their remaining time.

Pertinent Questions:

Knowledge: What are the ethical considerations of disclosing a terminal prognosis to a patient? (Autonomy, truth-telling, respecting the patient's right to information)

Attitude: How can doctors balance honesty with sensitivity when communicating with terminally ill patients? (Empathy, using cautious language, acknowledging emotions)

Application: How might Dr. Singh explore the patient's understanding of their illness and their wishes for end-of-life care? (Ask open-ended questions, explain treatment options and palliative care, discuss preferences with family)

Communication Skill: What is a good follow-up question after Dr. Singh shares the prognosis? ("This news can be overwhelming. How are you feeling about what I've shared?")

Communication Skill: Can bad news be broken over the phone? (A definitive NO)

Cultural Sensitivity: How might Dr. Singh adapt their communication if the patient comes from a culture with specific practices surrounding death and dying? (Acknowledge cultural beliefs, involve family members in discussions, and respect cultural practices that do not conflict with medical care)

****

Respecting Religious Beliefs during Medical Care

During ward rounds, Dr. Sharma encounters a 76-year-old patient who shares that he had a powerful religious vision while praying. The patient, who adheres to a different faith tradition than Dr. Sharma, then asks the doctor to join him in prayer. Dr. Sharma understands the importance of respecting the patient's spiritual beliefs. MCQ: Dr. Sharma says, "That must have been a very important moment for you." **What is the key aspect of Dr. Sharma's response?**

a) **Pressuring the patient to discuss the details of the vision:** Dr. Sharma focuses on acknowledging the experience.
b) **Discouraging the patient from talking about religion:** Healthcare is not limited to just physical needs; spiritual well-being matters too.
c) **Sharing his own religious beliefs:** Dr. Sharma respects the patient's right to his own faith tradition. (Correct)
d) **Feigning belief in the patient's vision:** Honesty is important, even when navigating religious conversations.
e) **Attempting to explain the vision scientifically:** Dr. Sharma avoids dismissing the patient's spiritual experience.

Explanation: Dr. Sharma's response emphasizes **respecting the patient's belief system**. By acknowledging the significance of the religious vision, Dr. Sharma demonstrates empathy and creates a safe space for the patient to share his spiritual experiences.

Additional Communication Aspects:

- **Non-verbal communication:** Maintain eye contact and a warm, receptive demeanour.
- **Active listening:** Encourage the patient to elaborate on his experience if he feels comfortable.
- **Respectful language:** Avoid making judgments or dismissive comments about the patient's faith.
- **Avoid using mobiles or gadgets during interview:**

Pertinent Questions:

Knowledge: How can healthcare professionals ensure respectful communication when encountering patients with different religious beliefs? (Understanding common religious practices, avoiding religious bias, focusing on patient-centered care)

Attitude: Why is it important for doctors to acknowledge the role of spirituality in a patient's overall well-being? (Spirituality can provide comfort, strength, and hope, impacting mental and emotional health)

Application: How might Dr. Sharma explore the impact of the religious vision on the patient's coping mechanisms or treatment preferences? (Ask open-ended questions, inquire if the vision offers comfort or guidance related to his illness)

Communication Skill: What is a good follow-up question after Dr. Sharma acknowledges the vision? ("Would you like to tell me more about how this vision has affected you?")

Cultural Sensitivity: How might Dr. Sharma adapt his communication if the patient comes from a culture with strong emphasis on religious rituals or practices? (Acknowledge cultural practices)

****

Maintaining Patient Confidentiality - Respecting Autonomy

During ward rounds, Dr. Mehta meets with a 60-year-old wealthy woman with terminal lung cancer. The woman is competent and has not authorized her brother to receive medical information. When the brother enters the room and asks for a diagnosis and prognosis update, Dr. Mehta prioritizes patient confidentiality. Dr. Mehta says, "Please ask your sister." **What is the primary focus of Dr. Mehta's response?**

- **Shifting responsibility to the patient:** Dr. Mehta protects patient confidentiality. (Correct)
- **Disregarding the concerns of the patient's family:** Open communication with families is important, but confidentiality takes precedence without patient consent.
- **Providing a vague or dismissive answer:** Direct and honest communication is necessary, while respecting confidentiality.
- **Pressuring the patient to share information with her brother:** The decision to share information rests with the patient.
- **Sharing the diagnosis and prognosis without permission:** Confidentiality can only be breached in exceptional circumstances and with patient consent.

Explanation: Dr. Mehta's response emphasizes **protecting patient confidentiality**. By directing the brother to the patient herself, Dr. Mehta ensures the woman retains control over her medical information.

Additional Communication Aspects:

- **Non-verbal communication:** Maintain a professional and respectful demeanour.
- **Explanation:** Briefly explain the importance of patient confidentiality and the need for the woman's authorization.
- **Offering support:** Offer to answer any questions the brother might have after speaking with the patient, if she chooses to share information.
- **Respectful boundaries:** Set clear boundaries regarding medical information and the need for patient consent.

Pertinent Questions:

Knowledge: What are the ethical and legal principles governing patient confidentiality? (Informed consent, regulations, protecting patient privacy)

Attitude: How can doctors balance patient confidentiality with the needs and concerns of family members? (Open communication, respecting patient autonomy, offering support to families)

Application: How might Dr. Mehta assess if the woman is willing to share her diagnosis and prognosis with her brother? (Ask the woman directly if she would like her brother present during discussions, explain the information being shared. In case, if she does not want it to be shared with family members, there shall be a written documentation to this effect – This is very crucial for medico-legal reasons, in future)

Communication Skill: What is a good follow-up question after Dr. Mehta asks the brother to speak with the patient? ("Is there anything I can do to support you or your sister during this time?")

Cultural Sensitivity: How might Dr. Mehta adapt their communication if the family comes from a culture with strong family decision-making structures? (Explain confidentiality while acknowledging cultural values, explore if the patient would like a family member present with her consent)

****

When Tears Become Textbooks - Medical School Odyssey

Rohan, a third year medical student at the outpatient ward of a Medical College, nervously adjusted his white coat. Today was his first official patient interaction. He'd devoured textbooks, aced his exams, but facing a real person, their anxieties laid bare, felt like a whole new ball game.

The patient, Mrs. Patel, her eyes red-rimmed, voice wavering as she described her symptoms. As she spoke, tears welled up, threatening to spill over. Rohan, his palms turning clammy, felt a pang of helplessness. Should he, like some of his seniors suggested, steer the conversation back to the medical history, a safe, dry zone?

Question 1: In Rohan's situation, what might be some reasons to avoid acknowledging Mrs. Patel's emotions?

A. Fear of making things worse or appearing unprofessional.
B. Lack of experience navigating such emotional scenarios.
C. Both A and B.
(Answer at the end of the scenario)

Rohan wasn't alone in his dilemma. Many medical students grapple with the fear of upsetting patients or getting bogged down in emotions. Textbooks provided a clear path, a logical progression of symptoms and diagnoses. Tears, however, felt like an unwelcome detour. Dr. Khanna, their wise and experienced communication skills mentor, recognized this struggle. "Tears," he explained gently, "are a patient's way of expressing their vulnerability. A doctor who can create a space for those emotions fosters a stronger connection, leading to a more accurate diagnosis and better treatment outcomes."

Question 2: How can Rohan demonstrate to Mrs. Patel that it's okay to express her emotions?

Dr. Khanna offered a solution: view tears as an opportunity. A simple gesture like offering a tissue and a reassuring "Please take your time, Mrs. Patel. We're here to listen" could go a long way. This doesn't require Rohan to become a therapist, but simply acknowledges her emotional state and shows empathy.

Answers:

1. C. Both A and B. Fear of appearing unprofessional and lack of experience can make students hesitant to address emotions.
2. By offering tissues and a reassuring statement like "It's okay to take a moment. We're here to listen when you're ready," Rohan shows Mrs. Patel that her feelings are valid.

Rohan understood. Effective communication wasn't just about flawless medical knowledge. It was about building trust, understanding the AETCOM needs behind the illness. By embracing emotions, Rohan could bridge the gap between a textbook and a real patient, transforming his journey from a nervous student to a healer with a human touch.

****

Beyond the Script: When Textbooks Don't Speak the Patient's Language

Dr. Anya, a brilliant medical student at Mumbai's Medical College, felt a surge of frustration. She'd aced her interview skills course, mastering the textbook approach - open-ended questions, active listening. But during her first clinical rotation, facing real patients, the script crumbled. Dr. Kapoor, a seasoned physician, used a more informal, conversational style, seemingly at odds with everything Anya had learned.

Question 1: How might Anya feel in this situation?

A. Confused and unsure of the right approach.

B. Confident in her textbook knowledge.
C. Impressed by Dr. Kapoor's communication skills.
(Answer at the end of the scenario)

Disheartened, Anya confided in her friend Rohan, "What we learn in class feels so different from real medicine." This wasn't uncommon. Many students grappled with reconciling theory and practice. The textbook approach felt sterile, robotic, while Dr. Kapoor's conversational style seemed to build a genuine rapport with patients.

Dr. Mehta, their insightful professor, understood the dilemma. He explained, "Different interviewing styles (unstructured/semi-structured or structured) have their merits. The textbook approach lays a strong foundation, but real patients respond best to genuine conversations. The key is to be flexible and adapt your communication to the individual."

Question 2: What skill can Anya develop to bridge the gap between theory and practice?
(Answer at end of the scenario)

Dr. Mehta proposed a solution: Analyse the strengths and weaknesses of various interviewing styles. Anya could observe Dr. Kapoor's interactions, identify the techniques that fostered trust and openness, and integrate them into her own approach. This wouldn't mean abandoning the core principles learned in class, but rather weaving them into a more natural, patient-centered conversation.

Answers:

1. A. Confused and unsure of the right approach. Anya's textbook knowledge clashes with Dr. Kapoor's style, creating uncertainty.
2. Adaptability. By observing and analysing different styles, Anya can learn to adjust her communication to best suit each patient.

Learning effective communication isn't about memorizing scripts. It's about understanding the patient's history, adapting to their needs, and building trust. Anya's journey from frustrated student to a well-rounded communicator highlights the importance of bridging the gap between theory and practice. This allows medical students to create a language that not only speaks the science, but also speaks to the human heart, in the process she learns to prioritize system specific, relevant questions.

****

From Talking Heads to Healers: A Medical Student's Awakening

Akash, a second-year medical student at Bangalore Medical College, slumped in his chair after another lecture on communication skills. It felt like a lecture on etiquette – "maintain eye contact," "use clear language." While the information was useful, Akash couldn't shake the feeling of being talked at, not talked to. "Don't they realize we already know how to have conversations?" he grumbled to his friend Priya.

Question 1: Why might Akash feel this way about the communication skills lecture?
A. The lecture content seems obvious and unnecessary.
B. He craves more practical application of the skills.
C. He feels like his communication skills are being micromanaged.
(Answer at the end of the scenario)

Priya, ever the pragmatist, offered a different perspective. "Maybe they're not trying to teach us basic conversation, but how to have effective conversations with patients in a medical setting." Akash, however, remained unconvinced. Many students shared his sentiment, feeling patronized by the lecture format.

Dr. Rao, their innovative professor, recognized the need for a change. She replaced lectures with interactive workshops. "Imagine you're the patient," she'd say, "What would make you feel comfortable opening up about your health concerns?" Students then role-played scenarios, identifying communication pitfalls, and devising solutions together.

Question 2: How can this new workshop approach benefit Akash's communication skills?
A. It fosters empathy by allowing him to see things from the patient's perspective.
B. It encourages critical thinking and problem-solving in real-time communication.
C. Both A and B
(Answer at the end of the scenario)
This shift from passive learning to active engagement made a world of difference. Akash found himself genuinely invested in understanding patient communication. Akash wasn't lectured anymore. He felt excited to learn how to talk to patients better, not just give orders.

Answers:

1. B. Akash craves practical application. The lecture format feels theoretical and doesn't translate to real patient interactions.
2. C. Both A and B. By putting himself in the patient's shoes, Akash develops empathy and learns to adapt communication based on the situation. The workshop format encourages critical thinking and real-time problem-solving in communication scenarios.

Effective communication isn't a one-size-fits-all formula. Dr. Rao's approach highlights the importance of student engagement and active learning. By transforming students from passive listeners to active participants, medical schools can bridge the gap between theory and practice, fostering a generation of healers who not only have the knowledge, but also the communication skills to truly connect with their patients.

****

The Paralysis of Perfection: When Rules Silence the Healer

Priya, a meticulous medical student at Tamil Nadu's Medical College, meticulously reviewed her communication skills notes. Dozens of highlighted rules stared back – "maintain open posture," "use active listening techniques," "avoid medical jargon." The sheer volume of information overwhelmed her. "What if I mess up?" she worried, her confidence waning.

Question 1: How might Priya's fear of making mistakes be impacting her communication skills development?
A. It leads to overthinking and hinders her ability to connect with patients.
B. It motivates her to study harder and learn all the rules perfectly.
C. It makes her a more cautious and careful communicator, which is always a good thing.
(Answer at the end of the scenario)

Priya wasn't alone. Many students felt paralyzed by the pressure to follow a rigid set of interviewing rules. The fear of making a mistake loomed large, hindering their ability to connect with patients on a human level. Dr. Paraman, their inspiring professor, understood this struggle. "Communication isn't about following a script," he explained. "It's about understanding the patient and adapting your approach." He proposed a novel solution: Students would work together to formulate their own interviewing "styles or approach" not rigid rules. They would analyse strengths and weaknesses of different approaches, learning to choose the most effective one for each situation.

Question 2: How can Dr. Paraman's approach help Priya overcome her fear of mistakes?
A. By focusing on the "why" behind the rules, it empowers her to adapt and improvise.
B. By creating a collaborative learning environment, it reduces the fear of judgment.
C. Both A and B
(Answer at the end of the scenario)

This shift from rule-following to informed decision-making was a revelation for Priya. Experimenting with different communication styles in a safe environment fostered confidence. She learned that effective communication wasn't about perfection, but about connecting with patients with empathy and understanding.

Answers:

1. A. Priya's fear of mistakes leads to overthinking. She's so focused on following the rules that she struggles to connect with the patient as a person.
2. Both A and B. By understanding the purpose of communication strategies, Priya can adapt them to different situations. The collaborative environment reduces the fear of judgment, allowing her to experiment and learn from mistakes.

Dr. Paraman's approach highlights the importance of empowering students to become active participants in their learning. By moving beyond a rigid rulebook, medical schools can foster a generation of adaptable communicators, doctors who can not only diagnose illnesses but also connect with patients, transforming their fear of mistakes into a driving force for growth and empathy.

****

From Lost in Translation to Healing Conversations: When Words Aren't Enough

The frustration was etched on Rahul's face, a medical student. He'd diligently followed Dr. Menon's lectures on communication skills, absorbing every word about active listening and open-ended questions. Yet, during his first patient interaction, he felt lost. Dr. Menon's instructions, clear in the sterile classroom environment, seemed to evaporate in the face of a real patient's anxieties. "Only now do I understand what you meant by..." he stammered to Dr. Menon later, feeling utterly unprepared.

Question 1: Why might Rahul feel unprepared despite attending communication skills lectures?
A. The lectures focused too much on theory and not enough on practical application.
B. He struggled to remember the specific details of Dr. Menon's instructions.
C. He underestimated the complexity of real-world patient interactions.
(Answer at the end of the scenario)

Rahul's experience resonated with many students. While lectures provided valuable knowledge, the leap to real-world communication felt daunting. Textbooks couldn't replicate the nuances of human interaction, the unspoken anxieties that swirled beneath a patient's words. Dr. Menon, a seasoned physician with a passion for communication, recognized this gap. "Imagine you're learning a new language," she explained to the class. "You wouldn't just memorize vocabulary, you'd practice speaking and listening." This semester, things would be different. Dr. Menon incorporated live demonstrations, role-playing scenarios where students could put theory into practice. She'd act as the patient, showcasing various communication techniques, from active listening to building rapport.

Question 2: How can Dr. Menon's live demonstration approach benefit Rahul's communication skills?
A. It allows him to observe effective communication techniques in action.
B. It provides a safe space to practice and receive immediate feedback.

C. Both A and B
(Answer at the end of the scenario)

The shift from theory to practice was transformative. Seeing communication skills come alive, Rahul grasped the nuances Dr. Menon had emphasized in her lectures. The classroom transformed into a safe space to experiment, make mistakes, and receive constructive feedback. No longer lost in translation, Rahul was on his way to mastering the language of healing.

Answers:

1. The lectures focused on theory, but Rahul needed practical application to bridge the gap between theoretical knowledge and real-world communication.
2. Both A and B. Observing Dr. Menon's demonstrations allows Rahul to see communication techniques in action. The live role-playing provides a safe space to practice and receive immediate feedback, improving his communication skills.

Dr. Menon's approach highlights the importance of moving beyond theory. By incorporating live demonstrations and practical exercises, medical schools can bridge the gap between knowledge and application. This fosters a generation of medical professionals who can not only understand communication concepts but also effectively use them to connect with patients on a deeper level.

****

Beyond the Band-Aid: When Practice Makes Imperfect

A sense of complacency hung in a Medical College's communication skills class. "We've done enough practice interviews," grumbled Sameer, echoing a common sentiment. While the initial role-playing exercises were helpful, they felt repetitive, lacking the complexity of real-world scenarios. Sameer craved a challenge, a chance to truly test his communication skills.

Question 1: Why might Sameer feel this way about the communication skills practice sessions?
A. He finds the role-playing scenarios unrealistic and inauthentic.
B. He lacks confidence in his communication skills and wants more practice.
C. He feels the practice sessions haven't progressed beyond basic interviewing techniques.
(Answer at end of scenario)

Sameer wasn't alone. Many students often feel disconnect between the classroom exercises and the real complexities of patient interactions. While the initial practice was valuable, there was a sense of stagnation, a lack of growth. Dr. Shanmugam, their insightful in-charge professor, recognized this challenge. "Communication is a lifelong journey," he explained, "and like any skill, it requires consistent practice with increasing difficulty." Dr. Shanmugam proposed a revamped curriculum. The initial sessions would focus on core communication techniques. Gradually, the complexity of the role-playing scenarios would increase, introducing "difficult patients" with anxieties, cultural differences, or communication barriers.

Question 2: How can Dr. Shanmugam's approach benefit Sameer's communication skills development?
A. It exposes him to a wider range of communication challenges, preparing him for real-world scenarios.
B. It fosters critical thinking and problem-solving skills in navigating complex patient interactions.
C. Both A and B
(Answer at end of scenario)

This shift in focus was a game-changer for Sameer. The new scenarios pushed him beyond his comfort zone, forcing him to adapt his communication style based on the patient's needs. He learned to navigate cultural nuances, address anxieties, and manage communication breakdowns. The sessions became a safe space to experiment, make mistakes, and receive constructive feedback.

Answers:

1. C. Sameer feels the practice sessions haven't progressed beyond basic techniques. He craves a challenge that reflects the increasing complexity of real-world communication.
2. Both A and B. Dr. Shanmugam's approach exposes Sameer to a wider range of communication challenges, preparing him for real-world difficulties. It also fosters critical thinking as he learns to adapt his communication and problem-solve in complex situations.

Dr. Shanmugam's approach highlights the importance of structured, progressive practice. By gradually increasing the complexity of communication challenges, medical schools can foster a generation of adaptable communicators, doctors who are not only equipped with the theoretical knowledge but also have the practical skills to navigate the complexities of real-world patient interactions. This ensures their communication skills go beyond a mere "band-aid solution" and become a cornerstone of their practice.

****

Bridging the Communication Gap: From Know-It-All's to Healers

Smriti, a bright-eyed first-year student at Kolkata Medical College, raised her hand during a communication skills lecture. "These rules feel restrictive," she argued. "Don't we already know how to have conversations?" A murmur of agreement rippled through the class. The professor's lecture on maintaining eye contact and active listening felt patronizing, a clash with their existing social skills.

Question 1: Why might Smriti disagree with the communication skills lecture?

A. She believes communication skills are innate and can't be taught.

B. The lecture format feels passive and doesn't encourage active participation.

C. She feels the rules are too basic and don't address the complexities of patient interactions.

(Answer at the end of the scenario)

Smriti's sentiment resonated with many students. They weren't blank slates; they possessed existing communication skills honed through years of social interaction. Being told how to "behave" felt off-putting. Dr. Khanna, their professor, recognized the resistance. "Communication in a medical setting is different," he explained. "It's about creating a safe space for patients to share their vulnerabilities." He scrapped the lecture format, opting for an interactive approach. He presented real-world communication challenges – a hesitant patient, a cultural barrier – and invited students to brainstorm solutions.

Question 2: How can Dr. Khanna's interactive approach benefit Smriti's communication skills development?

A. It fosters critical thinking and problem-solving skills in navigating communication challenges.

B. It allows students to see the practical applications of communication techniques

C. Both A and B

(Answer at the end of the scenario)

This shift from passive learning to active problem-solving was a revelation for Smriti. Engaging with real-world scenarios ignited her curiosity. Instead of feeling lectured at, she felt empowered to develop her communication skills as a doctor, not just a social butterfly. The classroom transformed into a collaborative space where students could challenge assumptions, devise solutions, and learn from each other.

Answers:

1. C. Smriti feels the lecture format is too basic and doesn't address the complexities of patient interactions. She believes her existing communication skills need to be adapted for a medical setting.
2. Both A and B. Dr. Khanna's approach encourages critical thinking as students analyze communication challenges and brainstorm solutions. It also allows them to see the practical application of communication techniques, making them more relevant and engaging.

Dr. Khanna's approach highlights the importance of moving beyond a "one-size-fits-all" model. By fostering student participation and critical thinking, medical schools can bridge the gap between theory and practice. This empowers students to transform from know-it-alls to healers, equipped with the communication skills to not only diagnose illnesses but also connect with patients on a human level.

****

Unscripted Success: When Grades Don't Tell the Whole Story

A wave of anxiety among final MBBS students rippled through Assam Medical College as final exams loomed. For Aditi, a bright but insecure student, the communication skills assessment was particularly daunting. "What exactly are they looking for?" she fretted to her friends. The lack of clear criteria left her feeling like she was winging it, unsure of how to translate textbook knowledge into real-world communication.

Question 1: Why might Aditi feel insecure about the communication skills assessment?

A. The assessment format is subjective and lacks clear guidelines for success.

B. She worries about memorizing facts and figures instead of focusing on genuine communication.

C. The pressure of high stakes testing is hindering her ability to perform at her best.

(Answer at the end of the scenario)

Aditi's anxieties mirrored those of many students. The current assessment system, focused on a single high-stakes test, felt like a gamble. There was no clear roadmap for success, no opportunity to receive feedback and course-correct. This, in some cases, led students to prioritize rote memorization and "playing the test" over developing genuine communication skills. Dr. Ramani, their professor, recognized the limitations of the existing system. "Communication is a journey, not a destination," she explained. "We need to assess progress, not just a final product." Dr. Ramani proposed a revolutionary change – replacing the summative assessment with regular, one-on-one formative discussions. Students would be observed during clinical rotations, and Dr. Ramani would provide constructive feedback, tailored to their strengths and weaknesses.

Question 2: How can Dr. Ramani's approach benefit Aditi's communication skills development?

A. It provides a safe space to receive personalized feedback and address communication challenges.

B. It fosters a growth mind-set, encouraging continuous learning and improvement.

C. Both A and B

(Answer at the end of the scenario)

This shift from a test-oriented approach to ongoing dialogue was a game-changer for Aditi. Dr. Ramani's personalized feedback shed light on her strengths – her empathetic listening skills – and areas for improvement – maintaining eye contact during conversations. The pressure of a single exam vanished, replaced by the opportunity to learn and grow in a supportive environment.

Answers:

1. A. The assessment format is subjective and lacks clear guidelines for success. Aditi feels unsure of what behaviours are considered desirable and how to translate theoretical knowledge into real-world communication.

2. Both A and B. Dr. Ramani's approach provides a safe space for Aditi to receive personalized feedback on her communication, allowing her to address challenges and improve her skills. It also fosters a growth mind-set by focusing on continuous learning and improvement rather than a single high-stakes test.

Dr. Ramani's approach highlights the importance of on-going feedback and personalized mentorship. Medical schools can empower students to develop their communication skills with confidence. This ensures their communication isn't just about performing well on an exam, but about becoming effective healers who can truly connect with their patients.

****

Beyond the Honeymoon Phase: When First Impressions Don't Tell the Whole Story

The mood in a Medical College's communication skills class was celebratory. Students, fresh from their first patient interactions, buzzed with excitement. "It went great!" they chorused, their enthusiasm echoing through the classroom. Dr. Subramani, the professor, basked in the positive feedback, a sense of satisfaction settling over him.

Question 1: Why might Dr. Subramani's focus on positive feedback be a cause for concern?
A. It can mask underlying communication issues that students might be facing.
B. Students are more likely to remember negative feedback, so positive reinforcement is essential.
C. Positive feedback demotivates students and hinders their growth.
(Answer at the end of the scenario)

While Dr. Subramani's enthusiasm was understandable, it masked a potential pitfall. The initial excitement of meeting patients could overshadow deeper communication challenges. A student might feel they've "aced" the interaction, while missing crucial nonverbal cues or failing to delve deeper into the patient's concerns.

Dr. Priya Peter, a visiting communication skills expert, observed this dynamic. "Positive feedback is important," she acknowledged, "but so is constructive criticism." She suggested a shift in focus – Dr. Subramani would actively solicit critical feedback, even if it came from a minority of students. This would ensure a more nuanced understanding of each student's communication strengths and weaknesses.

Question 2: How can Dr. Priya Peter's approach benefit the students' communication development?
A. It encourages students to self-evaluate and identify areas for improvement beyond the initial positive experiences.
B. It exposes them to different perspectives on communication effectiveness, fostering critical thinking.
C. Both A and B
(Answer at the end of the scenario)

Dr. Priya Peter's suggestion sparked a lively discussion. Students who initially felt their communication was flawless started re-evaluating their interactions. They considered nonverbal cues, the flow of conversation, and whether they had truly addressed the patient's anxieties. The classroom transformed from an echo chamber of positivity into a space for critical reflection and growth.

Answers:

1. A. Dr. Subramani's focus on positive feedback might mask underlying communication issues that students are facing but haven't identified yet. The initial excitement can overshadow the need to develop communication skills further.
2. Both A and B. Dr. Priya Peter's approach encourages students to self-evaluate and identify areas for improvement beyond their initial positive experiences. It also exposes them to different perspectives on

communication effectiveness, fostering critical thinking and a well-rounded understanding of successful communication in a medical setting.

****

Bridging the Gap: When Teachers Don't Speak the Same Language

Disappointment clouded Maya's face as she exited Mumbai Medical College's Clinical communication skills class. Professor Desai's lecture on disease-centered interviewing, while informative, felt disconnected from reality. During her clinical rotations, Dr. Shah, her mentor, prioritized the patient's story and concerns. The inconsistency left Maya ambivalent. "Who am I supposed to learn from?" she lamented to her friends.

Question 1: Why might Maya feel confused about communication styles?

A. She lacks the experience to navigate different interviewing approaches.

B. The inconsistency between classroom teachings and real-world practice is creating uncertainty.

C. Both A and B

(Answer at the end of the scenario)

Maya's experience resonated with many students. Disconnect between the disease-centered approach emphasized in lectures and the patient-centered approach observed in clinical settings sowed seeds of ambivalence. This inconsistency made it difficult for students to develop a cohesive communication style.

Dr. Kapoor, the head of the communication skills department, recognized this challenge. The root cause, was the lack of standardized training for clinical tutors. "Our professors are excellent doctors," he explained, "but they may not all be equipped to teach communication skills effectively." Dr. Kapoor proposed a solution – tailored workshops for clinical tutors, equipping them with the tools to role-model effective patient-centered interviewing techniques.

Question 2: How can Dr. Kapoor's approach benefit Maya's communication skills development?

A. It ensures consistency between classroom instruction and clinical mentorship, providing a clear roadmap for communication development.

B. It empowers clinical tutors to provide targeted feedback based on patient-centered interviewing techniques.

C. Both A and B

(Answer at the end of the scenario)

These workshops, focused on active listening, empathy building, and open-ended questioning, proved transformative. Clinical tutors, now equipped with a unified approach, became effective role models. Gone were the days of mixed messages. In their place emerged a clear and consistent communication philosophy, empowering students to develop a well-rounded approach to patient interactions.

Answers:

1. B. The inconsistency between the disease-centered approach taught in lectures and the patient-centered approach observed during clinical rotations is creating uncertainty for Maya. She's unsure of which style to prioritize.
2. Both A and B. Dr. Kapoor's approach ensures consistency between classroom instruction and clinical mentorship. This provides Maya with a clear roadmap for communication development. Empowered clinical tutors can provide targeted feedback based on patient-centered interviewing techniques, further enhancing her communication skills.

****

3. Psychomotor Skills

How to Learn Motor Skills in MBBS

Fine Motor Skills	Medical-Specific Examples	Activities	Key Words
Imitation	Grasping, suturing patterns, instrument handling	Mimicking suturing techniques, practicing catheter insertion, using surgical instruments under supervision	Observe, replicate, follow, mirror, mimic
Manipulation	Suture tying, knot tying, tool use (forceps, scalpels)	Practicing various suture knots, manipulating surgical instruments, suturing practice pads	Craft, build, manoeuvre, execute, assemble, manage
Precision	Microdissection, injecting medications, suturing fine tissues	Dissection exercises with delicate structures, practicing injections on simulation models, suturing small wounds with precision	Handle, manipulate, control, calibrate, stabilize, refine
Articulation	Laparoscopic surgery, CPR, complex wound closure	Performing mock laparoscopic procedures, practicing CPR compressions and breaths, suturing complex wounds with multiple layers	Coordinate, sequence, plan, strategize, execute, maintain
Naturalization	Fluency in surgical techniques, suturing without looking, instrument handling second nature	Performing surgeries with minimal guidance, suturing wounds quickly and accurately, using instruments instinctively	Automate, optimize, refine, master, perfect, adapt

Psychomotor Skills that a MBBS Student Should Aspire to Learn in the Psychiatry Department

Nonverbal Communication:

- **Body Language:**
    - Posture: Open, relaxed, and leaning slightly forward to show interest.
    - Gestures: Natural, non-aggressive, used sparingly to emphasize points.
    - Facial expressions: Warm, welcoming
    - Eye contact: Maintained but not overly intense, respecting patient comfort.
- **Maintaining boundaries:** Appropriate physical distance, avoiding touching unless explicitly permitted.
- **Nonverbal cues:** Observing and interpreting patient's nonverbal communication (e.g., fidgeting, blushing) for deeper understanding.

Verbal Communication:

- **Active listening:** Focusing intently, giving verbal and nonverbal cues of attentiveness.
- **Empathy:** Using tone, word choice, and phrases that convey understanding and compassion.
- **Clear and concise speech:** Avoiding jargon, explaining complex concepts in accessible language.
- **Open-ended questions:** Encouraging elaboration and deeper exploration of patient's experiences.
- **Reflective listening:** Summarizing key points and asking clarifying questions to demonstrate understanding.
- **Validation:** Acknowledging and accepting patient's feelings without judgment.
- **Nonverbal communication awareness:** Recognizing how your own vocal tone and pace impact the conversation.

Fine Motor Skills:

- **Note-taking:** Writing efficiently while maintaining eye contact and rapport.
- **Physical examinations (if applicable):** Performing assessments with dexterity, gentleness, and respect for patient privacy.
- **Technology use:** Operating computers, tablets, and other tools seamlessly while interacting with patients.
- **Expressive gestures:** Using hand movements to illustrate points with clarity and moderation.

Social Perception:

- **Emotional intelligence:** Identifying and understanding patient's emotions and responding appropriately.
- **Nonverbal communication decoding:** Accurately interpreting patient's body language and facial expressions.
- **Cultural sensitivity:** Recognizing and respecting diverse cultural values, beliefs, and communication styles.
- **Social cues:** Picking up on subtle social cues to gauge patient's comfort and understanding.

Overall:

- **Adaptability:** Adjusting communication and approach based on individual patient needs and cultural backgrounds.
- **Self-awareness:** Recognizing and managing one's own biases, emotions, and limitations.
- **Time management:** Efficiently utilizing session time to address patient needs while respecting boundaries.
- **Professionalism:** Maintaining a confident, composed, and ethical demeanour.
- **Stress management:** Utilizing healthy coping mechanisms to manage the emotional demands of the job.

Additional Skills:

- **Therapeutic touch (with consent):** Using touch in a therapeutic and culturally appropriate manner (e.g., handshake).
- **Creative expression:** Utilizing creative modalities (e.g., art therapy) to facilitate communication and exploration.
- **Humour (cautiously):** Using humour appropriately to build rapport and lighten the mood, considering cultural sensitivity.

Physical Examination in Psychiatry Practice

Why should psychiatrists be able to do a physical examination?

Psychiatric patients have significantly higher annual death rates from all causes compared to the general population, with a higher prevalence of physical disorders across various mental illnesses. Relying solely on the assumption that a patient's general practitioner or referring doctor has conducted a comprehensive physical examination is risky, as studies have shown that a significant percentage of patients with physical illnesses are misdiagnosed as having mental disorders. This is often due to the challenges faced by mentally disturbed patients in articulating their symptoms, even in the presence of life-threatening conditions.

Moreover, when patients are admitted to psychiatric units, physical diseases are frequently overlooked, leading to delayed recovery and extended hospital stays. Therefore, it is crucial for psychiatrists to conduct physical examinations as part of the psychiatric evaluation to differentiate between organic diseases and functional psychiatric disorders. Not only does this facilitate tailored drug use and reduce the risk of side effects, but it also establishes a baseline for monitoring changes in the patient's physical health and the effects of medication.

The evidence strongly suggests that holistic care for individuals with mental illnesses should encompass both physical and mental healthcare. However, achieving this integrated approach poses challenges and barriers that must be addressed. Overall, it is evident that allowing psychiatrists to perform physical examinations is essential for enhancing patient outcomes, improving overall health, and addressing the complex healthcare needs of individuals with mental disorders.

The General Physical Examination

The importance of conducting physical examinations in isolation from systemic inquiry cannot be under-estimated. A competent Indian medical graduate should have a decent good working knowledge of internal medicine, systemic inquiry, and medical history to focus the physical examination effectively. This knowledge selectively should be used to perform an efficient search for signs from different systems to confirm or support a diagnosis. The essence of a skilled physical examination, is not merely conducting a meticulous examination of various organs in isolation; rather, it involves using the clinician's knowledge to efficiently search for signs from different systems to support or confirm a diagnosis. **Remember – What your brain does not know, the eyes would not see.**

Additionally, he/she should take a reasonably sound psychiatric history reflecting on the examination of mental state and the role of internal medicine, systemic inquiry, and medical history in focusing the physical examination. The comprehensive understanding of internal medicine, systemic inquiry, and medical history is essential for conducting a skilled physical examination, and this knowledge supports an efficient search for signs from different systems to confirm or support a diagnosis.

Chaperones

Chaperones or attender or caregiver should always be present during any examination or any in-depth examination of a patient. Specifically, a female staff member should always accompany male doctors when they are examining female patients. The requirement for a chaperone should also extend to female psychiatrists examining male patients in order to prevent not only allegations of assault on the patient but also to avoid assault by the patient. This precaution is particularly important when dealing with intoxicated patients or those who may be sexually disinhibited due to substance abuse or elation.

General Observation

General observation is an important part of the physical examination in patients with mental illness. The significance of monitoring patients' weight, is critical not only in conditions like anorexia nervosa but also to confirm weight loss due to neglect in patients with psychosis and weight variation in depression. Observing cyanosis, especially central cyanosis, as it can indicate serious underlying physical problems requiring urgent medical intervention. Furthermore, the presence of a foreign body should be suspected in specific patient groups, such as the elderly or those with swallowing disorders.

Simple observation and work-up such as gait or laughter can convey more intricate details

What Gait can Convey

Gait Abnormality	Possible Underlying Conditions
Waddling gait	Primary muscle disease, congenital dislocation of hip
Spastic or Scissoring (legs cross midline when walking)	Bi-pyramidal lesions/ Cerebral palsy
High-stepping (excessive hip flexion during swing phase)	Foot drop, weakness in dorsiflexor muscles
High-stepping + Stamping gait	Posterior column lesion
Circumduction/hemiplegic gait (wide swinging motion of the leg)	Hemiparesis
Shuffling or Festinating gait (taking small, rapid steps with a hunched posture)	Parkinson's disease
Ataxic gait (uncoordinated walking, swaying- drunken or Sailor's gait)	Cerebellar dysfunction, multiple sclerosis, vitamin B12 deficiency

What Laughter can Convey

Type of Laughter	Description	Possible Associated Conditions
Pathological Laughter	Uncontrollable outbursts of laughter that don't match the situation or emotional state. Often described as sounding forced or hollow.	• Neurological disorders (stroke, tumors, multiple sclerosis) • Pseudobulbar affect (PBA) - damage to brain regions controlling emotions • Psychiatric conditions (schizophrenia, bipolar disorder)
Compulsive Giggling	Frequent and uncontrollable giggling, often triggered by social situations or mild amusement.	• Epilepsy (temporal lobe) • Geschwind-Schilder-Fohr syndrome (rare neurological disorder) • Psychiatric conditions (OCD)

Some Salient Points for Physical Examination from Psychiatry Point of View

Region	What to examine	Possible findings and significance
General	Body build	• Obesity: chronic psychotropic medications, myxedema, Cushing's syndrome • Low body weight: anorexia, depression, self-neglect due to chronic psychosis, chronic ill health, or dementia
General	Body asymmetry	• Strokes, old injuries
General	Smell	• Smell of alcohol or fetor hepaticus in alcoholics • Ketotic smell in diabetic ketoacidosis • Bad smell if poor self-care in depression and chronic psychosis • A smell of urine indicates incontinence (not necessarily from a physical problem - can also occur in self-neglect)
General	Gait	• Shuffling in Parkinson's disease (drug-induced or from the primary disease) • Impaired from strokes or other neurological problems
General	Tremors	• Lithium toxicity, Parkinson's disease, or drug-induced tremor
Skin	General appearance	• Rashes: Allergies, infections, autoimmune diseases. • Bruising: Bleeding or trauma. • Sores: Pressure, infection, poor circulation. • Changes in colour: Jaundice, anaemia. • Excoriations (scratch marks): OCD spectrum • Bruising/scars: Depression, self-harm disorder, borderline personality disorder. • Skin picking: Anxiety, BFRBs. • Pallor: Anaemia (common in depression, eating disorders). • Jaundice: Liver problems (alcohol abuse, medications-Chlorpromazine). • Others o Tattoos o Injection marks (Skin popping-Drug abuse) o Cut scars - Attempted suicide o Self-mutilating tendency o Caput medusae (distended veins) - Alcoholism (portal hypertension)
Hair	Quantity, texture, colour	• Lanugo (anorexia) • Piloerection (opiate withdrawal) • Loss: Stress, thyroid problems, malnutrition. • Changes in texture/colour: Malnutrition, hormonal problems.

Nails	Clubbing, brittleness, colour changes	• Clubbing: Lung or heart disease. • Brittleness: Malnutrition, dehydration. • Colour changes: Anaemia, infection.
Eyes	Redness, jaundice, pupil size changes	• Redness: Allergies, infections, dry eyes. • Jaundice: Liver problems. • Pupil size changes: Neurological problems, drug use.
Eyes	Constricted Pupil	• Heroin, Morphine, Oxycodone, Fentanyl, Methadone, Codeine, Hydrocodone
Eyes	Conjunctival redness	• Marijuana
Eyes	Dilated pupil	• Amphetamines, Hallucinogens, Opiates
Ears	Drainage, hearing loss	• Drainage: Infection. • Hearing loss: Age, noise exposure, infections.
Nose	Discharge, difficulty breathing	• Discharge: Allergies, infections, other conditions. • Difficulty breathing: Allergies, infections, structural problems. • Nasal septal defect (cocaine use) • Red, bulbous nose (alcoholism)
Mouth	Sores, bleeding gums, taste changes	• Sores: Infections, injuries, cancer. • Bleeding gums: Gingivitis, periodontitis. • Taste changes: Medications, infections, nerve damage. • Dry mouth: Anxiety, medication side effects. • Clenching/grinding teeth: Anxiety, sleep disorders.
Movement	Speed, restlessness, tremor	• Slowed down: Parkinson's disease, over-sedation, depression. • Restlessness/agitation: Anxiety, mania, ADHD. • Tremor: Anxiety, Parkinson's disease, medication side effects. • Tardive dyskinesia (involuntary movements) • Tardive dyskinesia (medication side effect).
Face	Expressions, asymmetry	• Blunted affect: Depression • Veraguths fold: Depression • Asymmetry: Bell's palsy, stroke (depression risk). • Moon-like face (Cushing's disease)
Neck	Thyroid enlargement	• Enlargement: Hyperthyroidism (anxiety, insomnia).
Skin (Neck)	Scars	• Scars (head injury, self-harm, accidents)
Parotid glands	Enlargement	• Enlargement: Anorexia, bulimia, alcoholism

Tongue, Teeth, Gums	Hygiene, condition	• Poor hygiene: Self-neglect. • Teeth eroded (inside): Bulimia (vomiting). • Broken teeth: Alcohol problems (falls, fights). • Dark line on gums: Lead poisoning. • Smooth/swollen/red tongue: Vitamin deficiencies, Anaemia • "Meth Mouth" • Candidal infection: Immune suppression • Clenching or grinding of teeth in anxiety and sleep disorders; MDMA use
Abnormal facial Movements	Tardive dyskinesia- Repetitive, involuntary movements of the face, tongue, or limbs	• Can be a side effect of long-term antipsychotic medication use
	Psychogenic movements- Functional movement disorders with no neurological cause	• Can mimic movement disorders like tremors or tics, often triggered by stress
	Stereotypes - Repetitive, purposeless movements such as rocking or head banging	• Can be seen in autism spectrum disorder or intellectual disability
	Tics - Sudden, brief, repetitive movements or vocalizations	• Characteristic symptom of Tourette's syndrome, may also occur in OCD or anxiety disorders

List is NOT exhaustive; Refer to standard Psychiatry, Neurology and General Medicine books for reference

Another classic issue, for a country like India is the need and the significance of identifying anaemia, which may be linked to chronic self-neglect and poor dietary intake, as commonly observed in patients with conditions like depression, schizophrenia, and anorexia nervosa.

One needs to identify and understand the significance of rashes due to medication and their association with mental health symptoms. Furthermore, it emphasizes the importance of examining the hands and arms for indicators of psychopathy, substance misuse, neural abnormalities and potential signs of liver disease.

The most neglected is cursory examination of the oral cavity, particularly in patients with mental illnesses and substance abuse, as dental hygiene is commonly neglected. [Meth mouth; Cocaine and MDMA causes bruxism and attrition]

Palpation

It is another integral part of clinical examination – For example potential information that can be gleaned from a simple handshake. For instance, a warm, sweaty palm may indicate endocrine disorders like thyroid disease or acromegaly, while a fine tremor can support a clinical diagnosis of thyrotoxicosis. Additionally, cold tremulous hands may be indicative of anxiety disorders, and tremors can also be caused by medication such as lithium and neuroleptics. Furthermore, symmetrical coarse tremors, bradykinesia, and rigidity may suggest iatrogenic

Parkinsonism, whereas, asymmetrical signs could point to primary Parkinson's disease, often associated with depressive disorder or Lewy body dementia.

Palpating lymph nodes might help to identify feature of tuberculosis, particularly in those susceptible due to self-neglect and living in institutional settings. Furthermore, tuberculosis and lymphoma are complications of HIV infection, which is known to be associated with cognitive impairment. The presence of an enlarged supraclavicular lymph node in a patient who smokes should raise suspicion of bronchogenic carcinoma, warranting close examination of the chest and chest X-ray. Moreover, axillary lymphadenopathy may indicate metastatic breast disease, highlighting the significance of breast examination as a crucial part of the physical examination.

Examination of Cardio-Vascular System

The examination of individual systems encompasses several key components. To begin, the jugular venous pressure (JVP) observation is a fundamental part of the cardiovascular examination and should be conducted with the patient lying at a 45° angle. In normal circumstances, the venous pulse should be observed just above the clavicle, and its prominence can increase with the patient lying flatter or with pressure applied over the right upper quadrant of the abdomen. Moreover, patients with congestive cardiac failure, causes of right heart failure, or vena caval obstruction may exhibit a raised jugular venous pressure. Additionally, the presence of edema is noteworthy as it is an important sign in congestive cardiac failure and can also be linked to hypoalbuminemia resulting from liver disease, and occasionally, anorexia nervosa.

Furthermore, baseline pulse, its rate, rhythm, and blood pressure hold significant importance in providing valuable information about the patient's physical well-being and serve as comparators for monitoring the patient's health status. The nature of the pulse and blood pressure can be particularly significant in various conditions.

To cite a few example,

- Hypertension can be associated with alcohol misuse, thyroid disorder, clozapine therapy, high doses of venlafaxine, and renal failure.
- Hypotension can be observed in anorexia nervosa, Addison's disease, and may signify autonomic dysfunction associated with diabetes mellitus and Lewy body dementia, or be a side-effect of certain medications.
- Swinging blood pressure in conjunction with other symptoms may indicate conditions such as acute intermittent porphyria or neuroleptic malignant syndrome or pheochromocytoma.

Additionally, the examination also includes the assessment of the apical beat, heart sounds, murmurs, and peripheral pulses for the comprehensive evaluation of the cardiovascular system and the presence of any vascular diseases.

Gastrointestinal System

The examination of the abdomen is crucial, and it should be carried out with the patient lying flat, except in cases of cardiac failure. It is particularly important in the case of suspected alcohol misuse.

- Distended veins around the umbilicus (caput medusae), can suggest portal hypertension due to cirrhosis.
- The abdomen itself may be distended owing to ascites, which can be confirmed by dullness on percussion in the flanks and a shift in the dullness when the patient moves onto one side.
- In the early stages of cirrhosis, the liver may be enlarged and tender, while in later stages, it can become hard and shrunken.
- Other signs of portal hypertension include splenomegaly and hemorrhoids.

These indicators can help in the diagnosis of gastrointestinal disorders and guide the appropriate treatment plan to address these conditions effectively. Therefore, recognizing these signs and symptoms during abdominal examination is of paramount importance in clinical practice. It allows for early intervention and management of gastrointestinal conditions, thereby improving patient outcomes and quality of life. Throughout the examination process, it is vital to consider these indicators and incorporate them into the patient's overall assessment and care plan.

Neurological Examination

The main objective of a neurological examination is to localize any potential neurological issues. Understanding neuroanatomy is crucial for clinicians conducting the examination, given its impact on the interpretation of findings. The neurological and mental state examinations overlap in assessing conscious level, orientation, memory, higher intellectual function, and speech. It is essential to record the conscious level on admission to establish a baseline for any changes. The Glasgow Coma Scale is a widely accepted tool for this purpose. Memory, intellectual function, and speech are pivotal in the assessment, with dysphasia being a significant localizing sign.

Conventional neuroleptics, anticonvulsants in high doses, cerebrovascular disease, multiple sclerosis, cerebellar disease, and tardive dyskinesia can all be associated with dysarthria. A full neurological examination, which takes about 40 minutes, should be conducted systematically, starting with cranial nerve examinations, followed by sensation, motor system, coordination, and reflexes. However, in practice, a more concise assessment is often performed, particularly in outpatient settings. Despite this, a brief assessment can still provide reasonable certainty regarding the absence of major brain pathology.

Neuroanatomy knowledge is crucial for effective neurological examination, which encompasses overlapping elements with mental state examination.

Memory, intellectual function, and speech play essential roles in the examination, and dysarthria can be a notable sign of various conditions. While a full neurological examination is ideal, practical limitations often lead to a more concise assessment, which can still provide valuable insights.

The 3-Minute Neurological Examination

The 3-minute neurological examination described in the research paper focuses on a concise assessment of various neurological functions.

- It begins with Romberg's test, intended to evaluate balance and proprioception.
- The heel-toe and tandem tests assess plantar and dorsiflexion, while the drift test examines for neurological deficits in muscle tone and coordination.
- Light touch and coordination are assessed by testing the patient's ability to touch their nose with specific fingers.
- The examination also encompasses assessments for extrapyramidal function, ataxia, facial nerve innervation, pseudobulbar palsy, visual fields, occulomotor function, reflexes, and signs of papilloedema, optic atrophy, and systemic vascular disease.

It serves as a valuable tool for triage and initial assessment, enabling timely and appropriate intervention for patients with potential neurological issues. This succinct examination demonstrates the efficiency and utility of a brief yet informative assessment of neurological function. It can be a valuable resource for healthcare professionals, particularly in scenarios where time is limited, allowing for a quick evaluation of a patient's neurological status and the identification of any potential concerns that may require further investigation or intervention.

The Extrapyramidal System

The extrapyramidal system is a crucial focus in the assessment of neurological impairment and the potential side effects of neuroleptic drugs.

- The examination of abnormal movements, poverty of movement, tone (specifically lead pipe or cogwheel rigidity), and gait (festinant) is emphasized, and abnormalities in these areas should be carefully noted.
- It has been observed that neuroleptic-naïve patients may exhibit abnormal involuntary movements and general neurological impairment. Furthermore, the presence of extrapyramidal signs has been linked to the acute extrapyramidal side effects of typical neuroleptic drugs, including rigidity, tremor, akathisia, and dystonia.
- It is noted that hyperkinetic signs in neuroleptic-naïve patients, along with abnormalities in manual dexterity and coordination, may be indicative of vulnerability to tardive dyskinesia.

These findings underscore the importance of thorough assessment of the extrapyramidal system in both identifying neurological impairment and predicting potential adverse effects of neuroleptic medications. Understanding the significance of these signs in neuroleptic-naïve patients can contribute to more effective assessments and interventions in clinical settings, particularly in the context of tardive dyskinesia vulnerability.

The Sensory System

The sensory system plays a crucial role in clinical examination, relying heavily on patient cooperation and subjective reporting rather than solely clinician observation. Sensation is typically tested in two main anatomical groups, with vibration and proprioception sensations conducted by neurons.

- Vibration sensation may be impacted by diabetic neuropathy, highlighting the importance of its assessment.
- The sensation of pain, pinprick, and light touch is carried out in the spinothalamic tracts.

Understanding the location of each dermatome is beneficial for localization purposes and can aid in distinguishing between functional and organic lesions, as the former may not adhere to a recognized dermatomal pattern. This underscores the significance of incorporating sensory system assessment into clinical practice to gain valuable insights into patients' neurological health and identifying potential lesions.

The Motor System

The motor system is crucial in diagnosing and understanding various neurological conditions. When assessing weakness in the motor system, the pattern of weakness is more important than its severity. Three essential patterns of weakness are highlighted: hemiplegia (weakness on one side of the body), paraparesis (weakness of both legs), and weakness limited to the distal portions of the limbs. These patterns can indicate site of lesions, such as contralateral brain damage, spinal cord damage, or peripheral nervous system damage.

In patients with medically unexplained hemiparesis, Hoover's sign is a valuable diagnostic tool. This test involves the patient lying supine on a couch and attempting to raise their affected and unaffected legs while the examiner assesses the strength and force exerted. Notably, if the examiner is able to raise the heel of the affected leg when the patient raises the unaffected leg, it reveals intact strength in the affected leg, indicating that the weakness may not be due to physical impairment but could be psychologically driven.

Overall, understanding the patterns of weakness in the motor system and utilizing diagnostic tools such as Hoover's sign can provide valuable insights into the underlying causes of motor deficits, ultimately aiding in the accurate diagnosis and management of neurological conditions.

Reflexes

The Reflexes assessment and interpretation of tendon reflexes is crucial – Distinguishing

- Sluggish reflexes, particularly those with a delayed relaxation phase, should prompt further investigations for hypothyroidism. Hyperreflexia, on the other hand, is associated with upper motor neuron lesions.
- Absence of reflexes may point to lower motor neuron lesions or peripheral neuropathy, which could be linked to conditions such as diabetes mellitus and alcohol misuse.
- Upgoing plantar response, known as Babinski's sign, indicates upper motor neuron pathology. This pathology may be localized in the spinal cord or brain.

Mental Status Examination:

The Mental Status Examination (MSE)—a structured assessment of client's behavioural and cognitive functioning—is a vital component of health examination that assists with evaluation of mental health conditions. The MSE is analogous to the physical examination. Specifically, the MSE assesses a patients current state including general appearance, mood and affect, speech, thought process and content, perceptual disturbances, impulse control, cognition, knowledge, judgment and insight. The MSE should and can be used across clinical settings, not just in a psychiatric context, takes only a few minutes to administer and can generate information that is crucial for creating a plan of care.

The acronym **BEST PICK** can assist with learning the main elements of an MSE. A brief description of the elements that are

- Behaviour and Appearance: This goes beyond just age and gender. It observes posture, how a person dresses and grooms themselves, their overall mannerisms, and alertness level. It also looks for signs of agitation, hyperactivity, or abnormal movements that could indicate underlying conditions.
- Emotions: This assesses a person's current mood (happy, sad, and anxious) and how well their emotions match their situation. It also considers the variability of their emotional state - do they swing rapidly between emotions, or remain stable?
- Speech: The examiner pays attention to how fast or slow someone speaks, how much they talk, and the overall style and tone of their speech. For instance, pressured speech (rapid and loud) or slow, mumbled speech can be indicators of different mental states.
- Thought Content and Processes: This explores a person's thought patterns and the content of their thoughts. Are there any obsessions or delusions present? Does the person express suicidal or homicidal thoughts? The doctor also looks for abnormalities in how thoughts are connected. For instance, "loose associations", "tangential thinking" "Word salad" "neologisms". The examination also considers whether thinking is circumstantial (focusing on irrelevant details) or abstract (considering broader concepts).
- Perceptual Disturbances: This assesses if someone is experiencing illusions (misinterpretations of real sensory stimuli) or hallucinations (seeing or hearing things that aren't there).
- Insight: Refers to the patient's understanding of their illness and functionality
- Cognition: This assesses a person's level of consciousness (alertness), orientation (to time, place, and person), concentration (ability to focus), and memory (immediate and long-term recall).
- Knowledge, and Judgment: This assesses a person's understanding of their situation, and the potential consequences of their actions. It also evaluates their ability to make sound decisions.

By examining all these aspects, the MSE builds a comprehensive picture of a person's mental state, providing crucial information for diagnosis and treatment planning. Learn the complete MSE from Standard Psychiatric Textbooks. **Remember skilful history taking is not only information gathering to diagnose but also a potential therapeutic opportunity.**

****

Studying Neurotransmitters Level for Diagnosis

Neurotransmitter	Metabolite	High levels in urine	Low levels in urine
Serotonin	5-HIAA	Depression, 5HTP use, anxiety	Autism spectrum disorder, depression, dysbiosis, irritability, low libido, oral contraceptives
GABA	Succinic semialdehyde	Sleep apnea, ovarian cancer, anxiety	Anxiety, sleep difficulties, adrenal distress, hypothalamic pituitary adrenal axis feedback dysfunction, ADHD, Tourette syndrome
Glycine	hippurate	Clinically suspected in anxiety	Diabetes, hypothyroidism, obesity, intense exercise, clinically suspected in depression
Glutamate	Alpha-ketoglutarate; Glutamine:	Celiac disease, hyperthyroidism, clinically suspected in anxiety, autism spectrum disorder, depression, sleep issues	Migraines, clinically suspected in depression, chronic fatigue, lack of concentration, low energy levels, sleep disturbances
Histamine	Methylhistamine	Cystitis, flushing disorder, food allergies, polycythemia, pregnancy	Fatigue, low libido, low productivity, mild depression, tension headaches, weight gain
Phenethylamine	Phenylacetic acid; Phenylpropionic acid	Bipolar major affective disorder, anxiety, insomnia, phenylketonuria, methylphenidate treatment	Autism spectrum disorder, ADHD, depression, inattentiveness
Dopamine	DOPAC, HVA	Anxiety, stress, paroxysmal hypertension, primary aldosteronism, PTSD, mercury toxicity	Alzheimer's disease, anorexia nervosa, fibromyalgia, hypertension, periodic limb movement disorder, sleep disturbances, hypoadrenergic orthostatic hypotension
Epinephrine	VMA	Anxiety, ADHD, bipolar disorder, depression, hyperglycemia, sleep apnea, PTSD, stress	Alzheimer's disease, metabolic syndrome, obesity
Norepinephrine	Normetanephrine, VMA	Anxiety, ADHD, bipolar disorder, depression, hyperglycemia, sleep apnea, PTSD, stress	Alzheimer's disease, metabolic syndrome, obesity

Source: Website of ZRTB labs

Additional tests

ADHD	Neurotransmitter assay + Diurnal Hormones test
Andropause	Neurotransmitter assay + Diurnal Hormones test
Children and Adolescents	Only Neurotransmitter assay - Urine
Establish a baseline for psychiatric disorder	Only Neurotransmitter assay - Urine
High androgen symptoms- acne, scalp hair loss, facial	Neurotransmitter + Hormone Metabolites

hair growth	
High or low androgen symptoms	Neurotransmitter assay + Hormones test
Hormone levels recently tested	Only Neurotransmitter assay - Urine
Low androgen symptoms- fatigue, foggy thinking, decreased stamina	Neurotransmitter + Hormone Metabolites
Managing psychiatric interventions	Only Neurotransmitter assay - Urine
Patients unable to use Hormone replacement therapy	Only Neurotransmitter assay - Urine
PCOS	Neurotransmitter assay + Diurnal Hormones test/ Hormone metabolites
PMS/PMDD	Neurotransmitter assay + Hormones test
Pre-menopause & menopause	Neurotransmitter assay + Diurnal Hormones test
Sleep problems	Neurotransmitter assay + Diurnal Hormones test
Suspected HPA axis dysfunction	Neurotransmitter assay + Diurnal Hormones test/ Hormone metabolites
Symptoms of estrogen dominance	Neurotransmitter assay + Diurnal Hormones test/ Hormone metabolites

Source: ZRTB labs

Patient Refferals - When & to Whom to Refer?

Domain	Advice	Counselling	Psychotherapy	Psychopharmacotherapeutics
Focus	Specific problem-solving	Specific problems or broader life challenges	Underlying causes of mental and emotional distress	Treatment of medical conditions and mental health disorders using medications
Goal	Provide a solution or suggestion	Facilitate understanding, exploration, and decision-making	Promote long-term healing and change	Improve or manage symptoms, address underlying biological factors
Provider	Anyone with expertise or experience	Trained counsellor or therapist	Licensed psychotherapist or Clinical psychologist	Registered Psychiatrist (MD/DPM)
Approach	Directive, focused on quick fixes	Collaborative, supportive, focused on client empowerment	In-depth exploration of thoughts, feelings, and behaviours	Medically-supervised use of medications to achieve therapeutic effects
Structure	Informal, may be one-time or ongoing	Structured sessions, typically weekly or biweekly	Structured sessions, often over a longer period of time	Prescriptions, medication monitoring, and adjustments as needed
Techniques	Offering suggestions, sharing opinions	Active listening, exploring options, providing resources	Using therapeutic techniques like CBT, psychodynamic therapy, or EMDR	Selection, administration, and monitoring of medications
Types of issues addressed	Specific problems, decisions, or dilemmas	Wide range of life challenges, including relationships,	Mental health disorders, trauma, chronic emotional distress	Medical conditions with mental health symptoms (e.g., depression, anxiety), treatment-resistant mental health disorders

		career, stress, grief, and addiction		
Depth	Shallow	Moderate	Deep	Focuses on biological and physiological aspects of mental health
What is it about	Specific issue or question	Broader life challenges	Mental health conditions, emotional distress, trauma	Medical conditions and their associated symptoms, mental health disorders
Where it happens	Informal setting	Counselling centre, school, community centre	Therapist's office, hospital	Doctor's office, hospital
Why seek it	Need a solution or suggestion	Explore options, gain clarity, manage challenges	Address underlying causes of distress, improve mental well-being	Manage symptoms, improve function, address underlying biological factors
When to seek it	Faced with a specific problem	Feeling overwhelmed, need support	Experiencing mental health symptoms	When symptoms are severe, psychotherapy is not effective alone, or there's a biological component to the condition
How much it costs	Varies depending on the provider	Variable fees, may have insurance coverage	Typically higher fees than counselling, may have insurance coverage	Varies depending on medication, dosage, and insurance coverage
Minimum Qualifications	No formal qualifications required	Master's degree in counselling or related field	Varies depending on the profession (MD in Psychiatry, Master's in Psychology/Social Work + professional training)	Doctor of Medicine (MD) or DPM degree
Legal Requirements & Registrations	None required	No specific legal requirement, but ethical practice guidelines exist	Mandatory registration with relevant Rehabilitation Council of India	Mandatory registration with NMC

4. Ethical Component in Mental Health Clinic & Wards

Mental Illness	**Ethical Issues with**		
	Interaction-Communication	**Case History & Record Maintenance**	**Referral issues**
Major Depressive Disorder	Confidentiality breaches; Stigma reduction, patient autonomy	Proper documentation of sensitive information including suicide.	Collaborative decision-making with mental health professionals
Schizophrenia	Informed consent challenges; Managing potential social isolation	Secure storage of detailed psychiatric evaluation	Ensuring timely and appropriate medical evaluation
Anxiety Disorders	Cultural competence; Balancing patient disclosure and privacy	Appropriate sharing of information with consent	Referring for psychotherapy or counselling as needed
Bipolar Disorder	Disclosure of diagnosis; Addressing medication non-adherence	Integration of psychiatric history in health records	Collaborating with medical professionals on medication adjustments
Substance Use Disorders	Confidentiality vs. safety; Non-judgmental approach to addiction	Documenting substance abuse history	Facilitating referrals to addiction specialists and rehabilitation centers
Substance-Induced Psychotic Disorder	Assessing substance use impact on mental health; Supporting withdrawal and managing substance-induced symptoms	Documenting substance use history and associated psychosis	Referring for injection drug users and coordinating care with addiction specialists
Neurocognitive Disorders	Capacity assessment; Empathetic communication with caregivers	Managing legal implications of cognitive decline	Ensuring patient and caregiver involvement in decision-making

Eating Disorders	Body image sensitivity; Avoiding reinforcement of unhealthy behaviours	Documenting nutritional and psychological aspects	Coordinating care with dieticians and mental health specialists
Personality Disorders	Boundary violations; Establishing therapeutic rapport	Ethical handling of challenging behaviours	Coordinating care with psychologists and psychotherapists
Antisocial Personality Disorder	Balancing safety concerns with therapeutic rapport; Establishing boundaries while promoting rehabilitation	Documenting antisocial behaviours and risk assessments	Coordinating care with legal authorities and mental health professionals
Borderline Personality Disorder	Managing potential self-harm risks; Establishing and maintaining therapeutic boundaries	Documenting self-harm risk assessments and safety plans	Collaborating with psychologists
Post-Traumatic Stress Disorder	Trauma-informed care; Providing a safe space for disclosure	Recording trauma history appropriately	Referring for trauma-focused therapy and support services
Obsessive-Compulsive Disorder	Balancing reassurance; Respectful engagement in exposure therapy	Documenting treatment plans and progress	Ensuring collaboration with psychologists and behavioural therapists
Child and Adolescent Issues	Consent and confidentiality; Building trust with both child and caregiver	Safeguarding minors' information	Collaborating with child psychiatrists and paediatricians
Sleep Disorders	Sleep hygiene; Evaluating lifestyle factors affecting sleep	Documenting sleep patterns and disturbances	Referring to sleep specialists and conducting sleep studies
Chronic Pain disorders	Opioid prescribing ethics; Addressing the psychosocial impact of pain	Properly documenting pain assessments	Coordinating care with pain specialists and physiotherapists

Somatoform Disorders	Empathetic communication; Validating patient experiences; Never say “nothing wrong” or “no illness”	Avoiding unnecessary medical interventions	Collaborating with psychologists for therapy
Terminal Illness	Truth-telling and empathy; Addressing end-of-life decisions	Recording advanced care directives	Collaborating with palliative care specialists and counsellors
Conversion Disorder	Sensitive diagnosis; Supporting patients without scepticism	Documenting psychological factors	Coordinating care with psychiatrists and neurologists
Sexual Dysfunction	Confidential sexual history; Creating a non-judgmental atmosphere	Documenting sexual history appropriately	Referring to sexual health specialists and therapists
Adjustment Disorders	Coping strategies; Offering emotional support	Documenting stressors and coping mechanisms	Referring for counselling and psychological support
Psychosomatic Disorders	Holistic approach; Recognizing the mind-body connection	Documenting both physical and psychological aspects	Coordinating care with specialists in psychosomatic medicine
Intimate Partner Violence	Safety concerns; Providing resources for support and safety	Documenting injuries and safety plans	Collaborating with domestic violence counsellors and legal services
Attention-Deficit/Hyperactivity Disorder	Disclosure to schools and workplaces; Creating supportive environments for academic and professional success	Record confidentiality in educational and occupational settings	Coordinating care with educators and employers for necessary accommodations
Autism Spectrum Disorder	Communication strategies with patients on the spectrum; Sensory considerations and social interaction challenges	Record communication preferences and sensory needs	Collaborating with special educators and therapists for tailored support

Dissociative Disorders	Establishing trust with patients experiencing dissociation; Avoiding retraumatization and understanding dissociative amnesia	Documenting dissociative episodes and triggers	
Conduct Disorder	Balancing confidentiality with the safety of others; Providing guidance on appropriate behaviour and consequences	Documenting behavioural interventions and consequences	Collaborating with school, child psychiatrists, and legal authorities
Acute Stress Disorder	Timely intervention following traumatic events; Providing emotional support and coping strategies	Documenting acute stress reactions and triggers	Referring for trauma-focused therapy and support services
Specific Phobias	Gradual exposure techniques; Addressing fears without causing distress	Documenting specific phobias and progression in treatment	Collaborating with psychologists for exposure therapy and behavioural interventions
Social Anxiety Disorder	Creating supportive environments for social interactions; Encouraging social participation while respecting patient comfort	Documenting social anxiety triggers and avoidance behaviours	Referring for cognitive-behavioural therapy and social skills training
Seasonal Affective Disorder	Addressing the impact of seasonal changes on mood; Encouraging lifestyle adjustments for seasonal affective symptoms	Documenting seasonal patterns of mood changes	Referring for light therapy
Body Dysmorphic Disorder	Addressing distorted body image concerns; Minimizing reinforcement of appearance-related obsessions	Documenting body dysmorphic concerns and associated behaviours	Referring to therapists specializing in body dysmorphic disorder treatment

Hoarding Disorder	Balancing autonomy with safety concerns ;Providing support for decluttering efforts	Documenting living conditions and safety assessments	Coordinating care with mental health professionals and social services
Trichotillomania	Sensitivity to shame and guilt associated with hair pulling; Encouraging alternative coping strategies	Documenting trichotillomania behaviours and triggers	Referring to therapists specializing in habit reversal therapy
Kleptomania	Addressing legal and ethical implications of stealing; Exploring motivations behind theft and impulse control	Documenting theft incidents and consequences; Past interactions with police/legal system	Coordinating care with legal authorities and mental health professionals
Factitious Disorder	Navigating deceptive behaviours and seeking genuine care; Establishing trust and understanding underlying motivations	Documenting patterns of deception and medical falsification	Coordinating care with psychiatrists and addressing underlying psychological issues; Involving risk management professionals
Paraphilic Disorders	Addressing stigma and discomfort around sexual behaviours; Offering non-judgmental support and appropriate interventions	Documenting paraphilic behaviours and associated distress	Referring to specialized therapists and sexologists for tailored interventions
Gaming Disorder	Balancing screen time concerns with autonomy; Addressing potential social isolation and withdrawal symptoms	Documenting gaming behaviours and associated impairments	Coordinating care with psychologists and incorporating family interventions
Premenstrual Dysphoric Disorder	Discussing hormonal influences on mood and behaviour; Providing support for emotional and physical symptoms	Documenting menstrual cycle-related symptoms and impact	Referring to gynaecologists and coordinating care with mental health specialists

Oppositional Defiant Disorder	Collaborating with caregivers and educators for support; Establishing clear boundaries and consequences for behaviour	Documenting disruptive behaviours and interventions	Coordinating care with educators, school counsellors, and mental health professionals
Gender Dysphoria	Affirming and respectful communication ;Supporting gender identity exploration and expression	Documenting gender identity concerns and related distress	Referring to gender-affirming healthcare and collaborating with gender specialists
Somatic Symptom disorder	Addressing health anxiety and excessive worry ;Offering reassurance while addressing underlying emotional distress	Documenting somatic symptoms and associated psychological factors	Coordinating care with psychologists and addressing underlying psychological concerns
Malingering	Balancing skepticism with maintaining patient trust; Conducting thorough assessments to distinguish genuine symptoms	Documenting inconsistencies and suspicions of malingering	Coordinating care with forensic psychologists and legal authorities
Stuttering	Creating a supportive and non-judgmental environment; Encouraging effective communication strategies	Documenting stuttering patterns and impact on daily life	Referring to speech therapists and incorporating communication support
Erotomania	Handling delusional beliefs about romantic relationships; Navigating potential legal and ethical concerns related to fixation	Documenting delusional beliefs and assessing potential risks	Coordinating care with mental health professionals and involving legal authorities
Postpartum Depression	Addressing cultural nuances around motherhood; Providing emotional support and understanding postpartum challenges	Documenting postpartum depressive symptoms and their impact	Referring to perinatal mental health specialists and involving family support

Acute Transient Psychotic Disorder	Navigating sudden onset of psychosis and distress; Offering support during acute episodes and understanding triggers	Documenting psychotic symptoms and associated stressors	Referral for neurology evaluation

5. Decoding Mind & Behaviour

Acting out - Masking Grief with Disruptive Behaviour

During ward rounds, Dr. Verma meets a teenage girl who has a younger sibling suffering from a terminal illness. While the family is much concerned, the teenager has begun exhibiting behavioural changes – declining grades at school and frequent arguments with her parents. Dr. Verma suspects these behaviours might be a way of coping with her difficult emotions. Dr. Verma recognizes the teenager's behaviour as a defense mechanism. **Which of the following is the most likely defense mechanism at play?**

a) **Denial**
b) **Displacement**
c) **Regression**
d) **Acting Out**
e) **Intellectualization**

Explanation: Acting out is the most fitting defense mechanism because the teenager's behaviour (declining grades, arguments) disrupts her normal routine and expresses her underlying emotional turmoil in a way that seeks attention. **Denial:** (Incorrect) The teenager is showing outward signs of distress through behavioural changes; **Displacement:** (Incorrect) Displacement redirects emotions towards a different target, but the teenager's behaviour seems directed at her immediate family; **Regression:** (Possible, but less likely) Regression is a return to earlier developmental stages. While emotional distress can manifest as regression, the school decline and arguments suggest a possible attempt to gain attention; **Acting Out:** (Correct) Acting out involves expressing unacceptable emotions through disruptive behaviour. The teenager's declining grades and arguments could be her way of expressing her grief and anger; **Intellectualization:** (Incorrect) Intellectualization involves overthinking and analysing emotions to detach from them. The teenager's behaviour suggests emotional expression, not detachment

Communication Aspects:

- **Empathy:** Acknowledge the difficulty of having a sibling suffering from a terminal illness.
- **Open-ended questions:** Encourage the teenager to express her feelings about her sibling's death.
- **Active listening:** Pay close attention to her verbal and nonverbal cues.
- **Validation:** Validate her emotions and let her know it's okay to feel sad, angry, or confused.
- **Support:** Offer support and resources for coping with grief, such as individual therapy or support groups.

Pertinent Questions:
Knowledge:
What are defense mechanisms and how do they function? (Unconscious psychological processes that protect the individual from overwhelming emotions)
How can acting out behaviour be a negative coping mechanism? (It can damage relationships, lead to academic decline)

Comment: Always rule out major depressive disorder as paediatric depression presents as irritability.

Attitude:

Why is it important to identify defense mechanisms in patients? (Understanding defense mechanisms helps address the underlying emotions causing the behaviour)

How can doctors balance empathy for a patient's emotional state with setting boundaries for disruptive behaviour? (Validate feelings while expressing clear expectations for appropriate behaviour)

Application:

How might Dr. Verma develop a plan to help the teenager cope with her situation in a healthier way? (Individual therapy, counselling, support groups, expressing emotions through creative outlets)

Communication Skills:

What is a good opening question for Dr. Verma to initiate a conversation about the teenager's concern? ("I know this must be a very difficult time for you. Can you tell me a little bit about how you're feeling since your sibling is suffering?")

How can Dr. Verma use active listening skills to understand the teenager's perspective? (Maintain eye contact, use encouraging nods, and summarize what she says to confirm understanding)

How can Dr. Verma validate the teenager's emotions without condoning her disruptive behaviour? (Acknowledge her sadness and anger, but also explain the importance of finding healthier ways to express those feelings)

****

Finding Purpose through Helping Others - Altruism and Self-Esteem

During outpatient, Dr. Rao meets with a woman who reported for stress and anxiety arising from multi-tasking. Patient appears to be quite dedicated to helping others. She works a demanding job but still volunteers all her free days at a local homeless shelter. Dr. Rao wonders if this strong commitment to helping others might be connected to the patient's own sense of self-worth. Dr. Rao suspects the woman's volunteer work might be serving a psychological purpose. **Which defense mechanism is most likely at play?**

a) **Denial**
b) **Projection**
c) **Reaction Formation**
d) **Altruism**
e) **Intellectualization**

Explanation: While the woman's volunteer work demonstrates genuine altruism, Dr. Rao recognizes that it might also serve the unconscious purpose of improving her self-image. Altruism best captures the concept of helping others while potentially addressing underlying emotional needs. **Denial** involves refusing to acknowledge a difficult reality. The woman is actively involved in helping the homeless; **Projection** attributes one's own unwanted feelings onto others. The woman is not attributing her struggles to the homeless population; **Reaction Formation** (Possible, but less likely) involves expressing the opposite of an unwanted feeling. While the volunteer work might mask negative self-esteem, other options fit more directly; **Altruism** is helping others with a genuine desire to improve their well-being. However, it can also serve an unconscious purpose, such as boosting self-esteem in someone struggling with self-image; **Intellectualization** involves overthinking and analysing emotions to detach from them. The woman's actions suggest an active approach to helping others, not emotional detachment

Communication Aspects:

- **Non-judgmental approach:** Acknowledge the positive aspects of the woman's volunteer work.
- **Open-ended questions:** Encourage the woman to talk about her motivations for volunteering and how it makes her feel.
- **Active listening:** Pay close attention to both verbal and nonverbal cues.
- **Exploration:** Gently explore the possibility of a connection between her volunteer work and her self-esteem.
- **Support:** Offer support and resources for improving self-esteem, if needed.

Pertinent Questions:
Knowledge:
What is altruism and how can it be a defense mechanism? (Unselfish helping behaviour that can also serve to alleviate negative self-feelings)
How can positive defense mechanisms, like altruism, benefit mental health? (They can provide a healthy outlet for emotions and foster a sense of purpose)

Attitude:
Why is it important to consider both conscious and unconscious motivations behind a patient's behaviour? (A complete understanding can lead to more effective treatment approaches)
How can doctors balance appreciating a patient's positive coping mechanisms with addressing any underlying emotional issues? (Acknowledge the benefits while exploring if there are healthier or more sustainable ways to manage self-esteem)

Application:
How might Dr. Rao explore the connection between the woman's volunteer work and her self-esteem without discouraging her from helping others? (Ask open-ended questions about her feelings of fulfilment and purpose)

Communication Skills:
What is a good opening question for Dr. Rao to initiate a conversation about the woman's volunteer work? ("Tell me about your work at the homeless shelter. What motivates you to volunteer your time?")
How can Dr. Rao use active listening skills to understand the woman's perspective? (Maintain eye contact, offer encouraging nods, and summarize her responses to confirm understanding)
How can Dr. Rao acknowledge the positive aspects of the woman's volunteer work while also exploring the possibility of a deeper purpose? (Express appreciation for her work, then ask open-ended questions about how volunteering makes her feel and if there are other areas where she might also want to focus on improving her self-esteem)

****

Denial in the ICU - A Patient in Distress

During rounds in the intensive care unit, Dr. Mehta is concerned about a 54-year-old man who recently suffered a myocardial infarction. Despite the seriousness of his condition and the presence of monitoring equipment, the patient insists on getting out of bed and even attempts to do push-ups. Dr. Mehta recognizes this behaviour as a potential defense mechanism. Dr. Mehta suspects the man's behaviour is a way of coping with his heart attack. **Which defense mechanism is most likely at play?**

a) **Altruism**
b) **Displacement**
c) **Dissociation**
d) **Intellectualization**

Explanation: Denial is the most fitting defense mechanism because the man's behaviour (push-ups) contradicts the reality of his critical illness. He is refusing to acknowledge the seriousness of his situation; **Altruism:** (Incorrect) Altruism involves helping others. The man's behaviour is focused on himself; **Displacement:** (Incorrect) Displacement redirects emotions towards a different target. The man's actions are not directed elsewhere; **Dissociation:** (Possible, but less likely) Dissociation involves a detachment from reality. While denial can be a form of dissociation, the man's physical actions suggest denial is more likely; **Intellectualization:** (Incorrect) Intellectualization involves overthinking and analysing emotions to detach from them. The man's behaviour suggests a lack of emotional processing, not overthinking.

Communication Aspects:

- **Calm and empathetic approach:** Acknowledge the seriousness of the situation while remaining calm and reassuring.
- **Validation:** Validate the man's fear or anxiety, even if he is not directly expressing it.
- **Simple explanations:** Use clear and concise language to explain his condition and treatment plan.
- **Open-ended questions:** Encourage the man to express his concerns and feelings when he is ready.
- **Patient-centred care:** Tailor communication to the patient's emotional state and cultural background.

Pertinent Questions:

Knowledge:

What is denial and how does it function as a defense mechanism? (Refusal to acknowledge a difficult reality to protect oneself from emotional distress)

What are the potential dangers of denial in medical situations? (Delaying treatment, hindering recovery, increasing risk of complications)

Attitude:

Why is it important to be patient and understanding when encountering denial in a patient? (Denial can be a coping mechanism, and addressing the underlying emotions is crucial)

How can doctors balance respecting a patient's autonomy with ensuring they receive necessary medical care? (Provide clear information, explain the risks of denial, and involve the patient in decision-making as much as possible)

Application:

How might Dr. Mehta develop a plan to help the man move beyond denial and adjust to his condition? (Provide education about heart disease, involve family members in support, and offer counselling)

Communication Skills:

What is a good opening question for Dr. Mehta to initiate a conversation about the man's condition? ("I understand this must be a difficult time for you. Can you tell me a little bit about how you're feeling since your heart attack?")

How can Dr. Mehta use reflective listening to validate the man's emotions? (Briefly summarize his statements and acknowledge the emotional subtext, e.g., "It sounds like you're feeling scared or overwhelmed right now.")

How can Dr. Mehta explain the importance of treatment while remaining respectful of the man's denial? (Focus on the benefits of treatment for his health and quality of life, e.g., "Following the treatment plan can help you recover and get back to doing the activities you enjoy.")

****

Dissociation and Coping with Trauma - A Patient's Emotional Disconnect

During rounds, Dr. Krishnan meets with a woman who seems to withdraw and become unresponsive when discussing her medical history. She has a history of sexual abuse as a child, and Dr. Krishnan suspects this experience might be affecting her current emotional state. The woman appears to "zone out" when under stress, which raises a concern about a possible defense mechanism. Dr. Krishnan suspects the woman's "zoning out" behaviour is a way of managing her emotions. **Which defense mechanism is most likely at play?**

a) **Dissociation**
b) **Reaction formation**
c) **Regression**
d) **Splitting**
e) **Sublimation**

Correct Answer: Dissociation. **Explanation:** Dissociation is the most fitting defense mechanism because the woman's "zoning out" describes a mental separation from her thoughts and emotions, particularly when discussing a potentially triggering topic (her childhood abuse).

Communication Aspects:

- **Empathy and safety:** Acknowledge the sensitivity of the topic and create a safe space for the woman to share as much as she feels comfortable.
- **Trauma-informed approach:** Use language that is respectful and non-judgmental.
- **Open-ended questions:** Encourage the woman to describe her experiences and coping mechanisms in her own words.
- **Active listening:** Pay close attention to both verbal and nonverbal cues, including signs of dissociation.
- **Validation:** Validate her emotions and experiences, even if she doesn't explicitly discuss the abuse.

Pertinent Questions:

Knowledge:

What is dissociation and how does it function as a defense mechanism? (Mental separation from thoughts, feelings, memories, or sense of identity to manage overwhelming emotions)

How can dissociation be a negative coping mechanism in the long term? (It can hinder emotional processing, healthy relationships, and overall well-being)

Attitude:

Why is it important to consider a patient's history of trauma when evaluating their behaviour? (Trauma can lead to various coping mechanisms, including dissociation, which need to be understood for effective treatment)

How can doctors balance respecting patient privacy with addressing potential consequences of dissociation? (Maintain confidentiality while exploring the impact of dissociation on the patient's daily life and offering support)

Application:

How might Dr. Krishnan develop a treatment plan to help the woman manage her dissociation and past trauma? (Trauma-focused therapy, relaxation techniques, building coping skills)

Communication Skills:

What is a good opening question for Dr. Krishnan to initiate a conversation about the woman's emotional well-being? ("I understand that talking about medical history can sometimes be stressful. Can you tell me a little bit about how you usually cope with stressful situations?")

How can Dr. Krishnan use active listening skills to identify signs of dissociation? (Observe for changes in eye contact, voice tone, or posture that might indicate emotional withdrawal)

How can Dr. Krishnan validate the woman's experience with dissociation without pressuring her to discuss her trauma? (Acknowledge the difficulty of her situation and help with grounding exercises to reconnect oneself with body, emotion and immediate external environment)

****

A Patient's Light-hearted Approach

In his OP, Dr. Patel encounters a man who is being treated for obesity. The man seems to make light of his weight with frequent jokes and humorous comments, even about himself. Dr. Patel wonders if this use of humour might be a way of coping with a sensitive topic. Dr. Patel suspects the man's use of humour is a defense mechanism. **Which of the following is most likely at play?**

a) **Denial**
b) **Humour**
c) **Intellectualization**
d) **Projection**
e) **Reaction formation**

Correct Humour. It is the most fitting defense mechanism because the man's jokes about weight, including jokes directed at himself, serve as a way to express his feelings (perhaps anxiety or embarrassment) about his obesity in a way that avoids causing discomfort. **Denial:** (Incorrect) Denial involves refusing to acknowledge reality. The man seems aware of his weight by his presence in the weight management program; **Intellectualization:** (Incorrect) Intellectualization involves overthinking and not processing emotions to detach from them. The man's humour suggests emotional expression, not detachment; **Projection:** (Incorrect) Projection attributes unwanted feelings onto others. The man's jokes are about himself, not others; **Reaction formation:** (Incorrect) Reaction formation involves expressing the opposite of an unwanted feeling. While humour can mask negative emotions, it's not necessarily the opposite; **Regression:** (Incorrect) Regression is a return to earlier developmental stages. The use of humour suggests a mature coping mechanism; **splitting:** (Incorrect) Splitting involves seeing things in extremes (all good or all bad). Humour is a more nuanced way of expressing complex emotions; **Sublimation:** (Incorrect) Sublimation channels unacceptable urges into socially acceptable outlets. While humour can be a healthy outlet, it's not necessarily about unacceptable urges in this case; **Suppression:** (Incorrect) Suppression involves pushing unwanted thoughts or feelings out of awareness. Humour suggests the man is acknowledging his weight, not suppressing it; **Undoing:** (Incorrect) Undoing involves symbolically repairing a mistake. Humour doesn't directly relate to repairing a mistake.

Communication Aspects:

- **Open-ended questions:** Encourage patient to elaborate on his use of humour and how he feels about his weight.
- **Reflective listening:** Summarize his jokes and comments to see if they accurately reflect his underlying feelings.
- **Normalization:** Acknowledge that weight management can be challenging and humour can be a coping mechanism.

- **Supportive environment:** Create a safe space for him to express his concerns without judgment.
- **Collaboration:** Develop a weight management plan that considers his individual coping style and preferences.

Pertinent Questions:
Knowledge:
What is humour as a defense mechanism and how does it function? (Using humour to express difficult emotions in a socially acceptable way)
How can humour be a positive coping mechanism? (It can help reduce tension, promote emotional expression, and foster social connection)

Attitude:
Why is it important to consider the context and function of humour in a patient's communication? (Humour can be a valuable tool for coping, but it can also mask deeper issues that need to be addressed)
How can doctors strike a balance between appreciating a patient's humour and addressing serious health concerns? (Acknowledge the humour while gently exploring the underlying emotions and offering support)

Application:
How might Dr. Patel help the man develop a healthy relationship with food and exercise, moving beyond just coping with his weight? (Explore his motivations for weight management, develop a personalized plan that incorporates healthy habits, and provide support for long-term success)

Communication Skills:
What is a good opening question for Dr. Patel to initiate a conversation about the man's weight management journey? ("I see you have a great sense of humour! Can you tell me a little bit about your goals for weight management?")
How can Dr. Patel use reflective listening to understand the man's perspective? (Briefly rephrase his jokes or comments in a neutral way to see if they accurately reflect his feelings, e.g., "It sounds like you might be feeling a little self-conscious about your weight at times.")

****

Detachment through Knowledge

Dr. Singh has just been diagnosed with malignant melanoma. During family gatherings and conversations with colleagues, she dominates discussions about the disease, focusing heavily on survival rates, treatment options, and various medical studies. This behaviour raises a concern for Dr. Rao, a friend and colleague, who wonders if Dr. Singh might be using a defense mechanism to cope with her emotions. Dr. Rao suspects Dr. Singh's behaviour is a way of managing her emotional response to her diagnosis. **Which defense mechanism is most likely at play?**

a) **Intellectualization**
b) **Reaction formation**
c) **Sublimation**
d) **Suppression**
e) **Undoing**

Explanation: Intellectualization is the most fitting defense mechanism because Dr. Singh's excessive focus on statistics and medical details (the mind's higher functions) serves as a way to avoid experiencing the difficult emotions (fear, anxiety) associated with her cancer diagnosis; **Reaction formation:** (Incorrect) Reaction formation involves expressing the opposite of an unwanted feeling. While intellectualization can be a way of detaching from emotions, it's not necessarily the opposite; **Sublimation:** (Incorrect) Sublimation channels unacceptable urges into socially acceptable outlets. Intellectualization is not about unacceptable urges, but managing emotions. **Suppression:** (Incorrect) Suppression involves pushing unwanted thoughts or feelings out of awareness. Intellectualization suggests Dr. Singh is actively analysing her situation, not suppressing it.

Communication Aspects:

- **Empathy and validation:** Acknowledge the seriousness of the situation and validate Dr. Singh's emotions, even if she doesn't explicitly express them.
- **Open-ended questions:** Encourage her to share her feelings and concerns beyond medical details.
- **Active listening:** Pay close attention to both verbal and nonverbal cues, such as hesitation or avoidance of emotional topics.
- **Supportive environment:** Create a safe space for her to express her vulnerabilities without judgment.
- **Offering resources:** Connect her with support groups or counsellors specializing in coping with cancer diagnoses.

Pertinent Questions:

Knowledge:

What is intellectualization as a defense mechanism and how does it function? (Using reason, logic, and analysis to distance oneself from difficult emotions)

How can intellectualization be both positive and negative in its effects? (Positive - organizing thoughts, negative - emotional detachment hindering coping)

Attitude:

Why is it important to recognize defense mechanisms in healthcare professionals? (They can hinder effective communication about their own health needs and well-being)

How can healthcare professionals create a culture of open communication and emotional support for their colleagues? (Normalize discussions about mental health, model healthy coping mechanisms, and offer resources for seeking help)

Application:

How might Dr. Rao support Dr. Singh in developing a healthy emotional response to her diagnosis? (Encourage expression of emotions, connect her with support groups, and explore stress management techniques)

Communication Skills:

What is a good opening question for Dr. Rao to initiate a conversation about Dr. Singh's well-being? ("I know this must be a very difficult time for you. Can you tell me a little bit about how you're coping with your diagnosis?")

How can Dr. Rao use active listening to identify Dr. Singh's underlying emotions? (Pay attention to nonverbal cues, validate the information she shares, and gently explore her feelings, e.g., "It sounds like you're gathering a lot of information. Are there any specific concerns you might have that you haven't shared yet?")

How can Dr. Rao offer support and resources without pressuring Dr. Singh to share more than she's comfortable with? (Acknowledge her strength in seeking knowledge, offer support groups or counselling as options, and let her know you're there to listen whenever she's ready)

****

Projecting Insecurity - A Misguided Suspicion

Mr. Patel, a newly married man, keeps accusing his wife of infidelity. He constantly checks her phone and monitors her whereabouts. During a clinic visit, Dr. Mehta notices Mr. Patel seems overly attentive to an attractive woman in the waiting room. Dr. Mehta wonders if Mr. Patel's accusations might be rooted in his own anxieties. Dr. Mehta suspects Mr. Patel's accusations are a defense mechanism. **Which of the following is most likely at play?**

a) **Reaction formation**
b) **Rationalization**
c) **Projection**
d) **Suppression**
e) **Undoing**

Explanation: Projection is the most fitting defense mechanism because Mr. Patel's accusations of infidelity (his unacceptable feelings) are being directed towards his wife (onto another person) This might stem from his own anxieties or potential attraction to someone else, which he is unable to acknowledge consciously; **Rationalization:** (Incorrect) Rationalization involves justifying unacceptable behaviour. Mr. Patel isn't justifying his accusations, but attributing them to his wife; **Reaction formation:** (Incorrect) Reaction formation involves expressing the opposite of an unwanted feeling. While jealousy can be a complex emotion, Mr. Patel's accusations aren't necessarily the opposite of attraction.

Communication Aspects:

- **Empathy and validation:** Acknowledge the pain of suspicion and the importance of trust in a marriage.
- **Open-ended questions:** Encourage Mr. Patel to explore the reasons behind his suspicions and his emotional state.
- **Active listening:** Pay attention to both verbal and nonverbal cues, such as signs of anxiety or discomfort.
- **Gentle exploration:** Carefully explore the possibility of his own anxieties or feelings of insecurity without directly accusing him.
- **Couples therapy:** If appropriate, suggest couples therapy to address communication issues and rebuild trust.

Pertinent Questions:

Knowledge:

What is projection as a defense mechanism and how does it function? (Attributing one's own unacceptable thoughts or feelings onto another person)

How can projection create problems in relationships? (It can damage trust, lead to accusations and arguments, and hinder open communication)

Attitude:

Why is it important to consider the underlying causes of jealousy in a patient? (Jealousy can be a symptom of deeper issues like insecurity or fear of abandonment, which need to be addressed)

How can healthcare professionals maintain a non-judgmental approach while addressing potentially sensitive topics like infidelity? (Focus on understanding the patient's perspective, validate their emotions, and offer support for exploring the root of the problem)

Application:

How might Dr. Mehta help Mr. Patel explore the possibility of his own anxieties and improve communication with his wife? (Encourage self-reflection, suggest communication exercises for couples, and explore potential underlying reasons for his insecurity)

Communication Skills:

What is a good opening question for Dr. Mehta to initiate a conversation about Mr. Patel's concerns? ("It seems like you're feeling very suspicious lately. Can you tell me a little bit about what's causing you to worry?")

How can Dr. Mehta use active listening to identify potential underlying anxieties in Mr. Patel? (Pay attention to hesitations or changes in tone when discussing his wife, and explore his emotional state, e.g., "You mentioned feeling worried. Are there any other emotions you might be experiencing?")

How can Dr. Mehta suggest couples therapy in a way that is supportive and non-blaming? (Frame it as a resource for improving communication and building a stronger relationship, emphasizing it can benefit both partners)

****

Reframing Failure - Downplaying the Importance

During rounds, Dr. Krishnan in his medical college, encounters a young woman alumni, who recently failed a crucial medical school entrance exam. The student seems nonchalant about the setback, even claiming she wasn't particularly interested in that specific specialization anyway. Dr. Krishnan suspects the student might be using a defense mechanism to cope with disappointment. Dr. Krishnan suspects the student's attitude is a defense mechanism. **Which of the following is most likely at play?**

a) **Reaction formation**
b) **Rationalization**
c) **Altruistic**
d) **Splitting**
e) **Sublimation**

Explanation: Rationalization is the most fitting defense mechanism because the student's explanation (disinterest in the specialization) provides a seemingly logical reason to downplay the importance of failing the exam (unacceptable feeling). This might help her manage the disappointment associated with not achieving her academic goal. **Reaction formation:** (Incorrect) Reaction formation involves expressing the opposite of an unwanted feeling. Disinterest isn't necessarily the opposite of wanting to succeed in the exam.

Communication Aspects:

- **Empathy and validation:** Acknowledge the difficulty of failing an important exam and the emotions it might evoke.
- **Open-ended questions:** Encourage the student to express her feelings about the situation beyond her initial nonchalance.
- **Active listening:** Pay attention to both verbal and nonverbal cues that might reveal underlying disappointment.
- **Exploring options:** Discuss alternative plans or strategies for achieving her academic goals.
- **Supportive environment:** Create a safe space for her to feel comfortable acknowledging her emotions and exploring next steps.

Pertinent Questions:

Knowledge:

What is rationalization as a defense mechanism and how does it function? (Providing seemingly logical reasons to justify unacceptable feelings or behaviours)

How can rationalization be both positive and negative in its effects? (Positive - maintaining self-esteem, negative - hindering healthy coping and motivation)

Attitude:

Why is it important to consider the potential use of defense mechanisms when interacting with patients who experience academic failure? (Defense mechanisms can mask underlying emotions that need to be addressed for healthy coping)

How can healthcare professionals strike a balance between acknowledging the disappointment of failure and promoting a growth mind set for future success? (Validate emotions, explore options for improvement, and offer support and encouragement)

Application:

How might Dr. Krishnan help the student develop a realistic and achievable plan to prepare for the next entrance exam? (Assess her strengths and weaknesses, explore different study strategies, and connect her with academic support resources)

Communication Skills:

What is a good opening question for Dr. Krishnan to initiate a conversation about the exam results? ("I understand failing an exam can be challenging. Can you tell me a little bit about how you're feeling about the results?")

How can Dr. Krishnan use active listening to identify the student's underlying emotions? (Observe nonverbal cues like sighs or hesitation, and explore her emotional state beyond her initial statement, e.g., "You mentioned not being very interested. Is there a particular specialization you were hoping to pursue?")

How can Dr. Krishnan offer support and encouragement without pressuring the student to disclose more than she's comfortable with? (Acknowledge the effort she put into studying, validate her feelings, and offer resources for academic support without demanding specific details about her future plans)

****

Unconscious Compensation

Mrs. Sharma recently gave birth to her first child. While she seems overjoyed and constantly showers the baby with expensive gifts and clothes, her husband notices she seems withdrawn and avoids spending extended periods holding the infant. Dr. Gupta, the paediatrician, wonders if Mrs. Sharma's behaviour might be a way of coping with an unexpected emotional response to motherhood. Dr. Gupta suspects Mrs. Sharma's behaviour might be a defense mechanism**. Which of the following is most likely at play?**

- **a) Regression**
- **b) Reaction formation**
- **c) Splitting**
- **d) Denial**
- **e) Anger**

Explanation: Reaction formation is the most fitting defense mechanism because Mrs. Sharma's excessive gift-giving (opposite behaviour) might be an unconscious way of compensating for underlying feelings of resentment (unacceptable feelings) towards the responsibilities of childcare; **Regression:** (Incorrect) It involves returning to earlier developmental stages. While Mrs. Sharma might be avoiding certain aspects of childcare, it's not necessarily a shift to a less mature behaviour; **splitting:** (Incorrect) Splitting involves seeing things in extremes (all good or all bad). Showering the baby with gifts doesn't necessarily reflect an extreme positive view of the child.

Communication Aspects:

- **Empathy and validation:** Acknowledge the challenges of new parenthood and the range of emotions women might experience after childbirth.
- **Open-ended questions:** Encourage Mrs. Sharma to express her feelings and experiences beyond the facade of constant gift-giving.
- **Active listening:** Pay attention to both verbal and nonverbal cues, such as hesitation or avoidance of certain aspects of childcare.
- **Normalization:** Reassure her that mixed emotions are common during this transition and offer support for navigating them.
- **Exploration of coping mechanisms:** Discuss healthy ways to manage stress and anxieties associated with parenthood.

Pertinent Questions:

Knowledge:

What is reaction formation as a defense mechanism and how does it function? (Expressing the opposite of an unwanted feeling or impulse)

How can reaction formation create problems in relationships and daily life? (It can mask underlying issues, hinder effective communication, and lead to inauthentic behaviour)

Attitude:

Why is it important to consider the potential use of defense mechanisms in postpartum mothers? (Unrecognized negative emotions can lead to maternal distress and affect parent-child relationship)

How can healthcare professionals create a safe space for new mothers to express their anxieties and challenges without judgment? (Normalize a range of emotions, practice active listening, and offer resources for support groups or counselling)

Application:

How might Dr. Gupta help Mrs. Sharma explore her underlying emotions and develop healthy coping mechanisms? (Encourage expression of emotions, normalize mixed feelings, and suggest relaxation techniques or support groups)

Communication Skills:

What is a good opening question for Dr. Gupta to initiate a conversation about Mrs. Sharma's emotional well-being? ("Motherhood can be a time of great joy and adjustment. Can you tell me a little bit about how you're feeling since the baby's arrival?")

How can Dr. Gupta use active listening to identify Mrs. Sharma's underlying emotions? (Observe nonverbal cues and explore her experiences beyond the gifts, e.g., "You mentioned getting the baby many gifts. Is there anything else you'd like to share about how you're adjusting to caring for a new-born?")

How can Dr. Gupta offer support and resources without pressuring Mrs. Sharma to disclose more than she's comfortable with? (Validate her challenges, acknowledge the complexity of emotions, and offer support groups or counselling as options for further exploration)

****

Disappointment Shatters the Ideal - From God to Villain

Ms. Singh has been raving about her cardiologist, Dr. Rao, calling him a "miracle worker" for successfully managing her heart condition. However, during a recent appointment, Dr. Rao is running behind schedule due to an emergency and Ms. Singh ends up waiting for over an hour. When Dr. Rao finally arrives, Ms. Singh is fuming and accuses him of being incompetent and uncaring. Dr. Rao wonders if Ms. Singh's drastic shift in perception might be a defense mechanism. Dr. Rao suspects Ms. Singh's behaviour might be a defense mechanism. **Which of the following is most likely at play?**

- **a) Anger**
- **b) Denial**
- **c) Splitting**
- **d) Suppression**
- **e) Humour**

Explanation: Splitting is the most fitting defense mechanism because Ms. Singh's view of Dr. Rao has shifted dramatically from "godlike" (all good) to "terrible" (all bad) This inability to tolerate any negativity towards someone previously idealized points to splitting as a way of coping with disappointment.

Communication Aspects:

- **Empathy and validation:** Acknowledge Ms. Singh's frustration and the importance of timely appointments.
- **Open-ended questions:** Encourage Ms. Singh to express her feelings about the wait time and the shift in her perception of Dr. Rao.
- **Active listening:** Pay attention to both verbal and nonverbal cues, such as anger or disappointment.
- **Explaining the situation:** Briefly explain the reason for the delay without going into unnecessary detail.
- **Rebuilding trust:** Focus on re-establishing a positive therapeutic relationship and open communication.

Pertinent Questions:

Knowledge:

What is splitting as a defense mechanism and how does it function? (Viewing people or situations in extremes of all good or all bad)

How can splitting create problems in relationships, both personal and professional? (It hinders open communication, fosters mistrust, and makes navigating conflict difficult)

Attitude:

Why is it important to consider splitting in doctor-patient relationships? (Splitting can lead to unrealistic expectations, emotional outbursts, and difficulty adhering to treatment plans)

How can healthcare professionals maintain a professional demeanour while addressing a patient's emotional response to a perceived slight? (Remain calm, validate their feelings, explain the situation factually, and focus on maintaining a therapeutic alliance)

Application:

How might Dr. Rao help Ms. Singh develop a more balanced view of their professional relationship? (Acknowledge her positive experiences, explain the challenges of managing a busy medical practice, and encourage open communication about any future concerns)

Communication Skills:

What is a good opening question for Dr. Rao to initiate a conversation about the situation? ("I understand you're upset about the wait today. Can you tell me a little bit about how you're feeling?")

How can Dr. Rao use active listening to identify the underlying reasons for Ms. Singh's anger? (Pay attention to her word choices and explore her emotional state beyond the immediate incident, e.g., "It sounds like you're very disappointed. Were you looking forward to discussing something specific today?")

How can Dr. Rao rebuild trust and maintain a positive therapeutic relationship? (Acknowledge her frustration, apologize for the inconvenience, and express his commitment to providing her with quality care going forward)

****

Push Away the Worry - A Time Limit for Ms. Kavitha

In the OPD of a General Hospital, Dr. Krishnan encounters a young woman named Ms. Kavitha who was recently diagnosed with breast cancer. While Kavitha appears calm and composed, Dr. Krishnan notices she steers clear of lengthy discussions about her illness and quickly switches topics whenever it's brought up. Dr. Krishnan wonders if Ms. Kavitha might be using a specific strategy to manage her emotional response. Dr. Krishnan suspects Ms. Kavitha's behaviour might be a defense mechanism. **Which of the following is most likely at play?**

- **a) Altruism**
- **b) Denial**
- **c) Reaction formation**
- **d) Dissociation**
- **e) Suppression**

Explanation: Suppression is the most fitting defense mechanism because Ms. Kavitha consciously tries to limit the amount of time she spends worrying about her illness (unwanted feelings). This allows her to function and cope with the situation without completely shutting down emotionally.

Communication Aspects:

- **Empathy and validation:** Acknowledge the difficulty of a cancer diagnosis and the spectrum of emotions Ms. Kavitha might be experiencing.
- **Open-ended questions:** Encourage Ms. Kavitha to express her feelings and concerns beyond the self-imposed time limit.
- **Active listening:** Pay attention to both verbal and nonverbal cues, such as hesitation or avoidance of discussing the illness.
- **Providing emotional support:** Offer resources for counselling or support groups to help her manage her emotional response.
- **Respecting boundaries:** Acknowledge her coping mechanism but gently encourage open communication when she feels ready.

Pertinent Questions:

Knowledge:

What is suppression as a defense mechanism and how does it function? (Consciously pushing away unwanted thoughts or feelings)

How can suppression be both positive and negative in its effects? (Positive - allows temporary relief from overwhelming emotions, negative - hinders healthy coping and can lead to emotional outbursts)

Attitude:

Why is it important to consider suppression in cancer patients? (Suppressing emotions can hinder communication about treatment options and emotional needs)

How can healthcare professionals strike a balance between respecting a patient's coping mechanisms and encouraging open communication about their illness? (Validate their coping strategies, offer support and resources, and create a safe space for them to express their emotions when they're ready)

Application:
How might Dr. Krishnan help Ms.Kavitha develop healthy coping mechanisms in addition to suppression? (Suggest relaxation techniques like yoga or pranayama, connect her with support groups, and encourage her to express her emotions in a safe space)

Communication Skills:
What is a good opening question for Dr. Krishnan to initiate a conversation about Ms. Kavitha's emotional well-being? ("A cancer diagnosis can be overwhelming, Ms. Kavitha. Can you tell me a little bit about how you're coping with everything?")
How can Dr. Krishnan use active listening to identify Ms. Kavitha's underlying emotions? (Observe nonverbal cues and explore her experiences beyond the time limit, e.g., "You mentioned setting a limit on worrying. Is there anything else you'd like to share about how you're feeling?")
How can Dr. Krishnan offer support and resources without pressuring Ms. Kavitha to disclose more than she's comfortable with? (Normalize a range of emotions, validate her coping mechanism, and offer support groups or counselling as options for further exploration if she's interested)

****

Seeking Redemption and a Second Chance after Quitting Smoking

Mr. Patel, a 60-year-old man with a long history of smoking, has been admitted to the hospital for advanced lung cancer. Despite his condition, Mr. Patel has become very health conscious. He has vehemently refused any cigarettes, actively participates in physiotherapy sessions, and even started juicing vegetables. Dr. Shah wonders if Mr. Patel's sudden shift towards a healthy lifestyle might be more than just a desire for improvement. **Dr. Shah suspects Mr. Patel's health behaviour might be a defense mechanism. Which of the following is most likely at play?**

a) **Denial**
b) **Identification**
c) **Projection**
d) **Undoing**
e) **Reaction formation**

Explanation: Undoing is the most fitting defense mechanism because Mr. Patel's drastic change in habits (quitting smoking, healthy diet, exercise) might be a way to symbolically "erase" his past smoking (negative past event) and potentially "earn" a better health outcome (reverse negative consequences). This behaviour reflects a belief that adopting positive actions now can somehow magically undo the damage caused by past choices.

Communication Aspects:

- **Empathy and validation:** Acknowledge the difficulty of his diagnosis and his desire to improve his health.
- **Open-ended questions:** Encourage Mr. Patel to express his thoughts and feelings about his health and lifestyle changes.
- **Active listening:** Pay attention to both verbal and nonverbal cues, such as guilt or regret related to smoking.
- **Realistic hope:** While offering support for his healthy choices, manage expectations about reversing the course of his illness.

- **Focus on present and future:** Help Mr. Patel focus on making the most of his remaining time and address any concerns he might have.

Pertinent Questions:

Knowledge:

What is undoing as a defense mechanism and how does it function? (Believing one can magically erase past mistakes through present actions)

How can undoing be both a positive and negative coping mechanism? (Positive - motivates positive behaviour change, negative - fosters unrealistic expectations and guilt)

Attitude:

Why is it important to consider undoing in terminally ill patients? (Undoing can provide a sense of control and purpose but might also lead to denial or anger if a miracle cure isn't achieved)

How can healthcare professionals balance offering hope with managing expectations for terminally ill patients? (Acknowledge their desire for improvement, explain the realities of their condition with empathy, and focus on optimizing their quality of life)

Application:

How might Dr. Shah help Mr. Patel cope with his diagnosis in a healthy way? (Encourage him to express his emotions, validate his efforts to improve his health, and offer support for end-of-life planning if appropriate)

Communication Skills:

What is a good opening question for Dr. Shah to initiate a conversation about Mr. Patel's lifestyle changes? (“I've noticed you've made some significant changes to your health habits recently. Can you tell me a little bit about what motivated you?")

How can Dr. Shah use active listening to identify Mr. Patel's underlying emotions? (Pay attention to nonverbal cues and explore his motivations beyond the physical benefits, e.g., "It sounds like you're putting a lot of effort into your health now. Is there anything else you're hoping to achieve with these changes?")

How can Dr. Shah offer support and manage expectations without diminishing Mr. Patel's hope? (Acknowledge his desire for improvement, explain the limitations of treatment, and offer support services like counselling or spiritual guidance)

****

6. Lessons from Psychiatrist Files….

Mrs. Patel and the Stubborn Blood Pressure

Dr. Rao, a young resident, couldn't figure out why Mrs. Patel's blood pressure wouldn't go down despite treatment. She ate healthy, took her meds, but nothing worked. Then, he realized she had anxiety and wondered if it was connected.

He talked to Dr. Sharma, a psychiatrist, who explained how stress and anxiety can raise blood pressure. She compared the body to an orchestra - when stressed, it's like a cymbal crash that disrupts the music. Medication helps fix the music, but the cymbal crash keeps happening. Dr. Rao understood. He saw Mrs. Patel not just as a patient, but as someone worried and stressed with generalized anxiety disorder. They worked together to create a new plan.

Dr. Rao discussed the anxiety-blood pressure link with Mrs. Patel and offered different anxiety medication. Dr. Sharma taught Mrs. Patel coping skills to manage stress and sleep better. It wasn't easy. There were ups and downs, but slowly, Mrs. Patel's health improved. Her anxiety calmed, and her blood pressure responded better to the medication.

This case changed Dr. Rao's view of medicine. He learned it's not just about pills, but understanding the mind-body connection. Dr. Sharma, the psychiatrist, helped connect these pieces to create a complete picture of Mrs. Patel's health.

Test Your Cognition:

Understanding:

- Why is it important for doctors to consider the patient's mental health alongside their physical health?
- What are the potential consequences of neglecting the mind-body connection in medical treatment?
- How can doctors advocate for better integration of mental and physical healthcare services?

Recall:

- What was the initial medical mystery Dr. Rao faced? How does HPAxis with Anxiety-Hypertension
- What are the tests that you would advise to explore and confirm mind-body connection in Mrs. Patel's case?
- What is the standard treatment plan for anxiety in Hypertensive patient?
- Is there a cause-effect relationship? If so, what is the cause? What is the effect?

Application:

- How could this case be relevant to other patients with seemingly unexplained health issues?
- What are some challenges faced in effectively managing a patient's mental and physical health together?
- How can doctors improve their communication with patients about the mind-body connection?

Doctor's Attitude:

- Empathy and understanding towards Mrs. Patel's anxiety and its impact on her health.
- Openness to collaboration with a psychiatrist for a holistic approach.

Ethical Aspects:

- Maintaining confidentiality of Mrs. Patel's medical information.
- Offering treatment options that align with Mrs. Patel's preferences and values.
- Avoiding stigmatizing language when discussing mental health.

Communication:

- Using clear and concise language that Mrs. Patel can understand.
- Checking for understanding and addressing any questions or concerns she may have.

- Encouraging open communication about her physical and mental health.

Understanding the correct approach in this case

1. Initial Observation: Mrs. Patel's blood pressure doesn't respond to conventional treatment despite adhering to a healthy diet and taking prescribed medications.
2. Recognition of Anxiety: Dr. Rao recognizes that Mrs. Patel's anxiety might be a contributing factor to her uncontrolled blood pressure.
3. Consultation with a Psychiatrist (Dr. Sharma): Dr. Rao seeks the expertise of a psychiatrist, Dr. Sharma, to explore the connection between stress, anxiety, and blood pressure.
4. Analogy of the Body as an Orchestra: Dr. Sharma uses the metaphor of an orchestra to explain the impact of stress on the body. Stress is likened to a disruptive cymbal crash, affecting the harmony (health) of the body.
5. Medication and Symptom Management: Medication is described as a way to "fix the music," addressing the symptoms, but the underlying stressors (symbolized by the cymbal crash) persist.
6. Holistic View of the Patient: Dr. Rao shifts his perspective, seeing Mrs. Patel not just as a patient with physical symptoms but as an individual with emotional concerns and stressors.
7. Collaborative Treatment Plan:
    - Dr. Rao and Dr. Sharma collaborate to create a comprehensive plan.
    - Dr. Rao addresses the physical symptoms by adjusting blood pressure medication.
    - Dr. Sharma focuses on treating the underlying anxiety with different medications and teaches coping skills for stress management and improved sleep.
8. Patient-Centred Approach: The treatment plan recognizes Mrs. Patel's unique needs, involving both medical and psychological interventions.
9. Progress and Challenges: The journey involves ups and downs, reflecting the complexities of addressing both physical and mental aspects of health.
10. Integrated Care and Improved Health: Through the integrated approach, Mrs. Patel's health gradually improves. Her anxiety reduces, and her blood pressure responds more effectively to medication.
11. Impact on Dr. Rao's Perspective: Dr. Rao undergoes a shift in his view of medicine, realizing the significance of understanding the mind-body connection for holistic patient care.
12. Collaborative Picture of Health: Dr. Sharma's expertise in psychiatry helps connect the pieces, creating a complete picture of Mrs. Patel's health that goes beyond just addressing physical symptoms.

For further reading: Qiu T, Jiang Z, Chen X, Dai Y, Zhao H. Comorbidity of Anxiety and Hypertension: Common Risk Factors and Potential Mechanisms. Int J Hypertens. 2023 May 25;2023:9619388. doi: 10.1155/2023/9619388. PMID: 37273529; PMCID: PMC10234733.

****

Mr. Rohan and Examinations

Dr. Gupta is taking a break when Mr. Kapoor rushes in, visibly distressed, bringing his son Rohan to the ward. Rohan appears pale, clammy, and hyperventilating. His eyes are wide, and he's gasping for air. Mr. Kapoor explains that Rohan was studying when he suddenly became breathless, started sweating profusely, and complained of chest tightness. They rushed to the hospital fearing a heart attack.

Dr. Gupta quickly examines Rohan and finds no signs of any physical emergency. An ECG confirms normal heart function. He notices Rohan trembling and asks him to describe his experience. Rohan, still breathless, speaks about a sudden wave of intense fear, feeling like he was choking, and fearing he'd lose control. He gives a history of similar brief episodes or chest pain.

Test Questions:

Comprehension: What are the key symptoms that suggest Rohan might be experiencing a panic attack?
The key symptoms that suggest Rohan might be experiencing a panic attack include intense fear, hyperventilation, sweating, chest tightness, and a feeling of choking. His symptoms started suddenly and he appears visibly distressed, lasting for few minutes

Recall: What are the diagnostic criteria for Panic Disorder as per the DSM-5?
The diagnostic criteria for Panic Disorder as per the DSM-5 include recurrent unexpected panic attacks, at least one of the attacks has been followed by one month (or more) of a) persistent concern about additional panic attacks, b) significant maladaptive change in behaviour related to the attacks, and c)the disturbance is not attributable to the physiological effects of a substance or another medical condition.

Application: If you were Dr. Gupta, what immediate steps would you take to manage Rohan's condition?
As Dr. Gupta, the immediate steps would be to calm Rohan, assess vital signs, perform a physical examination, and obtain a detailed history. It would also be important to rule out other medical conditions that could present with similar symptoms.

Psychomotor: Describe the physical examination process you would follow in this scenario.
The physical examination would include assessing vital signs, performing a thorough cardiovascular system examination, respiratory system examination, and a neurological examination (checking for signs of confusion, agitation, or other neurological symptoms).

Affective: How would you communicate with Rohan to ensure he feels safe and understood during this distressing experience?
It's important to use a calm and reassuring tone, maintain eye contact, and use simple and clear language. Validate his feelings and reassure him that he is in a safe place and that help is available.

Additional Questions and Answers:

What are panicogens? Substances that induce panic attacks are called panicogens.

- Respiratory, panic induced substances. They mediate panic responses primarily through respiration stimulation and shift in acid-base balance. Examples include:
  - Racemic Sodium Lactate
  - Carbon Dioxide (5-35%)
  - Bicarbonate
- Neurochemical-Related Panicogens: These panicogens induce panic responses through interaction with specific neurotransmitter systems. Some of the most common substances are:
  - Caffeine
  - Serotonergic Agents
  - Flumazenil
  - Adrenergic Agents such as Yohimbine
  - Cholecystokinin (CCK), especially the tetrapeptide and octapeptide fragments CCK-4 and CCK-8

Factors that can predispose to panic attacks. In teenagers, these can include:

- Family History: Teens with a family history of anxiety disorders or panic attacks are at a higher risk.
- Parenting Style: Having an overprotective or anxious parent can contribute to the development of panic disorder in teens.

- Personality Traits: Teens with an anxious, avoidant, or passive personality are more prone to panic attacks.
- Existing Mental Health Disorders: Teens already having an anxiety disorder or other mental health disorder are at a higher risk.
- Traumatic Experiences: Experiencing or witnessing something traumatic can trigger panic attacks.
- High Stress: High levels of stress can lead to panic attacks.
- Major Loss or Transition: A recent major loss or transition can trigger panic attacks.
- Abnormalities in Certain Substances: There is a suggestion that abnormalities in gamma-aminobutyric acid, cortisol (one of the body's stress hormones), and serotonin could lead to the development of a panic disorder.

****

Mr. Sharma's challenge with controlling his movements

A 65-year-old man, Mr. Sharma, is referred to the psychiatric consultation service from the medicine department. He was admitted for an uncontrolled diabetes and hypertension when the medical team noticed that Mr. Sharma seemed unusually slow in his movements and had a persistent tremor in his right hand. He also appeared anxious and reported having trouble sleeping. His daughter mentioned that he had been increasingly forgetful and had difficulty with tasks like buttoning his shirt or using utensils.

Questions and Answers:

Comprehension: What are the key symptoms that suggest Mr. Sharma might be experiencing a neurodegenerative disorder?

The key symptoms that suggest Mr. Sharma might be experiencing a neurodegenerative disorder include slowness in movements, persistent tremor, anxiety, sleep disturbances, forgetfulness, and difficulty with fine motor tasks.

Recall: What are the diagnostic criteria for Parkinson's disease?

The diagnostic criteria for Parkinson's disease include bradykinesia (slowness of movement) plus either resting tremor or rigidity. Non-motor symptoms such as anxiety, depression, sleep disturbances, and cognitive impairment are also common.

Application: If you were the consulting psychiatrist, what immediate steps would you take to manage Mr. Sharma's condition?

As the consulting psychiatrist, the immediate steps would be to collaborate with the neurology and medical teams. It would be important to confirm the diagnosis with a neurological examination and possibly imaging studies. Management of the anxiety symptoms and sleep disturbances would also be a priority. Rule out other co-morbid anxiety and Major depressive disorders.

****

Mr. Raj and Alcohol

A 24-year-old man, Raj, is referred to the psychiatric consultation service from the medicine department. He was admitted for dizziness and vomiting, when the medical team noticed that Raj seemed unusually anxious and restless. He also reported having trouble sleeping. His friend, who accompanied him, mentioned that Raj had been consuming alcohol heavily for the past few months and had recently tried to quit.

Questions and Answers:

Comprehension: What are the key symptoms that suggest Raj might be experiencing a substance-related withdrawal features?

The key symptoms that suggest Raj might be experiencing a substance-related withdrawal features include with drawal symptoms including but not limiting to anxiety, restlessness, sleep disturbances, nausea, sweating, after a history of heavy alcohol use and attempt to stop consuming alcohol

Recall: What are the diagnostic criteria for Substance Use Disorder as per the DSM-5?

The diagnostic criteria for Substance Use Disorder as per the DSM-5 include a pattern of substance use leading to clinically significant impairment or distress, manifested by at least two of eleven possible symptoms, occurring within a 12-month period. These symptoms include withdrawal symptoms, unsuccessful efforts to cut down or control substance use, and substance use in larger amounts or over a longer period than was intended, tolerance and craving etc.,

Application: If you were the consulting psychiatrist, what immediate steps would you take to manage Raj's condition?

As the consulting psychiatrist, the immediate steps would be to assess the severity of Raj's withdrawal symptoms and manage them appropriately, which could include medication for symptom relief. It would also be important to provide reassurance, counselling and support for his anxiety and sleep disturbances. If no comorbidities are there and ruling out organic causes of dizziness and vomiting, patient may be shifted to psychiatric ward, if inpatient management is required.

Additional Questions and Answers:

Attitude of Health Care Providers: How should healthcare providers approach patients presenting with symptoms potentially related to substance use?

Motivational interviewing. They should take the time to listen to the patient's concerns and reassure them that they are there to help. It's also important to avoid judgment or stigma related to substance use. Never confront the patient.

Ethical and Legal Aspects: **What are the ethical considerations when treating a patient with a potential substance use disorder?**

Ethical considerations include respecting the patient's autonomy, ensuring confidentiality, providing informed consent before any procedure, and ensuring the patient's welfare. It's also important to consider the legal aspects of substance use. Record any issues with legal entities as well as medico-legal issues, accidents, brawl, habitual confrontations with neighbours or non-acquaintances. Get an informed consent from legally valid primary caregivers for physical restraints, if Mr. Raj goes for complicated withdrawal states like delirium tremens.

Communication: How would you explain the diagnosis and treatment plan to Raj in a way that is respectful and understandable?

I would explain the diagnosis in simple terms, avoiding medical jargon. I would reassure Raj that substance use disorders are treatable conditions. I would outline the treatment plan, which may include medications to manage his symptoms, motivation enhancement therapy or therapy to address his substance use, and possibly referral to a support group. I would emphasize the importance of follow-up care and regular check-ups. I would also involve his family or friends in the discussions, with his consent, to ensure they understand his condition and how they can support him to prevent relapse.

****

Ms. Anjali's Problems

A 30-year-old woman, Anjali, is referred to the psychiatric consultation service from the medicine department. She was admitted for a recurrent abdominal pain, bloating, and altered bowel habits. Medical team noticed that Anjali seemed unusually anxious, having trouble sleeping and experiencing bouts of nausea. Her husband mentioned that Anjali had been visiting various doctors for the past few months for her abdominal discomfort but no physical cause has been identified.

Questions and Answers:

Comprehension: What are the key symptoms that suggest Anjali might be experiencing a gastrointestinal disorder?

The key symptoms that suggest Anjali might be experiencing a gastrointestinal disorder include recurrent abdominal pain, bloating, altered bowel habits, and nausea.

Recall: What are the diagnostic criteria for Irritable Bowel Syndrome (IBS)?

The diagnostic criteria for IBS, as per the Rome IV criteria, include recurrent abdominal pain, on average, at least 1 day/week in the last 3 months, associated with two or more of the following criteria: related to defecation, associated with a change in frequency of stool, and associated with a change in form (appearance) of stool.

Application: If you were the consulting psychiatrist, what immediate steps would you take to manage Anjali's condition?

As the consulting psychiatrist, the immediate steps would be to assess the severity of Anjali's anxiety and manage it appropriately, which could include cognitive-behavioural therapy or medication. It would also be important to collaborate with the gastroenterology team for further evaluation of her gastrointestinal symptoms.

Additional Points to Ponder:

- **Mind-Gut Connection:**

1 Be mindful of the bidirectional relationship: Stress and mental health issues can impact gut health, while gut imbalances can worsen mental health. Recognize this connection and screen for both aspects during assessments.

2 Validate the patient's experience: Don't dismiss gut-related complaints as "psychosomatic." Listen attentively and explore potential connections.

3 Psychoeducation is key: Explain the mind-gut connection and empower patients to understand how lifestyle changes can positively impact both their mental and gut health.

4 Consider incorporating relaxation techniques: Mindfulness, meditation, and deep breathing can help manage stress and improve gut motility.

5 Explore potential dietary modifications: Consider recommending a balanced diet rich in fruits, vegetables, and fermented foods, while limiting processed foods and sugary drinks. This can support a healthy microbiome.

6 Collaborate with other healthcare professionals: Consider referrals to gastroenterologists, dietitians, or naturopaths for specialized support depending on individual needs.

- **Microbiome Importance:**

1. Promote microbiome diversity: Encourage dietary changes like consuming prebiotics (found in fruits, vegetables, and fermented foods) and probiotics (yogurt, kefir) to foster diverse gut bacteria.
2. Minimize microbiome disruptors: Advise limiting processed foods, excessive antibiotics (except when medically necessary), and environmental toxins that can harm gut bacteria.
3. Consider personalized approaches: Emerging research suggests potential for microbiome-based interventions tailored to individual needs and mental health conditions. However, these are still in the early stages and require further exploration.

- **Additional Tips:**

A. Stay updated on research: The field of mind-gut interaction and microbiome research is rapidly evolving. Continuously update your knowledge to inform your practice.

B. Maintain a non-judgmental approach: Encourage open communication and avoid stigmatizing discussions about gut health and mental well-being.
C. Remember, it's a journey, not a destination: Supporting mind-gut health is an ongoing process. Encourage patients to be patient, consistent, and celebrate small improvements.

****

Mr. Kumar's Cancer Cauldron

A 45-year-old man, Mr. Kumar, is referred to the psychiatric consultation service from the oncology department. He was diagnosed with Acute Myeloid Leukemia (AML) six months ago and has been undergoing chemotherapy. The oncology team noticed that Mr. Kumar seemed withdrawn and reported having sleep disturbances. He also reported loss of appetite and significant weight loss. His wife mentioned that Mr. Kumar had been less interested in his usual activities and seemed persistently sad.

Questions and Answers:

Comprehension: What are the key symptoms that suggest Mr. Kumar might be experiencing a mood disorder?

The key symptoms that suggest Mr. Kumar might be experiencing a mood disorder include withdrawal, sleep disturbances, loss of appetite, significant weight loss, decreased interest in usual activities, and persistent sadness.

Recall: What are the diagnostic criteria for Major Depressive Disorder as per the DSM-5?

The diagnostic criteria for Major Depressive Disorder as per the DSM-5 include at least five of the following symptoms present during the same 2-week period and represent a change from previous functioning: depressed mood, markedly diminished interest or pleasure in all or almost all activities, significant weight loss or decrease in appetite, insomnia or hypersomnia, psychomotor agitation or retardation, fatigue or loss of energy, feelings of worthlessness or excessive guilt, diminished ability to think or concentrate, and recurrent thoughts of death.

Application: If you were the consulting psychiatrist, what immediate steps would you take to manage Mr. Kumar's condition?

As the consulting psychiatrist, the immediate steps would be to conduct a thorough psychiatric evaluation, including a detailed history of mood symptoms, their impact on functioning, and any thoughts of suicide. Collaboration with the oncology team would be crucial to rule out other secondary causes of depression. Management would likely involve a combination of pharmacotherapy and psychotherapy.

****

Mrs. Patel's Cancer & Further Complications

A 55-year-old woman, Mrs. Patel, is referred to the psychiatric consultation service from the oncology department. She was diagnosed with ovarian cancer 4 months ago and has been undergoing chemotherapy – 2 cycles completed. The oncology team noticed that Mrs. Patel seemed confused and disoriented. She has on and off episodes of fever. She also reported having hallucinations, and delusions. Her daughter mentioned that Mrs. Patel had been disrobing clothes and had faecal incontinence.

Questions and Answers:

Comprehension: What are the key symptoms that suggest Mrs. Patel might be experiencing a neuropsychiatric disorder?

The key symptoms that suggest Mrs. Patel might be experiencing a neuropsychiatric disorder include confusion, disorientation, hallucinations, delusions and disrobing clothes.

Recall: What are the diagnostic criteria for Autoimmune Psychosis?

The diagnostic criteria for Autoimmune Psychosis include new onset of psychosis, presence of neurological symptoms (like confusion or disorientation), and evidence of autoimmunity (like the presence of specific antibodies or response to immunotherapy).

Application: If you were the consulting psychiatrist, what immediate steps would you take to manage Mrs. Patel's condition?

As the consulting psychiatrist, the immediate steps would be to conduct a thorough psychiatric evaluation, including a detailed history of psychiatric symptoms, their impact on functioning, and any associated neurological symptoms to rule out a paraneoplastic syndromes- secondaries brain. The oncological drug must be revisited to ensure that there is possible psychiatric side effects. This is more important when employing the newer drugs. Collaboration with the oncology and neurology teams would be crucial. Management would likely involve a combination of pharmacotherapy and psychotherapy.

Psychomotor: Describe the physical examination process you would follow in this scenario.

The physical examination would include a general examination and a detailed mental status examination, assessing appearance, behaviour, speech, mood, affect, thought process, thought content, cognition, and insight/judgment.

Affective: How would you communicate with Mrs. Patel to ensure she feels safe and understood during this distressing experience?

Communication is difficult as patient is perplexed, does not have insight into the illness.

Additional Questions and Answers:

Attitude of Health Care Providers: How should healthcare providers approach patients presenting with symptoms potentially related to a neuropsychiatric disorder in the context of a serious medical illness?

Healthcare providers should approach patients with empathy, patience, and understanding. Psychoeducate the nursing team.

Ethical and Legal Aspects: What are the ethical considerations when treating a patient with a potential neuropsychiatric disorder in the context of a serious medical illness?

Ethical considerations include respecting the patient's autonomy, ensuring confidentiality, providing informed consent (always a challenge as the patient’s insight is compromised) before any procedure, and ensuring the patient's welfare. Record the primary caregivers – relationship, consent and statements, possibly documenting this as applicable as per institutional policies

Communication: How would you explain the diagnosis and treatment plan to Mrs. Patel in a way that is respectful and understandable?

I would explain the diagnosis in simple terms, avoiding medical jargon. Psychoeducation of the family to ensure they understand her condition and how they can support her.

****

The Unseen Storm: A Journey through Migraine and Derealization

A 23-year-old engineering student, Karan, is referred to the psychiatric consultation from the neurology department. He has been experiencing episodes of visual disturbances, described as seeing walls falling down brick by brick, sometimes erupting into flames or honey bees flying out. These episodes have been causing him significant distress, leading to feelings of unreality and detachment from his environment followed by headache. The team initially suspected visual hallucinations.

Questions and Answers:

Comprehension: **What are the key symptoms that suggest Karan might be experiencing a neurological rather than a psychiatric condition?**

The key symptoms that suggest a neurological condition include visual disturbances described as walls falling down brick by brick, erupting into flames, or honey bees flying out. These symptoms are characteristic of a migrainous aura. The feeling of unreality and detachment from the environment, known as derealization, can also occur in the context of a migrainous aura.

Recall: **What are the diagnostic criteria for Migraine with Aura?**

The diagnostic criteria for Migraine with Aura, as per the International Classification of Headache Disorders, include at least two attacks of reversible aura symptoms, at least one aura symptom developing gradually over more than 5 minutes, and/or different aura symptoms occurring in succession over more than 5 minutes, followed by a headache.

Application: **If you were the consulting psychiatrist, what immediate steps would you take to manage Karan's condition?**

As the consulting psychiatrist, the immediate steps would be to conduct a thorough psychiatric evaluation, including a detailed history of psychiatric symptoms, their impact on functioning, and any associated neurological symptoms. Collaboration with the neurology team would be crucial. Management would likely involve a combination of pharmacotherapy and psychotherapy.

Differential Diagnosis:

- Migraine with Aura
- Psychotic Disorder
- Dissociative Disorder
- Temporal Lobe Epilepsy

Psychiatrist Practice Pearls:

- Migrainous aura can present with complex visual phenomena that may be mistaken for visual hallucinations.
- Derealization can occur in the context of a migrainous aura.
- Collaboration with neurology is crucial in these cases.
- Management involves treating the migraine as well as addressing the associated psychiatric symptoms.

Specific Points for Proper Communication:

- Clear explanation of the nature of migrainous aura and its difference from psychiatric conditions like psychosis.
- Explanation of the treatment plan, including the role of medications and psychotherapy.
- Discussion of the importance of lifestyle modifications, such as stress management and avoidance of migraine triggers.
- Empathetic communication about the challenges of living with migraine and the importance of seeking help for associated psychiatric symptoms.
- Encouragement of open communication about any concerns or questions the patient may have.
- Involvement of family members in discussions, with the patient's consent, to ensure they understand the condition and how they can support the patient.
- Forewarning about the potential for recurrent episodes, but reassurance that these can be managed with adjustments to the treatment plan.
- Explanation of the importance of hope and positivity in managing a chronic condition, and reassurance that many people with his condition lead fulfilling and productive lives.
- Encouragement of the patient to educate himself about his condition and to be an active participant in his care, and reassurance that the healthcare team is there to help.

The Silent Struggle: Navigating the Storm of Bipolar Depression and Alexithymia

A 35-year-old software engineer, Mr. Verma, is referred to the psychiatric consultation from the medicine department. He has been experiencing episodes of extreme mood swings, ranging from periods of excessive energy, decreased need for sleep, and racing thoughts to periods of low mood, lack of interest in previously enjoyed activities, and significant fatigue. These episodes have been causing him significant distress, leading to difficulties at work and in his personal relationships. He is currently on a regimen of Olanzapine and Fluoxetine. Despite this, he reports persistent feelings of emotional emptiness and difficulty identifying and describing his emotions, a symptom known as alexithymia.

Questions and Answers:

Comprehension: What are the key symptoms that suggest Mr. Verma might be experiencing a mood disorder?

The key symptoms that suggest a mood disorder include extreme mood swings, periods of excessive energy, decreased need for sleep, racing thoughts, low mood, lack of interest in previously enjoyed activities, significant fatigue, and feelings of emotional emptiness.

Recall: What are the diagnostic criteria for Bipolar Disorder?

The diagnostic criteria for Bipolar Disorder, as per the DSM-5, include the presence of one or more Manic or Hypomanic Episodes, often alternated with Major Depressive Episodes. During the Manic Episodes, the individual experiences a period of abnormally elevated, expansive, or irritable mood and persistently increased activity or energy lasting at least one week.

Application: If you were the consulting psychiatrist, what immediate steps would you take to manage Mr. Verma's condition?

As the consulting psychiatrist, the immediate steps would be to conduct a thorough psychiatric evaluation, including a detailed history of mood symptoms, their impact on functioning, and any associated features such as alexithymia. Management would likely involve a combination of pharmacotherapy and psychotherapy.

Differential Diagnosis:

- Bipolar Disorder
- Major Depressive Disorder
- Generalized Anxiety Disorder
- Personality Disorders

Psychiatrist Practice Pearls:

- Bipolar depression can be challenging to manage due to the risk of triggering a manic episode with antidepressant treatment.
- Alexithymia can complicate the clinical picture and make emotional regulation more difficult for the patient.
- Management involves treating the mood symptoms as well as addressing the associated alexithymia.

****

The Hidden Battle: Navigating the Waves of Recurrent Depression, Galactorrhea, and Premenstrual Dysphoric Disorder

A 32-year-old school teacher, Mrs. Sharma, is referred to the psychiatric consultation. She has been experiencing episodes of low mood, lack of interest in previously enjoyed activities, and significant fatigue. These episodes have been causing her significant distress, leading to difficulties at work and in her personal relationships. She is a known case of recurrent depressive disorder, managed with Fluoxetine. She also reports experiencing an unusual symptom - milk production from her breasts, despite not being pregnant or breastfeeding. Additionally, she has a history of severe mood swings, irritability, and depression in the week or two before the start of her menstrual period.

Questions and Answers:

Comprehension: **What are the key symptoms that suggest Mrs. Sharma might be experiencing a mood disorder?**

The key symptoms that suggest a mood disorder include low mood, lack of interest in previously enjoyed activities, significant fatigue, feelings of sadness and hopelessness, galactorrhea, and severe mood swings, irritability, and depression before the start of her menstrual period.

Recall: **What are the diagnostic criteria for Recurrent Depressive Disorder and Premenstrual Dysphoric Disorder?**

The diagnostic criteria for Recurrent Depressive Disorder, as per the DSM-5, include the presence of at least two depressive episodes, separated by at least two consecutive months without a significant mood episode. For Premenstrual Dysphoric Disorder, the DSM-5 criteria include the presence of at least five symptoms (one of which must be a mood symptom) in the final week before the onset of menses, which start to improve within a few days after the onset of menses, and become minimal or absent in the week post-menses.

Application: **If you were the consulting psychiatrist, what immediate steps would you take to manage Mrs. Sharma's condition?**

As the consulting psychiatrist, the immediate steps would be to conduct a thorough psychiatric evaluation, including a detailed history of mood symptoms, their impact on functioning, and any causes for galactorrhea. Collaboration with the endocrinology team would be crucial. Management would likely involve a combination of pharmacotherapy and psychotherapy.

Differential Diagnosis:

- Recurrent Depressive Disorder
- Premenstrual Dysphoric Disorder
- Bipolar Disorder
- Major Depressive Disorder
- Generalized Anxiety Disorder
- Personality Disorders

Psychiatrist Practice Pearls:

- Galactorrhea can complicate the clinical picture and make emotional regulation more difficult for the patient.
- Collaboration with other medical teams is crucial in these cases.
- Management involves treating the mood symptoms as well as addressing the associated galactorrhea.

****

The Silent Struggle: A Journey through Sleepless Nights

Mr. Murugan, a 35-year-old man, has been managing hypertension for the past 2 years with propranolol. Recently, he has been experiencing poor and disturbed sleep. He reports feeling tired and irritable during the day, and his family has noticed changes in his mood and behaviour.

Examination and Diagnostic Process

What are the key aspects to consider during the physical examination of Mr. Murugan?

The physical examination should include vital signs, cardiovascular examination, ENT and a neurological examination to rule out any neurological causes of insomnia.

What diagnostic tests would be appropriate for Mr. Murugan?
Initial diagnostic tests could include a complete blood count, renal function tests, thyroid function tests, and a sleep study to evaluate for sleep disorders.

What factors should be considered when developing a diagnostic algorithm for Mr. Murugan's condition?
The diagnostic algorithm should consider Mr. Sharma's medical history, current medications, symptoms, physical examination findings, and results from diagnostic tests.

Differential Diagnosis

The differential diagnosis for Mr. Murugan's condition could include:

1. Primary insomnia
2. Sleep apnea
3. Restless legs syndrome
4. Depression
5. Anxiety disorder
6. Side effects of propranolol

Psychiatrist Practice Pearls: As a psychiatrist, it's important to note:

1. The importance of a comprehensive approach to diagnosis- Employing both diagnosis by exclusion (accounting for the fact that drugs can alter sleep architecture and mood disturbance) & inclusion (after tests)
2. The potential impact of chronic insomnia on Mr. Murgan's mental health.
3. The need to consider both psychiatric and medical causes of insomnia.

Ethical and Legal Aspects

What are the ethical considerations in Mr. Murugan's case?
Ethical considerations include respecting Mr. Murugan's autonomy in decision-making, ensuring informed consent for any proposed treatments, and maintaining confidentiality.

What are the legal aspects to consider in Mr. Murugan's case?
Legal aspects may include documenting all interactions and treatment plans, and ensuring that any necessary reporting requirements are met. Forewarning about all situations is a must.

Challenges: The main challenge in this case is to identify the underlying cause of Mr. Murugan's disturbed sleep and to develop an effective treatment plan that addresses both his physical and mental health needs. How would you approach this challenge?

****

The Foggy Trail: Unravelling the Mystery of Cognitive Deficit in a Cardiovascular Patient

A 68-year-old retired banker, Mr. Kapoor, is referred to the psychiatric consultation service from the cardiology department. He has never smoked in his life and is currently being investigated for cardiovascular disease. He was on statins until recently. His family has noticed significant changes in his behaviour. He has been forgetting things, has difficulty concentrating, and seems to be lost in his thoughts most of the time. These changes have been causing him significant distress, leading to difficulties in his daily activities.

Questions and Answers:

Comprehension: **What are the key symptoms that suggest Mr. Kapoor might be experiencing cognitive deficits?**

The key symptoms that suggest cognitive deficits include forgetfulness, difficulty concentrating, and being lost in thoughts.

Comprehension: What are the common causes of cognitive deficits in patients with cardiovascular disease?
Common causes of cognitive deficits in patients with cardiovascular disease include stroke, dementia (including Alzheimer's disease), and vascular cognitive impairment.

Application: **If you were the consulting psychiatrist, what immediate steps would you take to manage Mr. Kapoor's condition?**
Conduct thorough psychiatric evaluation. Shared risk factors should be assessed. Step wise approach advised.

Psychomotor: **Describe the specific examination process you would follow in this scenario.**
The examination would include a detailed mental status examination to assess cognition, including memory, attention, language, and executive functions. A physical examination focusing on the cardiovascular system would also be necessary given the existing diagnosis of cardiovascular disease.

Affective: **How would you communicate with Mr. Kapoor to ensure he feels safe and understood during this distressing experience?**
Speak clearly and slowly. Give time to respond. Be accommodative. It's important to use a calm and reassuring tone. Minimize distractions.

Differential Diagnosis:

- Vascular Cognitive Impairment
- Alzheimer's Disease
- Mild Cognitive Impairment
- Dementia due to General Medical Condition (Cardiovascular Disease)

Psychiatrist Practice Pearls:

- Cognitive deficits are common in patients with cardiovascular disease and can significantly impact their quality of life.
- Collaboration with other medical teams is crucial in these cases.
- Management involves treating the cognitive deficits (Intellectual stimulation) as well as addressing the underlying cardiovascular disease.

****

The Foggy Journey: Navigating the Labyrinth of the Mind

Mr. Ravi, a 45-year-old man, has been undergoing treatment for tuberculosis (MDR TB) for the past six months. His treatment regimen includes cycloserine. Recently, he has been exhibiting signs of confusion, disturbed sleep and seems preoccupied. His family reports that he seems to be lost in thought and is deluded that others are trying to harm him.

Examination and Diagnostic Process: During examination, Mr. Ravi appears disoriented and has difficulty in following instructions. His speech is coherent but slow, and delusion +. His motor skills seem unaffected, and his vitals are within normal limits.

Differential Diagnosis

1. Cycloserine-induced neuropsychiatric adverse effect
2. Central nervous system (CNS) TB
3. Metabolic encephalopathy
4. Delirium due to general medical condition
5. Substance-induced psychotic disorder

Psychiatrist Practice Pearls:

1. Cycloserine can cause CNS side effects including confusion and psychosis.
2. CNS TB, though less common, can present with similar symptoms and should be considered in patients with TB showing psychiatric symptoms.

Questions and Answers

What are the key steps in the diagnostic process for this case?

The key steps include a thorough psychiatric evaluation, a review of the patient's medical history and medications, laboratory tests to rule out metabolic causes, and potentially imaging studies to rule out CNS TB.

What are the key features of cycloserine-induced neurotoxicity?

Cycloserine can cause a range of CNS side effects including confusion, disorientation, psychosis, and even seizures in severe cases.

What are the key considerations in the management of this case?

Management should involve a multidisciplinary team including psychiatrists and pulmonologists. The patient's medications should be reviewed and potentially adjusted. Supportive care and monitoring are also crucial

Ethical and Legal Aspects

Informed consent should be obtained and documented for all procedures and changes in treatment. The patient and caregiver should be involved in the decision-making process. All facts should be documented in the case records. The patient and caregiver's wishes and versions should be respected and recorded. Any conflicts of interest should be declared and recorded.

****

Whispers of Despair

A 15-year-old adolescent, Rahul, is rushed to the Emergency Room by his parents. His parents report that lately, Rahul has been experiencing anxiety, constantly agitated, arguing, hitting and kicking that was unusual of him which has prompted them to seek immediate medical help. Rahul has a known allergy and has been treated with Montelukast for his allergic symptoms.

Presenting Complaints: Anxiety, Constantly arguing, hitting and kicking – unusual behaviour; History of Montelukast use for allergies; No prior psychiatric history

Clinical Presentation: Poor academic performance; Sleep disturbances; Fidgeting; Quarrelling; annoying

Differential Diagnosis:

1. Major Depressive Disorder
2. Adjustment Disorder with Depressed Mood
3. Medication-induced mood disturbance (Montelukast)
4. Other psychiatric conditions like bipolar disorder or attention-deficit/hyperactivity disorder (ADHD)

Psychiatrist Practice Pearls:

- Montelukast's association with neuropsychiatric events
- Family history of psychiatric disorders
- Any recent life stressors or changes
- Academic and social functioning

Relevant Questions for Examination and Diagnostic Process:

- Explore the patient's mood, affect, and thought content.

- Assess cognitive functions: attention, memory, and executive function.
- Inquire about any recent changes in sleep patterns.
- Explore any history of substance use or abuse.
- Assess for symptoms of ADHD or bipolar disorder.

Psychomotor Aspects of Examination:

- Observe for psychomotor agitation or retardation.
- Assess posture, gestures, and facial expressions for signs of distress.
- Evaluate speech patterns for rate and content.

Affective Domain and Attitude of Healthcare Providers:

- Demonstrate empathy and understanding.
- Discuss potential side effects of Montelukast, including mood disturbances.
- Address stigma and destigmatization surrounding mental health.
- Forewarn about potential challenges in the treatment process.

Ethical and Legal Aspects:

- Obtain informed consent for psychiatric evaluation.
- Involve the patient and caregivers in decision-making.
- Document facts in the patient's record, including Montelukast use.
- Record patient and caregiver wishes and versions.
- Declare and record any conflicts of interest.

Communication Points:

- Need to talk about the medication side effect and suggest alternate drugs.

Challenges and Questions:

- How can the psychiatrist differentiate between primary depression and Montelukast-induced mood disturbance?
- What are the ethical considerations when discussing mood disorder with an adolescent?
- How can healthcare providers navigate the delicate balance of addressing stigma and respecting cultural beliefs in mental health discussions?
- What are the potential challenges in obtaining informed consent from a minor for psychiatric evaluation and treatment?
- How can the healthcare team collaborate with the patient and caregivers in developing a comprehensive treatment plan?

****

The Phantom Menagerie: A Tale of Unseen Companions

Mr. Sharma, a 60-year-old gentleman, recently underwent surgery for a femur fracture. On the first post-operative day, he started reporting seeing rats and rabbits in his room, causing distress and confusion. Upon examination, Mr. Sharma appears anxious and repeatedly glances around the room. He insists on the presence of the animals and becomes agitated when staff members fail to acknowledge them. His vitals are stable, and there are no signs of infection or other post-operative complications.

Differential Diagnosis

1. Post-operative delirium
2. Medication-induced hallucinations
3. Early onset of a neurodegenerative disorder
4. Transient ischemic attack or stroke

Psychiatric Practice Pearls:

1. **ICU psychosis or Delirium** is common in elderly/ post-operative patients and can present with hallucinations.
2. Certain medications used for pain management post-surgery can cause hallucinations.
3. Sudden onset of hallucinations can be a sign of a neurological event like a stroke.

Questions and Answers

What are the key steps in the diagnostic process for this case?

The key steps include a thorough psychiatric evaluation, a review of the patient's medical history and medications, laboratory tests to rule out metabolic causes, and potentially imaging studies to rule out a stroke.

What are the key features of post-operative delirium?

Post-operative delirium can cause a range of symptoms including confusion, disorientation, hallucinations, and changes in consciousness.

What are the key considerations in the management of this case?

Management should involve a multidisciplinary team including physicians, psychiatrists, surgeons, and neurologists. The patient's medications should be reviewed and potentially adjusted. Supportive care and monitoring are also crucial.

Ethical and Legal Aspects

Informed consent should be obtained and documented for all procedures and changes in treatment. The patient and caregiver should be involved in the decision-making process. All facts should be documented in the case records. The patient and caregiver's wishes and versions should be respected and recorded. Any conflicts of interest should be declared and recorded.

Communication Points

1. Discuss the importance of involving caregivers in the treatment process.
2. Orientation strategies to be imparted
3. Provide reassurance and empathetic communication.
4. Discuss potential side effects of medications

Attitude of Health Care Providers

Health care providers, especially critical care nurses should demonstrate patience, empathy, and understanding. They should acknowledge the impact of the condition on the patient's life and discuss potential stigma and strategies for destigmatization.

How can health care providers ensure the best possible outcome for Mr. Sharma while navigating the complexities of his condition and treatment?

****

The Storm Within: A Voyage through Delirium

Mr. Kumar, a 40-year-old South Indian male, has been admitted for alcohol withdrawal treatment. On the third day after his last drink, he started seeing snakes and complained of incessant rains inside his room, causing distress and confusion. Upon examination, Mr. Kumar appears anxious and repeatedly glances around the room. He insists on the presence of the snakes and becomes agitated when staff members fail to acknowledge them. His vitals are stable, but he shows signs of tremors and increased perspiration.

Differential Diagnosis

1. Delirium Tremens
2. Alcohol induced psychotic disorder

3. Wernicke-Korsakoff Syndrome
4. Psychotic Disorder due to another medical condition

Psychiatric Practice Pearls:

1. **Delirium Tremens** is a complicated type of alcohol withdrawal that can cause vivid visual hallucinations, delusions, confusion, disorientation, hallucinations, hyperactivity, and extreme cardiovascular disturbances. Occurs 48-72 hours after the last drink
2. **Alcohol induced psychotic disorder** is a condition that can also cause hallucinations while drinking, withdrawal or between episodes.
3. **Wernicke encephalopathy**, caused by thiamine deficiency often seen in alcoholics, can present with confusion and hallucinations.

MNEMONIC: "GOA" – Global Confusion; Opthalmoplegia & Ataxia

4. **Alcohol withdrawal hallucinations**: This condition typically occurs within 12 hours after the last drink and can last a few days. Hallucinations are usually visual, but can also be auditory or tactile. Patients are usually oriented and alert.
5. **Psychotic disorder due to another medical condition**: This condition involves hallucinations or delusions due to medical conditions such as liver disease, kidney failure, brain tumours, or stroke.
6. Always consider the possibility of multiple overlapping conditions in patients with a history of alcohol abuse.
7. Early recognition and treatment of alcohol withdrawal syndromes can significantly reduce morbidity and mortality.
8. Regular monitoring of vital signs and mental status is crucial in managing these patients.

Questions and Answers

What are the key steps in the diagnostic process for this case?

The key steps include a thorough psychiatric evaluation, a review of the patient's medical history, other drug use and medications, laboratory tests to rule out metabolic causes, and potentially imaging studies to rule out a CVS accident and or head injury.

What are the key features of Delirium Tremens?

Delirium Tremens can cause a range of symptoms including confusion, disorientation, hallucinations, and changes in consciousness with tremors

What are the key considerations in the management of this case?

Management should involve a multidisciplinary team including psychiatrists, physician, and neurologists. The patient's medications should be reviewed and potentially adjusted. Supportive care and monitoring are also crucial.

Ethical and Legal Aspects

Informed consent should be obtained and documented for all procedures and changes in treatment. The patient and caregiver should be involved in the decision-making process. All facts should be documented in the case records. The patient and caregiver's wishes and versions should be respected and recorded. Any conflicts of interest should be declared and recorded. Prior consent should be secured for physical restraint, if it may be needed during the course of treatment

Communication Points

1. It is a medical emergency to be treated in ICU set-up.
2. Explain the potential need for changes in treatment.
3. Provide reassurance and empathetic communication.

4. Discuss the potential costs of treatment and diagnostic tests.
5. Discuss the importance of involving caregivers in the treatment process.
6. Discuss the potential impact of the condition on daily life and work.

Attitude of Health Care Providers

Health care providers should demonstrate patience, empathy, and understanding. They should acknowledge the impact of the condition on the patient's life and discuss potential stigma and strategies for destigmatization. They should involve the patient and caregiver in the decision-making process.

This case scenario ends with a challenge: How can health care providers ensure the best possible outcome for Mr. Kumar while navigating the complexities of his condition and treatment?

****

The Unseen Battle

A 32-year-old woman, Mrs. Anuradha, has been referred to the psychiatry department by the dermatologist. She has been suffering from persistent skin lesions on her arms and legs for the past six months. The lesions are irregular, varying in size, and appear self-inflicted. She reports increasing sense of tension before compulsion to scratch/pick, especially when she is stressed or anxious. She denies any history of allergies or exposure to irritants.What could be the possible causes of her symptoms?

Cognition Aspect

1. **Comprehension:** Explain the difference between excoriation disorder and Dermatitis Artefacta.
2. **Recall:** What are the common psychiatric comorbidities associated with excoriation disorder?
3. **Application:** How would you apply the biopsychosocial model to understand Mrs. Anuradha's condition?

Psychomotor Aspects

1. What specific signs would you look for during a physical examination?
2. How would you differentiate between self-inflicted lesions and lesions caused by a dermatological condition?

Affective Domain

Discuss the potential psychological impact of visible skin lesions on a patient's self-esteem and social interactions.

Differential Diagnosis

1. Dermatitis Artefacta
2. Body focussed repetitive behaviour disorder
3. Delusional Infestation/psychotic disorder
4. Substance use disorders
5. Dermatological conditions

Psychiatric Practice Pearls:

1. Excoriation disorders often coexists with psychotic disorders such as OCD, trichotillomania, depression and anxiety.
2. Patient education about the condition and its management is crucial.
3. Multidisciplinary approach involving dermatologists, psychiatrists, and psychologists can be beneficial.

Attitude of Health Care Providers

1. How would you address the stigma associated with psychiatric disorders in this case?
2. Discuss the importance of empathy in managing patients with Excoriation disorder

Ethical and Legal Aspects

1. Discuss the importance of informed consent in the management of excoriation disorder.

2. How would you handle a situation where the patient refuses a recommended diagnostic test?

Communication Points

1. Aim to provide the patient with relief of being understood. .
2. Strategies to manage stress and anxiety
3. Importance of regular follow-up visits.
4. The role of cognitive-behavioural therapy in managing the condition.

****

The Silent Struggle

A 22-year-old woman, Ms. Chandrika, has been referred to the psychiatric department by the dermatologist. She has been suffering from hair loss on her scalp and eyebrows for the past year. The hair loss is patchy and irregular, and she reports a compulsion to pull out her hair, especially when she is stressed or anxious. No history of any scalp diseases or exposure to hair-damaging chemicals. What could be the possible causes of her symptoms?

Cognition Aspect

Comprehension: Explain the difference between Trichotillomania and Alopecia Areata.

Trichotillomania is a psychiatry disorder where the patient pulls out their own hair with varying degrees of conscious awareness, pleasure/relief when pulling out hair while Alopecia Areata is an autoimmune disease that causes hair to fall out.

Recall: What are the common psychiatric comorbidities associated with Trichotillomania?

Common psychiatric comorbidities include OCD, Tourette's disorder, depression and anxiety.

Application: How would you apply the biopsychosocial model to understand Ms. Chandrika's condition?

The biopsychosocial model can be applied by considering biological factors (hair loss), psychological factors (stress, anxiety), and social factors (impact on work or relationships).

Psychomotor Aspects

What specific signs would you look for during a physical examination?

Look for patchy hair loss on the scalp and eyebrows, signs of regrowth, and any evidence of skin damage due to hair pulling.

How would you differentiate between hair loss caused by Trichotillomania and hair loss caused by a dermatological condition?

Hair loss in Trichotillomania is often in areas easily reached by the patient's hands and may have an irregular pattern. Hair loss caused by dermatological conditions usually follows a specific pattern or distribution and may be accompanied by other signs of the disease.

Affective Domain

Discuss the potential psychological impact of visible hair loss on a patient's self-esteem and social interactions.

Visible hair loss can lead to embarrassment, social withdrawal, and decreased self-esteem. It can also cause significant distress and impact the quality of life.

Differential Diagnosis

1. Alopecia Areata- Androgenic Alopecia, Telogen Effluvium
2. Chronic discoid lupus erythematosus, Lichen plano pilaris, folliculitis decalvans dissecting folliculitis

Psychiatric Practice Pearls

1. Trichotillomania often coexists with psychiatric disorders such as depression and anxiety.
2. Patient education about the condition and its management is crucial.

3. Multidisciplinary approach involving dermatologists, psychiatrists, and psychologists can be beneficial.

Attitude of Health Care Providers

How would you address the stigma associated with psychiatric disorders in this case?

Educate the patient and their family about the nature of the illness, emphasize that it's not a character flaw or weakness, and encourage open discussions.

Discuss the importance of empathy in managing patients with Trichotillomania.

Empathy is crucial in building trust, understanding the patient's experience, and providing effective treatment.

Ethical and Legal Aspects

Discuss the importance of informed consent in the management of Trichotillomania.

Informed consent ensures the patient understands the diagnosis, treatment options, risks, and benefits, allowing them to make an informed decision about their care.

How would you handle a situation where the patient refuses a recommended diagnostic test?

Respect the patient's autonomy, explore their reasons for refusal, provide further education if needed, and discuss alternative options.

Communication Points

1. Briefing about complications – trichophagia, trichobezoar
2. Importance of adhering to the treatment regimen.
3. Strategies to manage stress and anxiety/ Behavioural therapy
4. Importance of regular follow-up visits.

****

The Storm beneath the Skin

A 40-year-old man, Mr. Ganesh, has been referred to the psychiatric department by the dermatology department. He has been suffering from recurrent psoriasis flare-ups on his body for the past two years. The flare-ups appear to worsen during periods of high stress. He denies any history of allergies or exposure to irritants. What could be the possible causes of his symptoms?

Cognition Aspect

Comprehension: Can stress trigger psoriasis? Explain the mechanism? How stress triggers episodes?

Psoriasis is a chronic, relapsing skin disease with lesions characterized by silvery scales with Auspitz sign [HPA axis]

Recall: What are the common psychiatric comorbidities associated with stress and psoriasis?

Common psychiatric comorbidities include depression, anxiety, and stress-related disorders.

Affective Domain

Discuss the potential psychological impact of visible psoriasis on a patient's self-esteem and social interactions.

Visible psoriasis can lead to embarrassment, social withdrawal, and decreased self-esteem. It can also cause significant distress and impact the quality of life.

Differential Diagnosis

1. Eczema
2. Dermatitis
3. Pityriasis Rosea
4. Ringworm

Psychiatric Practice Pearls:

1. Stress triggered psoriasis often coexists with psychiatric disorders such as depression and anxiety.
2. Alcohol use may also trigger episodes.
3. Patient education about the condition and its management is crucial.
4. Multidisciplinary approach involving dermatologists, psychiatrists, and psychologists can be beneficial.

Attitude of Health Care Providers

How would you address the stigma associated with psychiatric disorders in this case?

Educate the patient and their family about the nature of the illness, emphasize that it's not a character flaw or weakness, and encourage open discussions.

Discuss the importance of empathy in managing patients with stress-induced psoriasis.

Empathetic confrontation for effective treatment.

Ethical and Legal Aspects

Discuss the importance of informed consent in the management of stress-induced psoriasis.

Informed consent ensures the patient understands the diagnosis, treatment options, risks, and benefits, allowing them to make an informed decision about their care.

How would you handle a situation where the patient refuses a recommended diagnostic test?

Respect the patient's autonomy, explore their reasons for refusal, provide further education if needed, and discuss alternative options.

Communication Points

1. Importance of adhering to the treatment regimen.
2. Strategies to manage stress and anxiety.
3. Importance of regular follow-up visits.
4. Potential side effects of prescribed medications.
5. The role of cognitive-behavioural therapy in managing the condition.

****

The Unseen Invaders and Phantom Pests

A 45-year-old man, Mr. Hakeem, has been referred to the psychiatric department by the dermatologist. He has been complaining of a sensation of worms crawling under his skin for the past six months. The sensation is persistent and seems to intensify during periods of high stress. He denies any history of travel or exposure to house hold pets. What could be the possible causes of his symptoms?

Cognition Aspect

Comprehension: Explain the difference between Delusional Parasitosis and Formication.

Delusional Parasitosis is a psychiatric condition where the patient has a fixed, false belief of being infested with parasites, while Formication is a sensation of insects crawling on or under the skin, which can be caused by various medical conditions or substance misuse (cocaine).

Recall: What are the common psychiatric comorbidities associated with Delusional Parasitosis?

Common psychiatric comorbidities include depression, anxiety, and obsessive-compulsive disorder.

Application: How would you apply the biopsychosocial model to understand Mr. Hakeeem's condition?

The biopsychosocial model can be applied by considering biological factors (sensation of worms), psychological factors (stress, anxiety), and social factors (impact on work or relationships).

Psychomotor Aspects

What specific signs would you look for during a physical examination?

Look for the absence of any physical signs of infestation, such as bites, rashes, or burrows. Also, note any signs of self-inflicted skin lesions due to scratching or picking.

How would you differentiate between Delusional Parasitosis and a genuine parasitic infestation?
Delusional Parasitosis is characterized by a fixed, false belief of infestation in the absence of any physical evidence. A genuine parasitic infestation would show physical signs such as bites, rashes, or burrows, and the parasites may be visible or detectable through laboratory tests.

Affective Domain
Discuss the potential psychological impact of Delusional Parasitosis on a patient's self-esteem and social interactions.
Delusional Parasitosis can lead to significant distress, social isolation, and decreased self-esteem due to the disturbing nature of the delusions and the stigma associated with mental health disorders.
Differential Diagnosis

1. Formication
2. Scabies
3. Pediculosis, cutaneous larvae migrans
4. Substance-induced Psychosis

Psychiatrist Practice Pearls:

1. Delusional Parasitosis often coexists with psychiatric disorders such as depression and anxiety.
2. Patient education about the condition and its management is crucial.
3. Multidisciplinary approach involving dermatologists, psychiatrists, and psychologists can be beneficial.

Attitude of Health Care Providers
How would you address the stigma associated with psychiatric disorders in this case?
Educate the patient and their family about the nature of the illness, emphasize that it's not a character flaw or weakness, and encourage open discussions.
Discuss the importance of empathy in managing patients with Delusional Parasitosis.
Empathy is crucial in building trust, understanding the patient's experience, and providing effective treatment.
Ethical and Legal Aspects
Discuss the importance of informed consent in the management of Delusional Parasitosis.
Informed consent ensures the patient understands the diagnosis, treatment options, risks, and benefits, allowing them to make an informed decision about their care.
How would you handle a situation where the patient refuses a recommended diagnostic test?
Respect the patient's autonomy, explore their reasons for refusal, provide further education if needed, and discuss alternative options.
Communication Points

1. As there **would be much resistance to diagnosis**, communication and convincing is necessary
2. Strategies to manage anxiety.
3. Potential side effects of prescribed medications.

****

The Sleepless Nights

A 16-year-old boy, Mr. Jeyakumar, has been referred to the psychiatric department by his family physician. He has been suffering from persistent insomnia for the past six months. His parents have noticed changes in his behaviour and suspect substance abuse. What could be the possible causes of his symptoms?

Cognition Aspect

Comprehension: Explain the difference between Insomnia due to Substance Abuse and Insomnia due to Anxiety.

Insomnia due to Substance Abuse is a symptom that occurs as a result of substance use or withdrawal. Insomnia due to Anxiety is a symptom where the individual has difficulty falling or staying asleep due to excessive worry or fear.

Recall: What are the common psychiatric comorbidities associated with Insomnia in teenagers?

Common psychiatric comorbidities include depression, anxiety, and substance use disorders.

Psychomotor Aspects

What specific signs would you look for during a physical examination?

Look for signs of substance abuse such as changes in physical appearance, unexplained injuries, or bloodshot eyes. Also, note any signs of fatigue or stress.

How would you differentiate between Insomnia due to Substance Abuse and Insomnia due to other causes?

Insomnia due to Substance Abuse often improves upon cessation of the substance and may be accompanied by other signs of substance abuse. Insomnia due to other causes would not show these patterns and may be associated with other symptoms depending on the underlying cause.

Affective Domain

Discuss the potential psychological impact of Insomnia on a teenager's self-esteem and social interactions.

Insomnia can lead to fatigue, difficulty concentrating, and mood changes, which can affect a teenager's academic performance, self-esteem, and social interactions.

Differential Diagnosis

1. Insomnia due to Anxiety
2. Insomnia due to Depression
3. Insomnia due to Substance Abuse
4. Delayed Sleep Phase Syndrome

Psychiatrist Practice Pearls:

1. Insomnia in teenagers often coexists with psychiatric disorders such as depression, anxiety, and substance use disorders.
2. Patient and parent education about the condition and its management is crucial.
3. Multidisciplinary approach involving family physicians, psychiatrists, and psychologists can be beneficial.

Attitude of Health Care Providers

How would you address the stigma associated with psychiatric disorders and substance abuse in this case?

Educate the patient and their family about the nature of the illness, emphasize that it's not a character flaw or weakness, and encourage open discussions.

Discuss the importance of empathy in managing patients with Insomnia due to suspected substance abuse.

Empathy is crucial in building trust, understanding the patient's experience, and providing effective treatment.

Ethical and Legal Aspects

Discuss the importance of informed consent in the management of Insomnia in teenagers.

Informed consent ensures the patient and their parents understand the diagnosis, treatment options, risks, and benefits, allowing them to make an informed decision about the care.

How would you handle a situation where the patient refuses a recommended diagnostic test?
Respect the patient's autonomy, explore their reasons for refusal, provide further education if needed, and discuss alternative options.

Communication Points

1. Importance of adhering to the sleep log, sleep training program etc.
2. Avoid social media
3. Behavioural sleep intervention
4. The role of cognitive-behavioural therapy (CBT-I) in management

****

Caught in the Web of Screens

A 15-year-old boy, Master. Lokesh, has been referred to the psychiatry department by his family physician. He has been suffering from sleep disrurbance for the past 1 year. His parents have noticed changes in his behaviour, irritability, falling grades and suspect substance abuse. However, upon further investigation, it is revealed that he has been spending excessive time on his digital devices due to fear of missing out (FOMO). What could be the possible causes of his symptoms?

Cognition Aspect

Comprehension: Explain the difference between Insomnia due to Substance Abuse and Insomnia due to excessive screen time.
Insomnia due to Substance Abuse is a sleep disorder that occurs as a result of substance use or withdrawal. Insomnia due to excessive screen time is a sleep disorder where the individual has difficulty falling or staying asleep due to excessive use of digital devices, often caused by FOMO.

Recall: What are the common psychiatric comorbidities associated with Insomnia in teenagers?
Common psychiatric comorbidities include depression, anxiety, and substance use disorders.

Application: How would you apply the biopsychosocial model to understand Master. Lokesh's condition?
The biopsychosocial model can be applied by considering biological factors (insomnia), psychological factors (FOMO, possible substance abuse), and social factors (impact on school performance or relationships).

Psychomotor Aspects

What specific signs would you look for during a physical examination?
Look for signs of fatigue, stress, or anxiety. Also, note any signs of substance abuse such as pin-prick marks, intra-oral pigmentation, physical appearance or bloodshot eyes.

How would you differentiate between Insomnia due to Substance Abuse and Insomnia due to other causes?
Insomnia due to Substance Abuse often improves upon cessation of the substance and may be accompanied by other signs of substance abuse. Insomnia due to other causes would not show these patterns and may be associated with other symptoms depending on the underlying cause.

Affective Domain

Discuss the potential psychological impact of Insomnia on a teenager's self-esteem and social interactions.
Insomnia can lead to fatigue, difficulty concentrating, and mood changes, which can affect a teenager's academic performance, self-esteem, and social interactions.

Differential Diagnosis

1. Insomnia due to Anxiety
2. Insomnia due to Depression
3. Insomnia due to Delayed Sleep Phase Syndrome
4. Insomnia due to Poor Sleep Hygiene

Psychiatric Practice Pearls:

1. Both conditions rely on dopamine reward circuit- hence pathophysiology remains the same.
2. Insomnia in teenagers often coexists with psychiatric disorders such as depression, anxiety, and substance use disorders.
3. Patient and parent education about the condition and its management is crucial.
4. Multidisciplinary approach involving family physicians, psychiatrists, and psychologists can be beneficial.

Attitude of Health Care Providers

How would you address the stigma associated with psychiatric disorders and substance abuse in this case?

Educate the patient and their family about the nature of the illness, emphasize that it's not a character flaw or weakness, and encourage open discussions.

Discuss the importance of empathy in managing patients with Insomnia due to suspected substance abuse.

Empathy is crucial in building trust, understanding the patient's experience, and providing effective treatment.

Ethical and Legal Aspects

Discuss the importance of informed consent in the management of Insomnia in teenagers.

Informed consent ensures the patient and their parents understand the diagnosis, treatment options, risks, and benefits, allowing them to make an informed decision about the care.

How would you handle a situation where the patient refuses a recommended diagnostic test?

Respect the patient's autonomy, explore their reasons for refusal, provide further education if needed, and discuss alternative options.

Communication Points

1. Importance of adhering to the sleep hygiene.
2. Digital detox
3. Strategies to manage stress and anxiety.
4. Importance of regular follow-up visits.
5. Addressing academics and family dynamics.

****

The Invisible Chains of the Digital World

A 16-year-old boy, Mr. Mani, has been referred to the psychiatric department by his family physician. He has been showing signs of self-social isolation for the past six months. His parents have noticed changes in his behaviour and suspect substance abuse. However, upon further investigation, it is revealed that he has been spending excessive time on his digital devices due to fear of missing out (FOMO). What could be the possible causes of his symptoms?

Cognition Aspect

Comprehension: Explain the difference between social isolation due to Substance Abuse and social isolation due to excessive screen time.

Social isolation due to Substance Abuse is a condition where the individual withdraws from social interactions as a result of substance use or withdrawal. Social isolation due to excessive screen time is a condition where the individual withdraws from social interactions due to excessive use of digital devices, often caused by FOMO.

Recall: What are the common psychiatric comorbidities associated with social isolation in teenagers?

Common psychiatric comorbidities include depression, anxiety, and substance use disorders.

Application: How would you apply the biopsychosocial model to understand Mr. Mani's condition?

The biopsychosocial model can be applied by considering biological factors (effects of screen time), psychological factors (FOMO, possible substance abuse), and social factors (impact on school performance or relationships).

Psychomotor Aspects

What specific signs would you look for during a physical examination?

Look for signs of fatigue, stress, or anxiety. Also, note any signs of substance abuse such as changes in physical appearance or bloodshot eyes.

How would you differentiate between social isolation due to Substance Abuse and social isolation due to other causes?

Social isolation due to Substance Abuse often improves upon cessation of the substance and may be accompanied by other signs of substance abuse. Social isolation due to other causes would not show these patterns and may be associated with other symptoms depending on the underlying cause.

Affective Domain

Discuss the potential psychological impact of social isolation on a teenager's self-esteem and social interactions.

Social isolation can lead to feelings of loneliness, difficulty in social skills, and mood changes, which can affect a teenager's self-esteem and social interactions.

Differential Diagnosis

1. Social Isolation due to Anxiety
2. Social Isolation due to Depression
3. Social Isolation due to Substance Abuse
4. Social Isolation due to Autism Spectrum Disorder

Psychiatrist Practice Pearls:

1. Social isolation in teenagers often coexists with psychiatric disorders such as depression, anxiety, and substance use disorders.
2. Patient and parent education about the condition and its management is crucial.
3. Multidisciplinary approach involving family physicians, psychiatrists, and psychologists can be beneficial.

Attitude of Health Care Providers

How would you address the stigma associated with psychiatric disorders and substance abuse in this case?

Educate the patient and their family about the nature of the illness, emphasize that it's not a character flaw or weakness, and encourage open discussions.

Discuss the importance of empathy in managing patients with social isolation due to suspected substance abuse.

Empathy is crucial in building trust, understanding the patient's experience, and providing effective treatment

Ethical and Legal Aspects

Discuss the importance of informed consent in the management of social isolation in teenagers.

Informed consent ensures the patient and their parents understand the diagnosis, treatment options, risks, and benefits, allowing them to make an informed decision about the care.

How would you handle a situation where the patient refuses a recommended diagnostic test?

Respect the patient's autonomy, explore their reasons for refusal, provide further education if needed, and discuss alternative options.

Communication Points

1. Stress that humans are social animals, need human interaction more.

2. Digital detox
3. Need for Screen vacation and quality family time.
4. Regular follow-up visits for preventing relapse and preservation of social relationship

****

The Unseen Journey

A 22-year-old man, Mr. Omar, has been referred to the psychiatric department by an ER physician from a hilly tourist place. He has been visiting the place with friends and has been complaining of persistent nausea for the past two days. He denies any alcohol or drug abuse and does not show symptoms of food poisoning. The ER physician suspects the use of psychedelic mushrooms. What could be the possible causes of his symptoms?

Cognition Aspect

Comprehension: Explain the difference between nausea due to Substance Abuse and nausea due to food poisoning.

Nausea due to Substance Abuse is a condition where the individual experiences nausea as a result of substance use or withdrawal. Nausea due to food poisoning is a condition where the individual experiences nausea due to the consumption of contaminated food or water.

Recall: What are the common psychiatric comorbidities associated with Substance Abuse?

Common psychiatric comorbidities include depression, anxiety, and substance use disorders.

Psychomotor Aspects

What specific signs would you look for during a physical examination?

Look for signs of dehydration, dilated pupils, increased heart rate, or tremors. Also, note any signs of substance abuse such as changes in physical appearance or bloodshot eyes.

How would you differentiate between nausea due to Substance Abuse and nausea due to other causes?

Nausea due to Substance Abuse often improves upon cessation of the substance and may be accompanied by other signs of substance abuse. Nausea due to other causes would not show these patterns and may be associated with other symptoms depending on the underlying cause.

Affective Domain

Discuss the potential psychological impact of Substance Abuse on a young adult's self-esteem and social interactions.

Substance Abuse can lead to feelings of guilt, difficulty in social interactions, and mood changes, which can affect a young adult's self-esteem and social relationships.

Differential Diagnosis

1. Anxiety
2. Gastroenteritis
3. Substance Abuse Withdrawal
4. Motion Sickness
5. **Substance-Induced Disorders:** Other substances of abuse, such as alcohol, cannabis, or stimulants, can also cause changes in perception, mood, and cognition. However, these substances often have additional effects that are not typically seen with psychedelics, such as sedation (alcohol), euphoria (stimulants), or paranoia (cannabis).
6. **Psychotic Disorders:** Conditions like schizophrenia can cause hallucinations and delusions. However, these symptoms are typically more persistent and are not associated with the recent use of a substance.
7. **Mood Disorders:** Conditions like depression or bipolar disorder can cause changes in energy levels and cognition. However, these symptoms are typically more persistent and are not associated with the recent use of a substance.

8. **Anxiety Disorders:** Conditions like panic disorder can cause heightened awareness and increased energy. However, these symptoms are typically triggered by specific situations and are not associated with the recent use of a substance.

Psychiatrist Practice Pearls:

1. Substance Abuse often coexists with psychiatric disorders such as depression, anxiety, and other substance use disorders.
2. Patient and parent education about the condition and its management is crucial.
3. Multidisciplinary approach involving family physicians, psychiatrists, and psychologists can be beneficial.

Attitude of Health Care Providers

How would you address the stigma associated with psychiatric disorders and substance abuse in this case?

Educate the patient and their family about the nature of the illness, emphasize that it's not a character flaw or weakness, and encourage open discussions.

Discuss the importance of empathy in managing patients with nausea due to suspected substance abuse.

Empathy is crucial in building trust, understanding the patient's experience, and providing effective treatment.

Ethical and Legal Aspects

Discuss the importance of informed consent in the management of nausea in young adults.

Informed consent ensures the patient and their parents understand the diagnosis, treatment options, risks, and benefits, allowing them to make an informed decision about the care.

How would you handle a situation where the patient refuses a recommended treatment?

Respect the patient's autonomy, explore their reasons for refusal, provide further education if needed, and discuss alternative options. Make a note of the same in patient words in the case records.

Clinical Presentation of Psychedelic Use: Psychedelic drugs, also known as hallucinogens, can cause a variety of physical and psychological effects. Some common signs and symptoms:

1. **Altered Perception of Time:** Individuals may feel as if time is moving slower or faster than usual.
2. **Difficulty Communicating Clearly:** They may have trouble expressing their thoughts or understanding others.
3. **Hallucinations:** This could include seeing, hearing, or feeling things that aren't real.
4. **Heightened Awareness or Understanding:** Individuals may feel more in tune with their surroundings or have profound insights.
5. **Increased Energy:** They may feel energetic or restless.
6. **Lack of Ability to Think Rationally:** Their thought processes may be disorganized or nonsensical.
7. **Mixed Sensory Experiences (Synesthesia):** They may "see" sounds or "hear" colors.
8. **Nausea:** Some psychedelics can cause nausea or vomiting.

****

The Colorful Symphony of the Mind

A 22-year-old man, Mr. Kannan, has been referred to the psychiatric department by a neurophysician. He has been experiencing episodes of unusual sensory experiences for the past two months. During these episodes, he reported seeing vibrant colours associated with certain sounds, perceiving music as a kaleidoscope of hues, and even associating specific tastes with particular words. These episodes lasted for approximately 10-15 minutes and occurred 2-3 times a week. Notably, there was no impairment in consciousness during these events. No significant past medical history, psychiatric disorders, seizures. Neurological examination revealed no abnormalities, and brain imaging (MRI) was unremarkable. What could be the possible causes of his symptoms?

Cognition Aspect

Comprehension: Explain the difference between hallucinations due to Schizophrenia, Synaesthesia, and hallucinations due to psychedelic substance use.

Hallucinations due to Schizophrenia is positive, persistant symptom which is a perceptual abnormality. Synaesthesia is a condition where stimulation of one sensory pathway leads to automatic, involuntary experiences in a second sensory pathway. Hallucinations due to psychedelic substance use are temporary and occur as a result of the substance's effects on the brain.

Recall: What are the common psychiatric conditions associated with hallucinations?

Common psychiatric comorbidities include Schizophrenia, Bipolar Disorder, Major Depressive Disorder with Psychotic Features, and Substance Use Disorders.

Psychomotor Aspects

What specific signs would you look for during a physical examination?

Look for signs of substance use such as changes in physical appearance, dilated pupils, or altered vital signs. Also, note any signs of psychosis such as disorganized speech or behavior.

Affective Domain

Discuss the potential psychological impact of hallucinations on a young adult's self-esteem and social interactions.

Hallucinations can lead to feelings of fear or distress, difficulty in social interactions, and mood changes, which can affect a young adult's self-esteem and social relationships.

Differential Diagnosis

1. Schizophrenia
2. Substance-Induced Psychotic Disorder
3. Temporal Lobe Epilepsy

Psychiatrist Practice Pearls:

1. Morbid Synesthesia is pathological
2. Patient and parent education about the condition and its management is crucial.
3. Multidisciplinary approach involving family physicians, psychiatrists, and psychologists can be beneficial.

Attitude of Health Care Providers

How would you address the stigma associated with psychiatric disorders and substance abuse in this case?

Educate the patient and their family about the nature of the illness, emphasize that it's not a character flaw or weakness, and encourage open discussions.

Discuss the importance of empathy in managing patients with hallucinations due to suspected substance abuse.

Empathy is crucial in building trust, understanding the patient's experience, and providing effective treatment.

Ethical and Legal Aspects

Discuss the importance of informed consent in the management of hallucinations in young adults.

Informed consent ensures the patient and their parents understand the diagnosis, treatment options, risks, and benefits, allowing them to make an informed decision about the care.

How would you handle a situation where the patient refuses a recommended diagnostic test?

Respect the patient's autonomy, explore their reasons for refusal, provide further education if needed, and discuss alternative options.

****

The Silent Battle of the Mind

A 20-year-old woman, Ms. Radhika, has been referred to the psychiatric department by her primary care physician. She has a known history of an eating disorder (anorexia nervosa) and has been experiencing premenstrual exacerbation of mood swings. What could be the possible causes of her symptoms?

Cognition Aspect

Comprehension: Explain the difference between mood swings due to Premenstrual Dysphoric Disorder (PMDD) and due to an eating disorder.

Mood swings due to PMDD occur in the final week before menstruation and resolve/reduce with menstruation. Mood disturbance due to an eating disorder may be related to body image (weight/shape) distress, or the psychological stress of behaviours that interfere with weight gain, persistence lack of recognition of seriousness of current low body weight.

Recall: What are the common psychiatric comorbidities associated with eating disorders?

Common psychiatric comorbidities include depression, anxiety disorders, and substance use disorders.

Application: How would you apply the biopsychosocial model to understand Ms. Radhika's condition?

The biopsychosocial model can be applied by considering biological factors (effects of malnutrition, hormonal changes), psychological factors (body image distress, fear of weight gain), and social factors (impact on relationships, societal pressure to be thin).

Psychomotor Aspects

What specific signs would you look for during a physical examination?

Look for signs of malnutrition such as low body weight, dry skin, or hair loss. Also, note any signs of self-induced vomiting such as calluses on the knuckles or dental erosion.

How would you differentiate between mood swings due to PMDD and mood swings due to other causes?

Mood swings due to PMDD are typically cyclical, occurring in the week or two before menstruation and resolving with menstruation. Mood swings due to other causes, such as an eating disorder, may not follow this pattern and may be associated with other symptoms such as changes in appetite or body weight.

Affective Domain

Discuss the potential psychological impact of an eating disorder on a young woman's self-esteem and social interactions.

An eating disorder can lead to feelings of shame, difficulty in social interactions, and mood changes, which can affect a young woman's self-esteem and social relationships.

Differential Diagnosis

1. Premenstrual Dysphoric Disorder (PMDD)
2. Major Depressive Disorder
3. Bipolar Disorder
4. Borderline Personality Disorder

Psychiatrist Practice Pearls:

1. Eating disorders often coexist with other psychiatric disorders such as depression, anxiety disorders, and PMDD.
2. Patient and parent education about the condition and its management is crucial.
3. Multidisciplinary approach involving primary care physicians, psychiatrists and dieticians can be beneficial.

Attitude of Health Care Providers

How would you address the stigma associated with psychiatric disorders and eating disorders in this case?

Educate the patient and their family about the nature of the illness, emphasize that it's not a character flaw or weakness, and encourage open discussions.

Discuss the importance of empathy in managing patients with eating disorders.

Empathy is crucial in building trust, understanding the patient's experience, and providing effective treatment.

Ethical and Legal Aspects

Discuss the importance of informed consent in the management of eating disorders in young adults.

Informed consent ensures the patient and their parents understand the diagnosis, treatment options, risks, and benefits, allowing them to make an informed decision about the care.

How would you handle a situation where the patient refuses a recommended diagnostic test?

Respect the patient's autonomy, explore their reasons for refusal, provide further education if needed, and discuss alternative options.

****

Navigating Neuropsychiatric Challenges

Mrs. Gupta, a 38-year-old woman, has been referred by an infectious diseases specialist for a liaison psychiatric consultation. She visited the infectious diseases clinic complaining of persistent headaches, fatigue, and muscle weakness. The infection specialist noticed neurological abnormalities during the examination. Mrs. Gupta also reported experiencing vivid and distressing dreams lately, accompanied by intermittent confusion and forgetfulness. Her medical history is unremarkable, with no significant psychiatric issues. During the infectious diseases evaluation, an MRI revealed focal lesions in the brain, raising concerns about a possible Toxoplasmosis infection. While awaiting the lab results, the infection specialist is puzzled by her neuropsychiatric symptoms. The liaison psychiatric team is called in for a comprehensive evaluation to explore potential psychiatric contributions.

Questions:

Comprehension: What are the key neuropsychiatric symptoms exhibited by Mrs. Gupta, and how might they be linked to infectious diseases?

Neuropsychiatric symptoms may include vivid dreams, confusion, and forgetfulness, which can be linked to the impact of Toxoplasma gondii on the central nervous system since it is a neurotrophic pathogen.

Recall: Can you recall the common ways Toxoplasmosis is transmitted, and how it may affect the central nervous system?

Toxoplasmosis, besides congenital transmission, is commonly transmitted through the ingestion of contaminated food or water, and it may affect the brain, causing neurological symptoms.

Psychomotor Aspects:

What specific neurological examinations would you perform to assess Mrs. Gupta's condition?

Neurological examination should always be a thorough detailed one. Imaging studies such as MRI can help visualize brain lesions

Affective Domain:

How might Mrs. Gupta's psychiatric symptoms impact her emotional well-being and overall quality of life?

Mrs. Gupta's psychiatric symptoms may significantly impact her emotional well-being, causing distress, anxiety, and potential challenges in daily life

Differential Diagnosis:

- Toxoplasmosis: Neurological symptoms, brain lesions on imaging.
- Autoimmune Encephalitis: Inflammatory markers, autoimmune antibodies.
- Primary Psychiatric Disorders: Detailed psychiatric evaluation ruling out organic causes.

****

Unveiling Shadows of the Mind - The Enigmatic Neurological Puzzle

Mr. Patel, a 42-year-old immigrant from a rural area, is referred by an Infectious disease specialist to the psychiatric liaison team due to an atypical presentation of neurological symptoms. The infection specialist suspect neurocysticercosis, given Mr. Patel's past travel history and food preferences(vegetarian). Mr Patel had recent onset of seizures, presented with Cognitive disturbances - memory lapses, and also Headache and visual disturbances. During the consultation, Mr. Patel appears distressed and mentions his recent difficulties in concentrating at work. He describes occasional episodes of forgetfulness and feeling "out of touch." His wife adds that he has been having seizures in the past few weeks, characterized by uncontrolled movements and loss of consciousness.

Questions/Challenges:

- What psychiatric history questions would you ask to understand the cognitive and emotional aspects of Mr. Patel's condition?
- How would you approach the patient and his family to discuss the potential psychiatric implications of his neurological symptoms?
- What challenges might arise in terms of stigma, cultural considerations, and the impact on Mr. Patel's daily life?

Cognitive Aspect Questions:

- Comprehension: Explain the pathophysiology of neurocysticercosis and its potential impact on cognitive function.
- Recall: List three common symptoms of neurocysticercosis.
- Application: Describe how neurocysticercosis could contribute to the development of psychiatric symptoms.

Psychomotor Aspect Questions:

- What specific neurological signs would you look for during the physical examination of Mr. Patel?
- How would you differentiate between various types of seizures through clinical assessment?
- Demonstrate the technique for performing a thorough neurological examination.

Affective Domain Questions:

- How would you approach the conversation about potential psychiatric symptoms with Mr. Patel and his family?
- Discuss the potential emotional impact of a neurocysticercosis diagnosis on the patient and family.
- How would you address cultural and stigma-related issues in the context of psychiatric consultation?

Differential Diagnosis:

- Epilepsy
- Meningitis
- Metabolic encephalopathy
- Neurocysticercosis
- Neurological sequelae of other parasitic infections

Psychiatry Practice Pearls:

- Psychiatric evaluation is crucial in cases with neurological symptoms to identify comorbid conditions.
- Consider cultural and social factors when addressing psychiatric concerns in diverse patient populations.
- Collaboration with other specialties, such as infectious disease and neurology, is vital for comprehensive patient care.

****

Delayed Language and Speech Development in a 2-Year-Old Boy

A 2-year-old boy is brought to the Psychiatrist by his parents due to concerns about his delayed language and speech development. He currently uses only about 10 words independently and has not yet started forming two-word sentences. Occasionally, he imitates what his parents say. Although he achieved the milestone of walking on time, he does not engage in pretend play and lacks interaction during playtime. The boy's preferred play activity involves toy key rings, which he holds and shakes his forearms up and down in a flapping motion. Additionally, he strongly dislikes loud noises and becomes upset when the vacuum cleaner or blender is turned on. His day-care provider has also observed similar behaviours.

Cognition Aspect

What are the typical speech milestones for a 2-year-old child?

- By age 2, children should have a vocabulary of approximately 50 to 100 words.
- They typically form two-word sentences (e.g., "more juice," "big dog").
- Comprehension includes following simple one-step directions (e.g., "pick up the block")

Psychomotor Aspects: Specific Examinations

During the physical examination, what specific signs should you assess?

1. Speech Assessment:
    - Observe the child's ability to imitate sounds and words.
    - Assess expressive language (number of words used independently).
    - Note any speech repetition or echolalia.
2. Fine Motor Skills:
    - Evaluate hand movements during play (e.g., shaking toy key rings).
    - Assess coordination and fine motor control.
3. Sensory Examination:
    - Observe the child's reaction to loud noises (e.g., vacuum cleaner, blender).
    - Assess sensory sensitivities (e.g., aversion to certain stimuli).

Affective Domain: Emotional and Behavioural Aspects

How might this child's behaviour impact his emotional well-being and family dynamics?

- Parental Concerns:
    - Parents may experience anxiety and frustration due to the child's delayed speech.
    - They may seek reassurance and guidance from healthcare providers.
- Child's Emotional State:
    - The child's frustration at being unable to express needs verbally.
    - Emotional distress related to sensory sensitivities (e.g., loud noises).

Differential Diagnosis: Diagnostic Pointers

Possible Diagnoses:

1. Autism Spectrum Disorder (ASD):
    - Delayed language and social communication.
    - Repetitive behaviours (e.g., flapping).
    - Lack of pretend play.
2. Expressive Language Disorder:
    - Limited vocabulary and difficulty forming sentences.
    - Normal cognitive development.
3. Selective Mutism:
    - Child speaks in some situations but remains silent in others.

  - Anxiety-related.
4. Hearing Impairment: Rule out hearing deficits affecting speech development.

Psychiatric Practice Pearls

- Early Intervention:
  - Timely referral for speech therapy is crucial.
  - Address parental concerns and provide support.
- Individualized Approach:
  - Understand the child's unique needs and strengths.
  - Collaborate with other professionals (speech therapists, educators).
- Family Education:
  - Educate parents about developmental milestones.
  - Discuss strategies for communication and play.

Healthcare Provider Attitude: Empathy and Stigma

How can healthcare providers approach this case with empathy and understanding?

- Patience:
  - Acknowledge parental worries and provide reassurance.
  - Understand that progress may be gradual.
- Stigma-destigmatization:
  - Avoid labelling; focus on strengths.
  - Educate parents about common developmental variations.
- Cost Considerations:
  - Discuss available resources (public programs, insurance coverage).
  - Address financial concerns related to therapy and assessments.

Ethical and Legal Aspects

Informed Consent: Obtain informed consent for assessments and interventions.

Confidentiality: Safeguard patient information; Discuss privacy and sharing of diagnostic information.

****

The Case of the Salesman

A 25-year-old man visits a sleep clinic accompanied by his wife. She informs the doctor that her husband has been experiencing disturbing dreams that abruptly wake him up during the past 2 months. Interestingly, the patient himself has no memory of these episodes; he only becomes aware of them because his wife has been complaining about his unusual behaviour including walking at night. The man works in a marketing company and admits to heightened stress levels due to an important work deadline. His usual bedtime is around 11 p.m., and he believes he falls asleep shortly after. Although he occasionally wakes up at night to use the restroom, he promptly returns to bed and falls back asleep. In the morning, around 7 a.m., he feels refreshed overall and denies significant daytime sleepiness.

While the patient's parents and wife have previously complained about his snoring, there is no evidence of observed apnea episodes. During the night, approximately 3 to 4 times a week, shortly after falling asleep, he sits up in bed, walks, appearing confused with open eyes and staring blankly. However, any attempts to interact with him during these episodes result in a blank stare, after which he typically falls back asleep almost immediately. Interestingly, the patient recalls having similar episodes during childhood but has not experienced them since starting middle school.

Cognition:

Comprehension: Can you explain the difference between REM and NREM sleep stages, and how might this be relevant to the case?

Sleep cycles through stages of Non-Rapid Eye Movement (NREM) sleep and Rapid Eye Movement (REM) sleep. NREM sleep has 4 stages [Currently 3 stages with the 3rd and 4th merged], with increasing depth. Sleepwalking typically occurs during NREM stages (old stages 3 and 4), when the brain is less responsive to external stimuli. REM sleep is characterized by rapid eye movements, increased brain activity, and dreaming. Nightmares typically occur during REM sleep, Sleep terrors occur during NREM sleep

Recall: List some risk factors for sleepwalking (somnambulism)

Several factors can increase the risk of sleepwalking, including:

- Age: Sleepwalking is most common in children but can persist into adulthood.
- Family History: Having a family member with sleepwalking increases the risk.
- Sleep Deprivation: Not getting enough sleep can make sleepwalking more likely.
- Stress: Increased stress can be a trigger for sleepwalking episodes.
- Certain Medications: Some medications can disrupt sleep patterns and increase the risk of sleepwalking.
- Alcohol or Drug Use: Substance use can interfere with sleep and make sleepwalking more likely.
- Medical Conditions: Certain medical conditions, like sleep apnea, can sometimes be confused with sleepwalking.

Application: Given Patient's childhood history and the characteristics of the episodes, how might this information influence the differential diagnosis?

Childhood history suggests a possible predisposition. The characteristics of the episodes (walking, confusion, amnesia, occurring shortly after falling asleep) point towards sleepwalking as the most likely diagnosis. However, other conditions like night terrors or REM sleep behaviour disorder (RBD) warrant consideration.

Psychomotor Skills (Examination):

History: What additional historical details might be helpful in reaching a diagnosis?

- Frequency and duration of episodes
- Activities during episodes (walking, talking, eating etc.)
- Presence of injuries or potential dangers during episodes
- Sleep quality (difficulty falling asleep, frequent awakenings)
- Use of medications, alcohol, or drugs
- Presence of daytime sleepiness

Physical Exam: What physical exam findings might be relevant to rule out or support specific diagnoses?

A general physical exam is important to rule out underlying medical conditions. A neurological exam may be performed if other conditions are suspected.

Investigations: Are there any initial investigations that could be considered in this case?

In some cases, a sleep study (polysomnography) may be recommended. This involves monitoring brain activity, muscle activity, breathing, and eye movements during sleep to differentiate other pathologies. `

Affective Domain (Emotions):

How might patient family be feeling emotionally about this situation? What are some potential psychosocial impacts?

Patient might feel embarrassed or frustrated about his sleepwalking episodes. He may also worry about potential dangers or injuries that could occur during an episode.

Patient's wife is likely experiencing sleep disruption due to patient episodes. She may also feel worried about patient safety and frustrated by the lack of control over the situation. Both may be feeling anxious or stressed about the situation.

Differential Diagnosis:

- Sleepwalking (Somnambulism): This is the most likely diagnosis based on the clinical presentation.
- Night Terrors: While less common than sleepwalking, night terrors share some similar features, but typically involve intense fear and confusion upon waking.
- REM Sleep Behaviour Disorder (RBD): This condition involves dream-acting behaviors during REM sleep. Given John's age, RBD is less likely, but should be considered.
- Psychiatric Disorders: Certain psychiatric disorders can manifest with sleep behaviors.

Psychiatric Practice Pearls

- A detailed sleep history obtained from both the patient and bed partner is crucial for diagnosis.
- Ruling out medical conditions like sleep apnea is important.
- Treatment for sleepwalking often involves optimizing sleep hygiene and creating a safe sleep environment.
- In some cases, medications may be considered.

Healthcare Provider Considerations:

- Empathy and Understanding: It's important to acknowledge the distress this is causing.
- Destigmatization: Sleepwalking is a common condition, and reassurance can be helpful.
- Cost Considerations: Discuss potential costs of investigations and treatment plans with the patient.

Ethical and Legal Aspects:

- Informed consent must be obtained for any investigations or treatment interventions.
- Involving both of them in the decision-making process is crucial.
- Documentation of the history, examination findings, and treatment plan is essential.

Communication for Improved Outcomes:

- Clearly explain the diagnosis and treatment options.
- Emphasize the importance of medication adherence (if applicable).
- Discuss lifestyle modifications that may improve sleep quality.
- Provide empathetic communication and acknowledge the challenges associated with sleepwalking

****

Managing the monthly Rollercoaster: PMS

(Contributed by: Dr. Charanya Kaliamoorthy, Assistant Professor, SSSMCRI)

Miss Sridevi, a 25 years old, unmarried female comes to her primary care physician with complaints of recurring physical and emotional symptoms that occur before her menstrual period each month. She reports that these symptoms have been affecting her daily life and relationships. Her menstrual history is of regular cycles with an average length of 28 days and normal flow. No significant medical conditions or previous mental health diagnoses. Miss Sridevi leads a healthy lifestyle and works as a teacher which can be stressful at times, especially around exam periods. She reports feeling overwhelmed and irritable in the days leading up to her period which affects her interaction with colleagues and students. She noticed the onset of symptoms about 6 months ago attributing to mood swings, irritability and fatigue to work stress and lack of sleep. She feels guilty and frustrated and struggles to control her emotions and behaviors. Dr Krishnamoorthy assessed Miss Sridevi and investigated her on certain blood parameters like thyroid function test, complete blood picture to rule out the other medical causes of her clinical presentation. Dr Krishnamoorthy after discussing with a psychiatrist implemented a comprehensive treatment plan for Miss Sridevi that includes lifestyle modification, medication, therapy and support.

Test your cognition

Recall:

- Why did Dr Krishnamoorthy discuss this case with a psychiatrist?
- What is the need for blood investigations in this case?

Application:

- What are the medical conditions that mimic or commonly associated with PMS?
- What is the biological purpose of PMS?
- Symptom diary to track the timing, duration, and severity of PMS symptom.

Understanding:

- What is the impact of PMS in women's physical health, mental well-being, quality of life and overall productivity?
- How common is PMS?
- What is the prognosis of PMS?
- What is the impact on relationships?

Doctor's Attitude:

- Non-judgmental attitude with support and empathy is recommended.
- Holistic approach considering Miss Sridevi's overall health and well-being.
- Collaborative decision making with patient education and empowerment.

Ethical Aspects:

- Reducing stigma and misconceptions
- Privacy and confidentiality
- Avoiding overmedicalization
- Informed use of medications

Communication:

- Encourage open discussion.
- Use descriptive language to convey the intensity and impact of symptoms.
- Empathetic listening

For further reading: Takeda T. Premenstrual disorders: Premenstrual syndrome and premenstrual dysphoric disorder. J Obstet Gynaecol Res. 2023 Feb;49(2):510-518. doi: 10.1111/jog.15484. Epub 2022 Nov 1. PMID: 36317488

****

Navigating the Intersection: Perinatal Psychiatric Disorders and Medical Comorbidities

(Contributed by: Dr. Charanya Kaliamoorthy, Assistant Professor, SSSMCRI)

Mrs. Priya, 32-year-old woman, is currently in her third trimester of pregnancy with her first child. She has a history of generalized anxiety disorder (GAD) and has been managing it with cognitive-behavioral therapy (CBT) and occasional use of benzodiazepines under the supervision of her psychiatrist Dr Menon. Additionally, she was diagnosed with gestational diabetes mellitus (GDM) during her pregnancy.

Mrs. Priya presents to the obstetric clinic with complaints of increased anxiety, frequent panic attacks, and difficulty controlling her blood sugar levels despite dietary modifications and insulin therapy. She reports feeling overwhelmed by the impending responsibilities of motherhood and worries excessively about her ability to care for her baby.

Physical examination reveals no significant abnormalities other than Priya's elevated blood pressure and blood glucose levels consistent with her gestational diabetes. She appears visibly distressed and reports feeling constantly on edge.

Diagnostic Workup:

Perinatal Psychiatric Evaluation: Mrs. Priya undergoes a comprehensive psychiatric evaluation to assess the severity of her anxiety symptoms, screen for depressive symptoms, and evaluate her risk of postpartum psychiatric complications.

Obstetric Evaluation: Obstetric evaluation includes monitoring fetal growth, assessing uterine contractions, and evaluating Priya's overall maternal-fetal health.

Endocrinological Assessment: Given Priya's history of gestational diabetes mellitus and difficulty controlling her blood sugar levels, an endocrinologist evaluates her insulin regimen, dietary intake, and glycemic control.

Mrs. Priya's treatment is planned with close collaboration between her psychiatrist, obstetrician, endocrinologist, and other healthcare providers involved in her care. Postpartum, Priya receives continued support to address the challenges of transitioning to motherhood and to mitigate the risk of postpartum psychiatric complications.

Test Your Cognition

Recall:

- What are the challenges in dealing with Mrs Priya?
- What are the various aspects Dr Menon should consider in diagnosing and treating Mrs Priya?
- What is the postpartum support that should be ensured to Mrs Priya?

Application:

- Collaboration of various departments in evaluating and treating this case.
- To take adequate precautions to avoid adverse reactions.

Understanding:

- Multidisciplinary Approach to Care
- The presence of medical comorbidities can complicate the management of psychiatric symptoms and vice versa.
- Addressing perinatal psychiatric disorders with medical comorbidity complications is paramount to safeguarding the health and well-being of both the mother and the developing child.

Doctor's Attitude:

- Doctors should adopt a holistic approach to care that considers the interconnectedness of physical, psychological, and social factors influencing maternal and fetal health.
- Healthcare providers should prioritize patient-cantered care, involving patients in decision-making processes, respecting their preferences and values, and addressing their individual needs and concerns.

Ethical Aspects:

- Principles of autonomy, beneficence, non-maleficence, justice, and confidentiality.

Communication:

- Using plain language and avoiding medical jargon can help patients better understand their conditions, treatment options, and the rationale behind medical recommendations.
- Empathetic communication involves active listening, showing empathy towards patients' emotional experiences, and providing reassurance and support.
- Establishing Trust and Rapport

For further reading: Meltzer-Brody S, Stuebe A. The long-term psychiatric and medical prognosis of perinatal mental illness. Best Pract Res Clin Obstet Gynaecol. 2014 Jan;28(1):49-60. doi: 10.1016/j.bpobgyn.2013.08.009. Epub 2013 Aug 27. PMID: 24063973; PMCID: PMC3947371.

Unveiling the challenges: A case scenario of Postpartum Psychosis

(Contributed by: Dr. Charanya Kaliamoorthy, Assistant Professor, SSSMCRI)

A 29-year-old female, Mrs Suja, was brought to emergency on her 10th postpartum day with irritability and agitated behaviour. Vitals were stable, Dr Helen, patient's treating gynaecology doctor was called. Mrs Suja had undergone Caesarean Section for a transverse lie. Her male infant was born healthy with no complications. Doctor noticed Mrs Suja to be disturbed and talking out of context and muttering to self. Her husband reported that she was pulling off her clothes and throwing away her baby's clothes. She was fisting her hands on and off and staring at the family members. The above symptoms lasted for the last 3 days. She had no history of chronic illnesses including diabetes mellitus or hypertension. No substance uses. She had a well-adjusted premorbid personality and no past h/o mood disorder. Her first pregnancy was uneventful and no similar complaints in the previous pregnancy.

After assessing the patient, Dr Helen asked for psychiatry opinion. Baseline investigations (Complete Blood Count, Renal Function Test, Urine Routine, ECG, serum electrolytes and Thyroid Function Test) were normal. On her mental state examination, she was irritable with increased psychomotor activity, hallucinatory behaviour, and persecutory idea without insight. The Brief Psychiatric Rating Scale (BPRS) score was 48 and Clinical Global Impressions-Severity (CGI-S) score was 6. She was treated with antipsychotics and appropriate breastfeeding measures were taken.

Test Your Cognition

Recall:

- Why did Dr Helen ask for Psychiatry opinion? What is the challenge Dr Helen was facing?
- Why is the postpartum day important?
- What is the relevance of past h/o mood disorder?
- How is the history of previous pregnancy important?

Application:

- What are the appropriate breastfeeding measures that should be taken?
- Why are the baseline investigations important in this patient?
- What are the challenges faced in treating a postpartum patient?
- What are the measures taken to control an agitated female who is on breastfeeding?

Understanding:

- What are the risk factors for postpartum psychosis?
- Why is it important to know about postpartum psychosis?
- How common is postpartum psychosis?

Doctor's Attitude:

- Postpartum psychosis is considered a medical emergency, and prompt treatment is crucial for the safety of both the mother and the baby.
- Non-judgmental attitude with support and empathy is recommended.

Ethical Aspects:

The ethical aspects of postpartum psychosis require multidimensional approach that considers the rights, well-being, and dignity of the patient, the child and the family. It involves promoting autonomy, ensuring access to care, reducing stigma, respecting cultural beliefs and providing compassionate and comprehensive support.

Communication:

- Using clear and simple language that Mrs Suja can understand.

- Providing information about postpartum psychosis, its symptoms, prognosis and treatment options to Mrs Suja's husband.
- Communicating about safety planning is essential, especially if Mrs Suja is experiencing thoughts of harm to themselves, others or the baby.

For further reading: Friedman SH, Reed E, Ross NE. Postpartum Psychosis. Curr Psychiatry Rep. 2023 Feb;25(2):65-72. doi: 10.1007/s11920-022-01406-4. Epub 2023 Jan 13. PMID: 36637712; PMCID: PMC9838449.

****

Beyond the Baby Blues- Post Partum Depression

(Contributed by: Dr. Charanya Kaliamoorthy, Assistant Professor, SSSMCRI)

Mrs. Renette, 28 years old female working as a marketing manager has delivered a female child 6 weeks ago, she presents to her doctor with feelings of sadness, overwhelming anxiety, and a sense of disconnection from her new born daughter. She reports difficulty bonding with the baby and experiencing intense guilt and shame about her emotions. She had no significant medical history. Her pregnancy was uneventful, although she experienced mild anxiety during the third trimester.

In the first few weeks after delivery, Mrs. Renette felt a surge of love and joy. However, these feelings were quickly overshadowed by intense anxiety and sadness. She found herself crying frequently for no apparent reason. She struggled to sleep and felt overwhelmed by the demands of motherhood and guilty for not feeling the joy she expected. She began avoiding calls and visits from friends and family.

During her visit to doctor, she breaks down in tears and expresses feelings of hopelessness, worthlessness and fear that she is failing as a mother. She admits that she had thoughts of wanting to disappear and run away from her responsibilities.

Dr Krishnan, her consulting psychiatrist diagnosed her as Postpartum Depression and discussed the severity of symptoms with the family. Risk assessment was done as Mrs. Renette is at increased risk of self-harm due to presence of suicidal ideation. She was put on both pharmacotherapy and psychotherapy.

Test your cognition

Recall:

- Why is Mrs Renette feeling guilty and what might be the consequences of her symptoms?
- What are the risks that Dr Krishnan should address?
- How important is the support system?
- What is the need for this case to be treated as an emergency condition?

Application:

- What are the high-risk protocols that should be taken in this case?
- Relevance of informed consent with suicidal patients.
- What are the appropriate breastfeeding measures that should be taken?
- Why are the baseline investigations important in this patient?
- What are the challenges faced in treating a postpartum depressive patient?

Understanding:

- The difference between postpartum depression and 'baby blues'
- The significance of fluctuation in hormones after childbirth.
- Why is it important to know about postpartum depression?

- Understanding the need for CBT (Cognitive Behavioural Therapy) and IPT (Interpersonal therapy)

Doctor's Attitude:

- Approach postpartum depression with empathy, understanding and commitment to providing comprehensive care.
- By validating Mrs Renette's experiences, offering treatment options and supporting her well-being, Dr Krishnan plays a crucial role in helping her to navigate this challenge period and achieve recovery.
- It's a delicate balance of medical intervention, emotional support and ongoing management.

Ethical Aspects:

- Protecting the confidentiality of Mrs Renette's medical information is important. However, sharing information with Mrs Renette's partner or family members may be necessary for her safety and wellbeing.
- Informed decision making about medication and breast feeding.
- Addressing the risk of harm.

Communication:

- Establish a safe, private and comfortable space for the conversation.
- Listen attentively to Mrs Renette's thoughts, feelings and concerns.
- Usage of non-judgmental language.
- Normalize her experience
- Educate about symptoms and treatment

For further reading: Gopalan P, Spada ML, Shenai N, Brockman I, Keil M, Livingston S, Moses-Kolko E, Nichols N, O'Toole K, Quinn B, Glance JB. Postpartum Depression-Identifying Risk and Access to Intervention. Curr Psychiatry Rep. 2022 Dec;24(12):889-896. doi: 10.1007/s11920-022-01392-7. Epub 2022 Nov 23. PMID: 36422834; PMCID: PMC9702784.

****

Double Vulnerability: Adolescent Pregnancy and Mental Health

(Contributed by: Dr. Charanya Kaliamoorthy, Assistant Professor, SSSMCRI)

Miss Maria is a 16-year-old high school student who presents to a clinic for a prenatal check-up. She recently discovered that she is pregnant and is unsure about how to cope with the pregnancy and its impact on her life. Maria comes from a low-income family and lives with her parents and two younger siblings in a small apartment. She is in her second trimester of pregnancy and has not received any prenatal care thus far. She has a history of asthma and has been experiencing worsening symptoms since becoming pregnant.

Maria expresses feelings of confusion, fear, and uncertainty about her pregnancy. She is worried about how her family and peers will react to the news and feels overwhelmed by the prospect of becoming a mother at such a young age. Maria reports experiencing frequent mood swings, episodes of sadness, and difficulty sleeping since learning about her pregnancy.

Physical examination reveals signs of respiratory distress, including wheezing, shortness of breath, and decreased air movement in the lungs. She appears anxious and emotionally distressed during the assessment.

Mental health professionals, obstetricians, and pulmonologists, ensures comprehensive and integrated care throughout Maria's pregnancy.

Test your cognition

Recall:

- What are the challenges in dealing with Miss Maria?
- What are the expected complications in this case?
- How to deal with Miss Maria's family?

Application:

- Collaboration of various departments in evaluating and treating this case.
- Disorders such as depression, anxiety, and stress can negatively affect Miss Maria's physical health, leading to difficulties in managing medical conditions such as asthma during pregnancy.
- Untreated maternal mental health disorders and poorly managed medical conditions during pregnancy are associated with adverse fetal and neonatal outcomes, including preterm birth, low birth weight, and developmental delays.

Understanding:

- Mental health disorders can exacerbate medical conditions and vice versa, leading to a vicious cycle of poor health outcomes if left untreated.
- Adolescent pregnancy and its associated mental health and medical comorbidities can have long-term implications for the health and well-being of both the mother and her child.

Doctor's Attitude:

- Responsibility to advocate for adolescent mothers and ensure they have access to the resources, support services, and healthcare they need to navigate pregnancy and parenthood successfully.
- Holistic approach to care that addresses the physical, emotional, and social needs of young mothers.

Ethical Aspects:

- Ensure that adolescent mothers understand the nature of their conditions, the risks and benefits of treatment options, and any alternatives available to them.
- When adolescent mothers are minors, healthcare providers should obtain informed assent from the adolescent and informed consent from their legal guardians, balancing the adolescent's autonomy with their need for parental support and guidance.
- Protection of Children from Sexual Offences (POCSO) Act requires medical providers to report pregnancies to the police when a pregnant minor is involved. Section 19(1) of the POCSO Act requires the reporting of all sexual offenses against a child to law enforcement authorities, and failure to do so may lead to punitive consequences.
- The POCSO Act also treats all pregnant minors as rape survivors, which conflicts with the confidentiality clause under the Medical Termination of Pregnancy (MTP) Act. The MTP Act allows doctors to terminate a pregnancy of less than 24 weeks without a court order. The Supreme Court has also ruled that doctors do not need to disclose the name and identity of the minor girl in the information given to police.

Communication:

- Building trust and rapport with adolescent mothers is crucial in fostering a therapeutic relationship and facilitating open communication.
- Doctors should deliver culturally sensitive communication that acknowledges and respects the cultural backgrounds and traditions of adolescent mothers, incorporating their cultural perspectives into treatment planning and decision-making.

For further reading: Siegel RS, Brandon AR. Adolescents, pregnancy, and mental health. J Pediatr Adolesc Gynecol. 2014 Jun;27(3):138-50. doi: 10.1016/j.jpag.2013.09.008. Epub 2014 Feb 20. PMID: 24559618.

****

HPT and Psychiatry – Hypothyroidism

(Contributed by: Dr. Mukhil Sakthi P, Senior Resident, SSMCRI)

Mrs. Amaira, 38 years old female, presented to Dr. Gaurav, a budding resident with complaining that she was feeling weak, low and had gained weight considerably over the past few months despite being therapy for newly diagnosed hypothyroidism.

She reported feeling constantly tired, lacking the energy to be involved in routine chores, and was finding it difficult to concentrate at work, along with a demotivating lack of interest in the activities that she previously used to enjoy. Her symptoms have been significantly impacting her quality of life, interpersonal relationships and disturbed her to the extent of her losing the interest to take her Thyroid supplementation.

Dr. Gaurav was confused, as her latest Thyroid profile revealed she had attained euthyroid state and during his initial assessments, she had presented with classical features of hypothyroidism. In his quest to clarify, he got in touch with Dr. Alok, a psychiatrist who was his good friend, and discussed with him regarding the persisting low mood and other associated symptoms.

He was then enlightened about how a deficit of thyroid functioning can disrupt the brain's serotonergic system, and cause symptoms of depression, revealing how the mind-body connect works. And further, he was advised to start antidepressants as adjunctive therapy to treat the patient. Within a few weeks, Mrs. Amaira reported back to him, saying her life has gotten so much better, and profusely thanked him for helping her out.

Test Your Cognition:

Recall:

- What confounded Dr. Gaurav with regards to Mrs. Amaira? How does HPT axis relate with Hypothyroidism and depression?
- What is the standard treatment plan for depression in Hypothyroidism patient?
- Is there a cause-effect relationship? If so, what is the cause? What is the effect?

Application:

- What are the specific tests you can use to assess the severity of such symptoms? What tests will you suggest for this patient?
- Do all patients of Hypothyroidism develop depression? If not, suggest measures to identify at risk patients and patients with comorbid depression.
- How will you explain the reason for such symptoms to Mrs Amaira, given her present mental state?

Understanding:

- Why is it important for doctors to consider the patient's mental health alongside their physical health?
- What are the potential consequences of neglecting the mind-body connection in medical treatment?
- How can doctors advocate for better integration of mental and physical healthcare services?

Doctor's Attitude:

- Empathy and understanding towards Mrs. Amaira's Depression and its impact on her prognosis.
- Openness to collaboration with a psychiatrist for a holistic approach.

Ethical Aspects:

- Maintaining confidentiality of Mrs. Amaira's medical information.
- The need for an inclusive approach towards preparing a treatment plan for this patient.
- Avoiding stigmatizing language when discussing mental health.

Communication:

- Using clear and concise language that Mrs. Amaira can understand.

- Checking for understanding and addressing any questions or concerns she may have.
- Encouraging open communication about her physical and mental health.

****

HPT and Psychiatry – HYPERTHYROIDISM

(Contributed by: Dr. Mukhil Sakthi P, Senior Resident, SSMCRI)

47 years old Mr. Vincent is brought to Dr. Santhosh, the emergency physician by his worried family members with complaints of extreme and scary changes in his behavior over the past week. Mr. Vincent consistently spoke about feeling very energetic, expressed a decreased need for sleep when asked to sleep at night, and often mentioned that he was "chosen by god" and was "hunted for by demons". He was found to be talking faster than usual, seen engaging in risky, reckless behaviors such as rash driving, spending money excessively, and frequently praying to god. He became increasingly irritable and agitated when confronted, with episodes of anger and hostility towards them.

Dr. Santhosh, while taking a detailed history, concurrently calls Dr. Mayank, the Psychiatrist to the ER, to help with managing the behavioral disturbance. Dr. Mayank advised to isolate the patient straight away. Upon evaluation, Mr. Saha expressed an inflated sense of self-importance. He exhibited flight of ideas, distractibility, poor judgment and lacked insight regarding the abrupt change in his behavior. He was unable to sit still and constantly moved about the room, in an agitated fashion, amounting to hostility when he was tried to be calmed. Mr. Vincent had no previous psychiatric diagnoses or treatment. Dr. Santhosh's evaluation revealed that his mother was diagnosed as a case of hyperthyroidism and was taking treatment for it back in her days.

Mr. Vincent was managed with appropriate chemical restraints. He was tachycardic, and had fine tremors in bilateral upper extremities. Given the symptoms and family history, a comprehensive medical workup was initiated and in the meanwhile, Laboratory tests revealed elevated levels of thyroid hormones (T3 and T4) and decreased thyroid-stimulating hormone (TSH), consistent with hyperthyroidism, for which the endocrinologist was consulted.

Mr. Vincent was diagnosed with Bipolar and related due to another medical condition - thyrotoxicosis. Antithyroid medication was started along with a beta blocker as a part of treatment plan. He was started on Tab. Risperidone adjunctively, and 3 days later, due to unsatisfactory treatment response, a mood stabilizer was added for better outcome. 2 weeks later, He was discharged with appropriate dose tapering post attaining euthyroid state with significant reduction in symptoms, and visibly relieved family members.

Test your cognition:

Recall:

- What were the initial psychiatric symptoms observed by Mr. Vincent's caretakers? Why was there a need to isolate him?
- What is a chemical restraint? Name the drugs you shall use for this patient for this purpose.
- Why was Risperidone chosen to treat the patient in this case?
- Given the partial response, which mood stabilizer will you choose and which will you avoid for this patient?

Application:

- Endocrinology/Psychiatry. Which will be the specialty of choice to admit this patient under? Substantiate your choice with adequate reasoning.
- What other steps can be considered before considering chemical restraint for this patient?
- What other psychiatric manifestations can you possibly encounter in a case of thyrotoxicosis?

Understanding:

- Assume that the family history was unclear. What other investigations will you advise given the age of onset for the purpose of differential diagnosis?
- What is the role of a doctor in case of an agitated person (possibly a person with mental illness) in a different i.e public setting?

Doctor's Attitude:

- How will you approach Mr. Vincent, given his hostile behavior?
- Openness to collaboration with a psychiatrist and an endocrinologist for a holistic approach.

Ethical Aspects:

- Maintaining confidentiality of Mr. Vincent's medical information.
- Steps involved in preparing a treatment plan for such patient, from the initial presentation to discharge.
- Possible scenarios which may call for disclosure of patient information.

Communication:

- The family members understand the heritability, but are worried with regards to the change in his behavior as it wasn't noticed in his mother. Sensitize their understanding.
- Care to be taken while addressing the religious components of symptomatology given that they belong to an orthodox religious background.
- Psychoeducate the family members regarding the risks involved in confronting a patient with such clinical presentation.

****

Depression in diabetes mellitus

(Contributed by: Dr. Mukhil Sakthi P, Senior Resident, SSMCRI)

Mr. Abhay, a 55-year-old man had struggled with diabetes management for several years, experiencing frequent fluctuations in blood sugar levels despite medication and lifestyle modifications. He presented to Dr. Anand, an endocrinologist, complaining of a lack of motivation to adhere to his diabetes treatment regimen. He reported feeling overwhelmed by the daily demands of managing his condition, including medication adherence, dietary restrictions, and regular blood sugar monitoring. He told that he was constantly burned out, felt tired and irritability most of the time, and was losing hope regarding his ability to effectively control his diabetes. He also described a sense of isolation, being misunderstood by his family and friends, who struggled to comprehend the apparent complexities of living with diabetes, and was constantly frustrated and burdened by constant monitoring and lifestyle adjustment.

Physical examination revealed signs consistent with poorly controlled diabetes, such as elevated blood pressure and neuropathic symptoms. Laboratory tests confirm inadequate glycemic control with persistently elevated HbA1c levels despite adherence to oral hypoglycemic medications.

On further evaluation, Mr. Abhay reported experiencing symptoms suggestive of depression such as low mood, loss of interest in routine activities, and feelings of worthlessness. Dr. Anand then decided to consult Dr. Charan, the psychiatrist for his expert opinion, who then conducted a comprehensive assessment, exploring the interplay between Mr. Abhay's diabetes and mental health symptoms.

Both the doctors then together formulated a treatment plan focused on addressing both the physiological and psychological aspects of Mr. Abhay's condition, with interventions tailored to his individual needs. Pharmacotherapy was initiated to manage Mr. Abhay's depression, with close monitoring for potential interactions with his diabetes medications. Psychotherapy, such as cognitive-behavioral therapy (CBT) is employed to Mr. Abhay develop coping strategies for managing his diabetes distress and improving treatment adherence.

Test your cognition:

Recall:

- What deterred Mr. Abhay from sticking to his antidiabetic regime?
- What is the phenomenon mentioned by Mr. Abhay with regards to his fmaily members and friends? How will you address it?
- What is the standard treatment plan for depression in Diabetes for this patient?
- What cognitive restructuring can be done for this patient in CBT for a synergistic treatment with the antidepressant?

Application:

- Why does depression complicate other illnesses associated with it?
- Do all patients of Diabetes mellitus develop depression? If not, suggest measures to identify at risk patients and patients with comorbid depression.
- Is the relation between diabetes and depression that of a cause and effect or rather a comorbidity?
- What are the other Psychiatric illnesses that can possibly occur along with Diabetes mellitus?

Understanding:

- Why is it important for doctors to consider the patient's mental health alongside their physical health?
- What are the potential consequences of neglecting the Psychiatric symptomatology in medical treatment?
- How can doctors advocate for better integration of mental and physical healthcare services?

Doctor's Attitude:

- Empathy and understanding towards Mr. Abhay's Depression and its impact on his prognosis.
- Attitude towards addressing the family members' lack of understanding.
- Openness to collaboration with a psychiatrist for a holistic approach.

Ethical Aspects:

- Maintaining confidentiality of Mr. Abhay's medical information and alleviating stigma
- Inclusivity in preparing a treatment regime for Mr. Abhay

Communication:

- Using clear and concise language that Mr. Abhay can understand.
- Checking for understanding and addressing any questions or concerns he may have.
- Encouraging open communication about his physical and mental health.

****

Psychosis in Wilson's disease

(Contributed by: Dr. Mukhil Sakthi P, Senior Resident, SSMCRI)

12 years old Master Hrithik presented to Dr. Samar with complaints of abdominal distension associated along with continuous pain dull aching type for past 1 month. About a week following the onset of pain in the abdomen, his parents noticed changes in his behavior in the form of irritability, expressing feelings that his friends were mocking him in the corridor as he walked, secretly planning to steal his belongings and harm him in some way, associated with marked dysfunction in the form of refusal to attend school, secondary to the other symptoms. Over the next few days, the symptoms worsened, due to which he was even found to keep all his belongings under lock and key. Additionally, he developed frequent and severe mood swings and reduced appetite.

He was brought to the hospital primarily for the continuous abdominal pain. His routine investigations did not reveal any abnormality. However, ultrasound examination of the abdomen revealed parenchymal liver disease with portal hypertension and ascites. In view of the evidence of parenchymal liver disease, serum ceruloplasmin was investigated for and was found to be low, that is, 7.5 mcg/dl . Serum copper level and total urine copper level were also investigated for, reports of which were increased and consistent with a diagnosis of Wilson's disease. Slit lamp examination of the eyes showed the presence of Kayser–Fleischer ring. On the basis of clinical manifestations and laboratory findings, a diagnosis of Wilson's disease was made.

Tab penicillamine 250 mg along with zinc acetate 150 mg/day were started to treat Master Hrithik. After a week, Tab penicillamine was increased to 500 mg/day, with which his psychiatric symptoms worsened. In addition to the above-mentioned symptoms, Hrithik became very agitated and disinhibited, due to which he was admitted for inpatient care, and Dr. Samar sought the Psychiatrist, Dr. Ashok's opinion.

Upon doing a mental status examination, he was found to be conscious and oriented to time, place and person. He had psychomotor agitation, was anxious and fearful. He expressed delusion of reference and persecution. In view of the clinical picture, a diagnosis of organic delusional disorder due to Wilson's disease was considered. As there was some evidence for an increase in psychotic symptoms after increasing the dose of penicillamine, the dose of same was reduced to 250 mg/day. However, this did not lead to abatement of psychotic symptoms and Master Hrithik needed initiation of Tab risperidone 1 mg/day, after which, within a week the psychotic symptoms resolved, and he was discharged from the hospital.

Test your cognition:

Recall:

- What worried Master Hrithik's parents? What probably caused the delay in bringing him to the hospital initially?
- Why was penicillamine prescribed for this patient? What is its role in treatment of the disease?
- If penicillamine was administered to get the patient better, why did it worsen his psychiatric symptoms?

Application:

- What are the other possible psychiatric symptoms that can develop in a patient with Wilson's disease?
- Which among the Psychiatric manifestations are you most likely to encounter? Arrange in the order of most common to least common.
- Is the relation between Psychosis and Wilson's disease that of a cause and effect or rather a comorbidity?

Understanding:

- Why is it important for doctors to consider the patient's mental health alongside their physical health?
- What are the potential consequences of neglecting the Psychiatric symptomatology in medical treatment?
- Why was risperidone the choice of drug for this patient?

Doctor's Attitude:

- Empathy and understanding towards Mr. Hrithik's Psychosis and its impact on his prognosis.
- Openness to collaboration with a psychiatrist for a holistic approach.

Ethical Aspects:

- Maintaining confidentiality of Mr. Hrithik's medical information and alleviating stigma.
- How will you formulate the treatment plan for this patient and why?

Communication:

- Checking for understanding and addressing any questions or concerns they may have.
- Consider that Master Hrithik has a younger sibling. Prepare a sequential plan of action.

****

Mysterious pregnancy

(Contributed by: Dr. Vaishali Katchi Kannan, Senior Resident, SSSMCRI)

Mrs. Saradha presented with symptoms suggestive of urinary tract infection (UTI) to Dr. Zoe, including urinary frequency and urgency. Upon examination, no evidence of UTI was found. Further evaluation revealed pseudocyesis, manifesting as a false belief of pregnancy. Dr. Zoe referred the patient to psychiatrist Dr. Ben for comprehensive psychological assessment and management. Dr. Ben conducted thorough psychiatric evaluation, confirming the diagnosis of pseudocyesis.

Recall:

- What made you think it might be pseudocyesis instead of a real urinary tract infection for Mrs. Saradha?
- How did you decide between pseudocyesis and other medical conditions during the first check-up?

Attitude:

- How do you stay kind and understanding when talking about tricky diagnoses like pseudocyesis?
- How do you make sure patients feel like they're the focus of their care when dealing with complex conditions like pseudocyesis?

Application:

- How do you work with psychiatrists to help patients like Mrs. Saradha who have both medical and psychological issues?
- How do you make treatment plans for patients with pseudocyesis, using both medical and psychological help?

Understanding:

- How can you tell the difference between pseudocyesis and real medical issues like urinary tract infections at first?
- When do you decide to send patients for psychiatric help if you think they might have pseudocyesis?
- What makes people believe they're pregnant when they're not, like in pseudocyesis?

Ethical Aspects:

- How do you keep Mrs. Saradha's information private when talking about her pseudocyesis and psychiatric help?
- How do you make sure Mrs. Saradha gets to make choices about her care even with a tricky diagnosis like pseudocyesis?
- How do you deal with people may be thinking differently about Mrs. Saradha because she needs psychiatric help for her symptoms?

Communication:

- How do you explain pseudocyesis to patients like Mrs. Saradha in a way that's easy to understand and kind?
- How do you make sure everyone on the team knows what's happening when treating someone with pseudocyesis, so Mrs. Saradha gets good care?
- How do you talk to patients about why they might need help from both medical and psychiatric teams when they have something like pseudocyesis?

****

Mr. Pegs pelvic pain and Dr. Perks perplexity

(Role Play Contributed by: Dr. Vaishali Katchi Kannan, Senior Resident, SSSMCRI)

Mr. Peg, 35, presented to Dr. Perk with persistent pelvic pain, urinary urgency, frequency, and sexual dysfunction. Despite extensive medical evaluation, no structural abnormalities or infections were identified. Frustration led to feelings of hopelessness, anxiety, and depression, impacting work and relationships. Upon referral to Dr. Pound Perk, a Psychiatrist, a comprehensive assessment revealed the significant impact on patient pes's well-being. The diagnosis of chronic prostatitis/chronic pelvic pain syndrome (CP/CPPS) with concomitant anxiety and depression was established, emphasizing the importance of interdisciplinary collaboration in managing complex cases.

Recall:
- Dr. Perk, what tests did you do to check Mr. Peg's pelvic pain and urinary problems?
- What made you think Mr. Peg needed to see Dr. Pounds for more help with his feelings?

Attitude:
- Dr. Pounds, how do you make sure Mr. Peg feels cared for when you talk about his pelvic pain and feelings?
- Dr. Perk, how do you make sure Mr. Peg knows you understand his pain and feelings during your appointments?

Understanding:
- Dr. Perk, what did you learn from Mr. Peg's story that helped you understand his pelvic pain better?
- Dr. Pounds, how do you see how Mr. Peg's body pain and feelings are connected, and how does this help you help him?

Ethical Aspect:
- Dr. Perk, how do you make sure Mr. Peg gets to choose what treatment he wants for his pelvic pain and feelings?
- Dr. Pounds, how do you keep Mr. Peg's feelings private and make sure he's okay with the treatment choices you talk about?

Application:
- Dr. Perk, can you explain how you use different treatments and work with other doctors to help patients like Mr. Peg feel better?
- Dr. Pounds, how do you use talking and other treatments together to help patients like Mr. Peg with their body pain and feelings?

Communication:
- Dr. Perk, how do you make sure you and Dr. Pounds understand each other when you talk about how to help patients like Mr. Peg?
- Dr. Pounds, how do you make sure Mr. Peg understands what's going on with his body pain and feelings, and how you're going to help him?

****

Bladder Blues: Mrs. Olive's Journey with Dr. Ombré!

(Role Play Contributed by: Dr. Vaishali Katchi Kannan, Senior Resident, SSSMCRI)

Mrs. Olive, a 40-year-old woman, sought help from Dr. Ombré due to urinary urgency, frequency, and nocturia persisting despite lifestyle changes. Medical tests showed no abnormalities. Frustration and anxiety grew, impacting her social life and work. Referral to Dr. Ohambu, a psychiatrist, revealed the psychological toll of her symptoms. The diagnosis of overactive bladder with anxiety shed light on the complex interaction between physical and mental health in Mrs. Olive's case.

Recall:

- Dr. Ombré, what were Mrs. Olive's main problems when she first came to see you?
- Can you remember what tests Dr. Ombré did to check Mrs. Olive's bladder problems?

Attitude:

- Dr. Ohambu, how do you make sure Mrs. Olive feels listened to and supported when you talk about her bladder problems and feelings?
- Dr. Ombré, how do you show Mrs. Olive that you understand how her bladder problems are affecting her emotions?

Understanding:

- Dr. Ohambu, what did Mrs. Olive say about how her bladder problems make her feel?
- Dr. Ombré, how do you think Mrs. Olive's feelings are connected to her bladder problems, and how does that help you treat her?

Ethical Aspect:

- Dr. Ohambu, how do you make sure Mrs. Olive's private information stays private when you talk about her bladder and emotional problems?
- Dr. Ombré, how do you make sure Mrs. Olive feels respected and in control of her treatment choices when you talk about her bladder and feelings?

Application:

- Dr. Ohambu, can you explain how talking with patients like Mrs. Olive can help them feel better about their bladder and feelings?
- Dr. Ombré, how do you and Dr. Ohambu work together to help Mrs. Olive with her bladder and emotional problems?

Communication:

- Dr. Ohambu, how do you make sure Mrs. Olive feels okay talking to you about her bladder and feelings?
- Dr. Ombré, how do you make sure Mrs. Olive understands what's happening with her bladder and feelings, and how both of you are helping her?

****

Ambal's awful vaginal discharge

(Contributed by: Dr. Vaishali Katchi Kannan, Senior Resident, SSSMCRI)

Mr. Ambi and Mrs. Ambal, a couple married for 5 years from a rural area, visited Dr. Rani's psychiatry clinic for an evaluation. They were referred by a gynecology resident Dr. Jan who is treating them for infertility. 5 years ago, Mrs. Ambal developed recurrent white, clear, odorless vaginal discharge. Discharge worsened pre-menses, improved slightly after intercourse. She believes discharge caused weakness, also felt distressed and developed headaches, body aches, and fatigue. Friends/family confirmed her belief, worsening her distress. She developed a range of symptoms including mood swings, low energy, difficulty concentrating, and decreased appetite, which she linked to her existing concerns about vaginal discharge. Dr. Jan and her team ruled out gynecological or medical causes especially anemia as the symptoms shows similar clinical picture. Also, Mrs. Ambal urges for recurrent visits to Dr. Jan desperately seeking reassurance hence sorted for opinion. Mr. Ambi expressed his frustration for spending on hospital visits for the same. By history well-adjusted pre-morbidly personality and no past medical or psychiatric illnesses. physical examination no abnormality detected. Hence diagnosed to be Dhat syndrome.

Dr. Jan over phone expressed her misconceptions about Dhat syndrome to be seen only in men and never in women.

Recall

- What was the initial presentation of Mrs. Ambal to Dr. Jan resident Gynecologist?
- What was Ambal's belief about her bodily symptoms?
- Based on the scenario, what additional information would you seek from Mrs. Ambal to gain a more comprehensive understanding of her symptoms and concerns?
- Were there any cultural or social factors affecting the patient's presentation or understanding of the symptoms?

Application

- How would you approach a case of recurrent white, clear, odorless vaginal discharge that worsens pre-menstrually and improves slightly after intercourse, especially in the absence of gynecological or medical causes?
- What are the differential diagnoses for Mrs. Ambal's symptoms besides Dhat Syndrome? How would you rule out each diagnosis?
- Are you familiar with the concept of psychosomatic symptoms and their presentation in female patients?
- Are you aware of the potential cultural influences on symptom interpretation and diagnosis in different communities?

Understanding

- Have you encountered cases of Dhat Syndrome presenting in female patients similar to Mrs. Ambal's case?
- What are the diagnostic criteria for Dhat Syndrome in women, considering its typical association with men?
- How do you approach patients who frequently seek reassurance or express anxiety related to their gynecological health, similar to Mrs. Ambal's recurrent visits to Dr. Jan?

Doctor's attitude

- Seeking additional information and consulting with colleagues demonstrates a willingness to expand knowledge and expertise, ultimately benefiting patients.
- Acknowledging and understanding cultural beliefs and experiences can lead to more accurate diagnoses and effective treatment plans.

Ethical aspects

- Conduct thorough examinations and investigations to rule out underlying medical causes before attributing symptoms to cultural beliefs or psychological factors.
- Seek consultations with other specialists when encountering unfamiliar cases or atypical presentation like Mrs. Ambals.

Communication

- Actively listen, clarify concerns, acknowledge emotions, and avoid interrupting. Demonstrate empathy and understanding towards Mrs. Ambals concerns.
- Be sensitive to emotional responses, especially regarding sensitive topics like infertility to the couples. Offer emotional support and explore mental health resources if necessary.

****

Sebastin and the sudden onset of Psychotic symptoms

(Contributed by: Dr. Seytha Najva Naina Mohamed, Senior Resident, SSSMCRI)

Mr. Sebastin 44/M known case of ADS was brought by his wife for consultation with Dr. Joy, consultant psychiatrist to his OPD. Wife elaborates of complaints of suspiciousness that she is having extramarital affair, irritable, difficulty in recalling, hearing of voices that others can't hear and on and off confusions for past 4wks. She further reports his last intake of alcohol was 4weeks back.

Though Sebastin was a regular follow-up case for Dr. Joy, he had suspicions regarding sudden emergence of psychotic symptoms and cognitive decline. Pre-morbidly he was an impulsive, irresponsible, sensitive person with suspiciousness, poor moral values, combativeness, and tendency to blame others.

His general physical examination revealed BP-140/100mm of Hg; PR-100/min. Systemic examination revealed; CNS- disoriented, slowness of gait, mild abnormality in finger- nose test, & dysdiadokinesia present. Mental Status Examination revealed increased psychomotor activity; SPEECH: increase in tone, tempo, volume and decreased reaction time, AFFECT: lability present and restricted, THOUGHT: delusion of infidelity, PERCEPTION- Auditory & visual Hallucination present, COGNITION: attention not aroused/concentration not sustained, immediate & recent memory – mildly impaired with MMSE- 17/30.

Patient was initially diagnosed as a case of wernicke's encephalopathy and corresponding treatment was initiated. After 1 week on follow-up there was worsening of symptoms, immediate and recent memory was impaired, patient was disoriented with excessive salivation, crying spells, slowness of movements, decline in self-care, social and occupational functioning. Dr. Joy decided to rule out any organicity.

Following which MRI was done which revealed foci of T2W/FLAIR hyperintensities involving cortical & subcortical regions of bilateral frontal, temporal & deep white matter regions (possibly CADASIL).

Test your cognition:

Recall:

- What was the initial medical history given by Sebastin?
- What made Dr. Joy to suggest for an MRI?
- What are the MSE findings of Sebastin?
- What was the initial diagnosis made by Dr. Joy for Sebastin? What where the findings in favor of and against the initial diagnosis?

Application:

- How could this case be relevant to other patients with sudden onset of psychiatric symptoms?
- What are some challenges faced in managing patients whose clinical picture has a thin line of demarcation from organicity and psychiatry?
- What are other medical conditions which initially presents with psychiatric symptoms?

Understanding:

- Why is it important for psychiatrist to rule out any organicity before labelling them with psychiatric disorder?
- What are the potential consequences of neglecting underline organicity in psychiatric cases?

Doctor's Attitude:

- Empathy and understanding towards Mr.Sebastin and its impact on his health.
- Psychoeducation of Family members regarding the illness
- Appropriately substantiate the need for further investigations, which should be properly communicated to the family members.

Ethical Aspects:

- Maintaining confidentiality of Mr. Sebastin medical information.
- Having possible differential diagnosis and instigating essential investigations alone.

- Making the attenders take the decision for Mr.Sebastin for the best of his interest when he has poor insight about the illness.

Communication:

- Using clear and concise language so that Mr. Sebastin wife can understand the nature and prognosis of the illness.
- Checking for understanding and any clarification which the patient or his wife may have regarding his condition.
- Encouraging open communication about her physical and mental health.

****

Mary and Her Suspicious act

(Contributed by: Dr. Seytha Najva Naina Mohamed, Senior Resident, SSSMCRI)

Ms. Mary 23/F brought by family members to psychiatry OPD of Dr. Venu with c/o locking up cooking utensils in wardrobe, withdrawn behavior, suspiciousness that neighbors have kept black magic against her and her husband is trying to kill her, increased irritability, threatening others that she would bite them, wandering behavior and sleep disturbance. H/o staring at the mirror for abnormally long hours, associated with repetitive stereotypic movements of the hands and awareness of the surrounding and able to hear others questioning her but unable to give a reply. History of 6-7 similar episodes in the past 2 years and each episode lasting for 2-3months.

Pre-morbidly: responsible, impulsive, intolerant to frustration, religious with moral values GPE: BP-110/80mmHg; PR-82/min, CNS- rigidity + MSE- eye contact not sustained, rapport established with difficulty, PMA - ↓ SPEECH ↓ R/T/V; reaction time ↑,AFFECT: constricted, THOUGHT: delusion of persecution, PERCEPTION - NAD, COGNITION: attention aroused/concentration not sustained, immediate, recent and remote memory intact. Working diagnosis was Psychosis NOS.

Even though pt was started on antipsychotics according to prescribed guideline pt didn't exhibit significant improvement. Dr. Venu was confused of the clinical picture. He had a word with neurologist Dr. Kiran, who had suspected underlying neurological disorder and advised was advised MRI Brain MRI BRAIN: B/L symmetrical T1 hyperintensity seen involving B/L globus pallidus, substantia nigra & along dentate nucleus. Blooming on SWI sequence. (suggestive of Fahr's disease)

Test your cognition:

Recall:

- What was the initial clinical presentation of Mary?
- What are the MSE finding of Mary?
- What was the initial diagnosis made by Dr. Venu for Mary? What where the findings in favour the initial diagnosis?
- What did Dr. Kiran suggest for the Mary and what were its findings?

Application:

- What is the differential diagnosis for Fahr's disease?
- What are some challenges faced in managing patients whose clinical picture has a thin line of demarcation from psychiatric and neurologic case?
- What are other medical conditions which initially presents with psychiatric symptoms?

Understanding:

- Why is it important for psychiatrist to rule out any organicity before labelling them with psychiatric disorder?
- What are the potential consequences of neglecting underline organicity in psychiatric cases?

Doctor's Attitude:

- Empathy and understanding towards Mary and its impact on her health.
- Psychoeducation of Family members regarding the illness
- Appropriate and timely referral to neurologist or other consultation liaison for the best interest of the patient.

Ethical Aspects:

- Maintaining confidentiality of Mary's medical information.
- Having possible differential diagnosis and instigating essential investigations alone.
- Making the attenders take the decision for Mary for the best of his interest when he has poor insight about the illness.

Communication:

- Using clear and concise language to communicate the nature and prognosis of the illness.
- Checking for understanding and clarification by the patient or her family regarding her illness.
- Encouraging open communication about her physical and mental health.

****

7. Lived Experiences

Lost in the Lights: Helping a Young Man Find His Way

A 23-year-old man from Chennai visits a psychiatrist with a primary complaint of feeling low. He appears very anxious and visibly uncomfortable in the doctor's clinic. Which of the following actions should be taken to help establish a rapport with this patient?

a. Assure the patient that his problem is straightforward and can be resolved easily.
b. Show empathy towards the difficult situation the patient is in.
c. Share with the patient that you too feel nervous when you meet new patients.
d. Ask the patient why he is so unusually anxious about seeing a psychiatrist.
e. Immediately address the patient's complaint so that the patient can leave as soon as possible.

Explanation: The correct answer is b. A patient in this situation requires empathy for a successful rapport to be developed. Assuring the patient that his problem is straightforward and can be resolved easily might eventually bring some relief to the patient, but if stated early in the interview process can sound dismissive, as if the patient should not trouble the physician with such trivial things. Showing empathy for the difficult situation the patient finds himself in is showing true understanding of the patient's current discomfort. Sharing with the patient that you too feel nervous when you meet new patients could be seen as an expression of empathy with the patient, but may also make the patient feel dismayed, since he wants a confident and competent physician to treat him. Asking the patient why he is so unusually nervous will only make the patient more self-conscious, and it is not unusual for patients to be this nervous on a first visit to a psychiatrist (especially if they have never seen one before). Finally, immediately addressing the patient's complaint just ignores the uncomfortable feeling the patient has come in with, and this will not help the development of rapport (nor is it very observant of the psychiatrist).

Some related questions for the scenario:

1. How would you approach a patient who is visibly anxious during their first visit to a psychiatrist?
2. What strategies would you use to build rapport with a new patient?
3. How would you handle a patient who is reluctant to share their feelings or symptoms?

Practice Psychiatric Pearls:

- Empathy is key in building rapport with patients. It's important to validate their feelings and show understanding.
- Avoid making assumptions or minimizing the patient's feelings or experiences.
- Be patient and give the patient time to become comfortable. It's normal for patients to be anxious, especially during their first visit.
- Use open-ended questions to encourage the patient to share more about their feelings and experiences.
- Remember, building rapport is a process. It takes time and consistent effort.

****

From Loving Wife to ICU Nightmare: What Caused This Sudden Change?

A 45-year-old woman from Bengaluru is admitted to the hospital after her IT company Vice President Husband and entrepreneur son finds her with pain abdomen, vomiting and sleepiness at home. She is treated for diabetic ketoacidosis and her recovery is a challenging one, necessitating that she stay in the ICU. During this period of time, she is often irritable, irrational, and demanding, all of which are not her usual behaviour, according to her husband. What is the most likely explanation for the change in this woman's behaviour?

a. The fluid shifts that are occurring during the stabilization of her diabetes are causing an organic mood disorder.
b. Her fear of a newly diagnosed illness is causing her to dissociate.
c. The stress of her illness and hospital stay is causing her change.
d. She is delirious secondary to brain damage.
e. A previously unrecognized personality disorder is coming to the fore.

Explanation: The correct answer is c. Stress, such as this woman is experiencing secondary to her sudden illness and hospitalization, has long been known to cause an alteration in cognitive and emotional functioning. The clue here is that her previous functioning, as described by her husband, was normal in both the cognitive and the emotional realms, making a previously undiagnosed personality disorder unlikely. Delirium would be accompanied by waxing and waning of consciousness, which is not described in this case. A mood disorder secondary to an organic cause is likewise unlikely, since the patient is not described as depressed or manic in behaviour. Dissociation involves a person, under a sudden stressor that cannot be handled, switching to a distinctly different personality (indeed, the patient might not remember a sense of "who she was" prior to the switch).

Some related questions for the scenario:

1. How would you approach a patient who is displaying a change in behaviour during their hospital stay?
2. What strategies would you use to manage a patient who is irritable and demanding?
3. How would you handle a situation where a patient's behaviour is affecting their treatment plan?

Practice Psychiatric Pearls:

- Stress can cause a regression in cognitive and emotional functioning. It's important to recognize this and provide appropriate support as the language that health professional's use may affect the patient's willingness to talk abou challenges living with diabetes.
- Avoid making assumptions about a patient's behaviour without considering their current situation and stress levels.
- Be patient and empathetic with patients who are experiencing a high level of stress due to their illness and hospital stay.
- Use effective communication strategies to manage challenging behaviours and ensure the patient's needs are being met.
- Remember, changes in behaviour can be a sign of underlying issues. Always consider the context and seek further assessment if needed.

****

When Familiarity Fades

A 65-year-old man from Mumbai with a history suggestive of alcohol dependence cheerfully greets the resident doctor of his nursing home, whom he has met many times before, and calls him, "My dear friend Ravi." The physician, Dr. Sumeet Patel, explains who he is and tells the patient his name. Two minutes later, when he asks the patient if he knows who he is, he answers with a smile, "Of course, you are my cousin Anand from Delhi." What vitamin deficiency can cause this form of amnestic disorder?

a. Pantothenic acid
b. Folate
c. Thiamine
d. Riboflavin
e. Niacin

Explanation: The correct answer is c. Severe anterograde memory deficits with an inability to form new memories are the main feature of Korsakoff syndrome, or alcohol-induced persisting amnestic disorder. Retrograde amnesia is present (for recent events). Remote memories are relatively preserved. The disorder is because of dietary thiamine deficiency and subsequent damage to the mammillary bodies and the regions surrounding the third and fourth ventricles in the brain. Korsakoff syndrome can sometimes (though rarely) be attributed to other causes of thiamine deficiency, such as diseases that cause intractable vomiting, severe malabsorption etc.,

Some related OSCE questions for the scenario:

1. How would you approach a patient who is displaying signs of an amnestic disorder?
2. What strategies would you use to manage a patient with Korsakoff syndrome?
3. How would you handle a situation where a patient's behavior is affecting their treatment plan?

Practice Psychiatric Pearls:

- Thiamine deficiency can lead to severe cognitive disorders like Korsakoff syndrome, especially in patients with a history of alcohol dependence syndrome. .
- Patients with Korsakoff syndrome often present with severe anterograde and retrograde amnesia (recent memory) with or without confabulation.
- It's important to approach these patients with patience and empathy, as their condition can be distressing and confusing.
- Treatment involves thiamine supplementation and addressing the underlying cause, such as alcohol dependence.
- Remember, changes in behaviour can be a sign of underlying issues. Always consider the context and seek further assessment if needed.

****

Lost Boy or Lost Connection?

A 13-year-old boy from Delhi is brought to the psychiatrist because his mother says the boy is driving her "crazy." She reports that he constantly argues with her and his father, does not follow any of the house rules, and incessantly teases his sister. She says that he is spiteful and vindictive and loses his temper easily. Once he is mad, he stays that way for long periods of time. The mother notes that the boy started this behaviour only about 1 year previously. While she states that this behaviour started at home, it has now spread to school, where he argues with teachers, grades are dropping because he refuses to participate in academic activities. The patient maintains that none of this is his fault—his parents are simply being unreasonable. He denies feeling depressed and notes that he sleeps well through the night. Which of the following is the most likely diagnosis?

a. Oppositional Defiant Disorder (ODD)
b. Antisocial personality disorder
c. Conduct disorder
d. Childhood-onset schizophrenia
e. Mania

Explanation: The correct answer is a. This patient has Oppositional Defiant Disorder (ODD). The presence of the symptoms, including being angry, spiteful and vindictive, losing his temper quickly, and deliberately annoying others, for at least 6 months is characteristic of the disorder. It is also characteristic that the boy denies that he has a problem, blaming it instead on others. While sometimes the behaviour starts outside the home, other times, as in this question, the disorder starts at home and then is carried to school and other arenas. This patient has no history of aggressive behaviour toward animals or others and has not been destructive or in trouble with the law, making conduct disorder less likely. He is under the age of 18, the minimum age for which antisocial personality disorder may be diagnosed. He denies mood symptoms and is sleeping well through the night, making mania unlikely. No psychotic symptoms were noted, ruling out childhood schizophrenia.

Some related OSCE questions for the scenario:

1. How would you approach a patient who is displaying signs of Oppositional Defiant Disorder?
2. What strategies would you use to manage a patient with Oppositional Defiant Disorder?
3. How would you handle a situation where a patient's behaviour is affecting their academic performance?

Practice Psychiatric Pearls:

- Oppositional Defiant Disorder (ODD) is characterized by a pattern of angry/irritable mood, argumentative/defiant behaviour, or vindictiveness.
- It's important to approach these patients with patience and empathy, as their condition can be distressing and confusing.
- Treatment involves behavioural therapy and parent management training.
- Account for the adolescent developmental moratorium
- Remember, changes in behaviour can be a sign of underlying issues. Always consider the context and seek further assessment if needed.

****

Blindsided by Diabetes: Why Won't She Check Her Blood Sugar?

A 28-year-old woman with diabetic ketoacidosis is under the care of the internal medicine department. The doctors find her difficult to manage and request a psychiatric consult because she refuses to learn how to monitor her blood sugar levels, despite understanding the importance and not fearing the needles. Which of the following is the most likely reason for this patient's noncompliance?

a) Impaired judgment
b) Negative transference towards the physician
c) Desire for a longer hospital stay
d) Unknown primary gain (unconscious benefit from the illness)
e) Toxic reaction to insulin

Explanation: The most likely reason for the patient's noncompliance is **negative transference towards the physician.** This occurs when a patient unconsciously projects negative feelings from past experiences with authority figures onto their current doctor. This can lead to resistance towards treatment recommendations. Why the other options are less likely: Impaired judgment: The patient understands the need for blood sugar monitoring, making this less likely; Desire for a longer hospital stay: While possible, it's a less common reason compared to negative transference; Unknown primary gain: This is difficult to determine without further evaluation; Toxic reaction to insulin: There would likely be other physical symptoms present in this case.

Additional Questions and Answers:

Knowledge: Can diabetes mellitus trigger mental illness? Does it predispose to any conditions? If so, what is the relationship?

Diabetes mellitus does not cause or trigger mental illness, but may contribute to create a situation that predisposes people with diabetes to certain mental health conditions. **Increased Risk-** People with diabetes are 2 to 3 times more likely to develop depression and anxiety disorders compared to the general population; There's also a condition called diabetes distress specifically related to the stress and emotional burden of managing diabetes. It shares symptoms with depression and anxiety but is caused by the challenges of the disease itself. **Factors Contributing to Increased Risk:** Chronic Illness Burden: Living with a chronic condition like diabetes can be stressful. It can lead to feelings of isolation, frustration, and fear of complications; Blood Sugar Fluctuations: Swings in blood sugar levels can affect mood, energy levels, and concentration. This can contribute to symptoms of depression and anxiety; Lifestyle Changes: Diabetes often requires dietary and lifestyle modifications, which can be challenging and lead to feelings of restriction and loss of control.

Cognition:

What are the complications of diabetic ketoacidosis?

Coma, kidney failure, and even death.

How can a psychiatrist assess if a patient has impaired judgment?

Through a mental status examination, which evaluates orientation, memory, attention, and problem-solving abilities.

How can a doctor differentiate between a patient's fear of needles and negative transference?

By exploring the patient's past experiences with healthcare professionals and their feelings towards authority figures.

Attitude

How can a healthcare professional build trust with a patient who might have negative transference?

By actively listening, practicing empathy, and demonstrating genuine concern for the patient's well-being.

How can a medical team approach a patient who is difficult to manage?

With patience, clear communication, and a collaborative approach that respects the patient's autonomy

Application

What resources can a diabetic patient utilize to improve their self-care and disease management?

Support groups, diabetes education classes, online resources from reputable organizations, and consultations with a diabetes educator.

What are some strategies to improve a patient's self-management of diabetes?

Educating them on blood sugar monitoring, healthy eating habits, medication adherence, and exercise.

Psychiatric Practice Pearls

Negative transference towards the physician can emanate towards any one of the treating physician(s). All medical specialities, NOT only psychiatrist, should be watchful of this aspect. Effective communication is the key

****

Miracle Pill or Mind over Matter?

A man visits a doctor complaining of mild pain. He receives a sugar pill, which is inert and contains no pain-relieving medication. Surprisingly, just 15 minutes later, the man reports that his pain has completely vanished. What is the most likely explanation for this experience?

a) The man is drug-seeking.
b) The man is malingering.
c) The man has a factitious disorder.
d) The man is demonstrating a placebo response.
e) The man had no real pain to begin with.

Explanation: The most fitting choice is **the man is demonstrating a placebo response**. A placebo is a treatment that has no inherent medicinal properties but can still improve a patient's condition due to the power of belief. In this case, even though the sugar pill was inactive, the man's expectation of relief seems to have triggered a positive response, leading to a reduction in his pain perception. Why the other options are less likely: Drug-seeking: There's no indication the man requested medication specifically; Malingering: Malingering implies faking symptoms for a secondary gain, which isn't evident here; Factitious disorder: This involves deliberately creating or exaggerating symptoms for attention, which isn't suggested in this scenario; No real pain: While possible, the man's initial pain report suggests otherwise.

Additional Questions and Answers:

Knowledge

What are some physiological mechanisms involved in the placebo effect?

Release of endorphins (natural painkillers) from periaqueductal gray PAG – key structure in propagation and modulation of pain perception pathways.

What is the opposite of the placebo effect, and how does it manifest?

The nocebo effect. It's when a patient experiences negative side effects because they believe the treatment will cause them harm.

Attitude

How can doctors address a nocebo effect in their patients?

By openly discussing the patient's concerns, providing reassurance, and educating them about the true potential side effects of the medication

How can healthcare professionals utilize the placebo effect ethically?

By fostering a positive doctor-patient relationship, building trust, and providing clear explanations about treatment expectations.

Cognition

How can a doctor differentiate between a true response to a medication and a placebo effect in a clinical trial?

Through double-blind, randomized controlled trials where neither the patient nor the doctor knows who is receiving the active medication or placebo.

How can researchers account for the placebo effect when designing clinical trials for new medications?

By including a placebo control group alongside the group receiving the new medication. This allows researchers to compare the treatment's effectiveness against the potential influence of the placebo effect.

Application

Can the placebo effect be harnessed to enhance the effectiveness of actual medical treatments?

Yes, studies suggest that combining a placebo with a real medication can sometimes lead to better outcomes than the medication alone. This is likely due to the psychological boost provided by the placebo effect.

What are some ethical considerations when using a placebo in a clinical setting?

Patients should be informed of the possibility of receiving a placebo and have the option to withdraw from the study if they wish.

****

Diagnosis Diabetes: Denial's Prick

A 45-year-old man is diagnosed with diabetes and learns he'll need insulin. The doctor explains the medication and frequent follow-up appointments to monitor his blood sugar. Despite no prior negative experiences with doctors, the patient reacts angrily, accusing the physician of wanting to control his time, money, and actions. What's the most likely explanation for this outburst?

a. Delusions
b. Transference
c. Splitting
d. Mania
e. Anticipation of Rejection

Explanation: The most likely explanation is **Transference**. Transference, in psychology, is the unconscious projection of feelings and experiences from past relationships onto a present person or situation. In this situation, patient might be unconsciously projecting past experiences with controlling authority figures onto his current doctor. Why the other options are less likely: Delusions: are fixed false beliefs not based on reality. There's no indication of this here; Splitting: Splitting is a defence mechanism where people see things in extremes (all good or all bad). While possible, the outburst doesn't necessarily reflect this; Mania: Mania is a psychiatric disorder characterized by hyperactivity, elated mood or dysphoria. The anger suggests a different emotional state; Anticipation of Rejection- There's no evidence the patient expects rejection.

Additional Questions and Answers:

Knowledge

What are some other examples of how transference can manifest itself in a patient-doctor relationship?

Excessive idealization of the doctor, extreme dependency on the doctor, or feelings of intense dislike or distrust.

Is countertransference a real phenomenon? How can it impact therapy?

Yes, countertransference is a therapist's unconscious emotional reaction to a patient. It can cloud judgment and hinder therapy if left unaddressed.

Attitude

What are some strategies a health care professionals can use to manage their countertransference?

Seeking supervision, therapy for themselves, and practicing self-awareness to identify their own emotional responses to patients.

How can doctors recognize and manage transference in their patients?

By being aware of transference, maintaining professional boundaries, and fostering a safe space for open communication.

Cognition

How can a health care professional differentiate between transference and a genuine negative reaction to a therapist's personality or treatment approach?

Exploring the patient's past experiences with authority figures and considering the overall therapeutic relationship.

How can therapists differentiate between countertransference and a genuine concern for a patient's well-being?

Consulting with colleagues, considering the patient's objective needs, and reflecting on their own emotional state.

Application

Can transference be a positive force in therapy?

Yes, positive transference can create a sense of trust and safety, which can be a foundation for therapeutic progress

How can a therapist utilize transference to benefit the patient's therapy?

By identifying and working through the patient's underlying emotional conflicts related to past experiences.

****

Scars Deeper Than Skin: Healing Beyond Self-Harm

A 32-year-old woman enters the emergency room claiming to be suicidal. She has a past history of unnecessary surgeries and later was diagnosed with Munchausen syndrome. Which approach is most likely to be helpful in therapy for such a patient?

a) Assign a psychiatrist to control all medical and psychiatric treatments.
b) Use supportive strategies to encourage healing while avoiding blame by employing face-saving behavioural strategies.
c) Directly confront the patient about her behaviour and illness.
d) Discharge the patient from the hospital quickly.
e) Conduct extensive medical tests to quickly diagnose any physical issues.

Explanation: The most beneficial approach is **Use face-saving behavioural strategies to promote healing.** People with factitious disorder often have complex emotional needs and may react poorly to confrontation. A supportive and non-judgmental approach is more likely to build trust and encourage them to engage in therapy. Why the other options are less likely to be helpful: Gatekeeper Psychiatrist: While collaboration is important, restricting access to care can be counterproductive; Direct Confrontation: This could push the patient away from treatment; Early Discharge: Hospitalization may be necessary to ensure safety and initiate treatment; Extensive Testing: Excessive tests can reinforce the patient's desire for medical attention.

Additional Questions and Answers:

Knowledge

What are some of the challenges in treating patients with factitious disorder?

Building trust, addressing underlying emotional issues, reducing risk of mortality and morbidity while minimizing unnecessary medical interventions.

What are some potential underlying causes of factitious disorder?

A history of childhood abuse or neglect, a need for attention or sympathy, or a distorted sense of self-identity.

Attitude

How can family members be supportive of someone with factitious disorder?

By expressing concern and love, encouraging professional help, and avoiding enabling behaviours like seeking unnecessary medical care.

How can mental health professional maintain empathy and avoid enabling behaviour in patients with factitious disorder?

By focusing on the patient's emotional needs, setting clear boundaries, and offering support without condoning unnecessary medical procedures. Avoid aggressive, direct confrontation

Cognition

How can a mental health professional differentiate between factitious disorder and a genuine medical condition?

A thorough medical and psychiatric evaluation, considering the context and the patient's history of seeking unnecessary treatments.

How can mental health professional assess the risk of self-harm in a patient with factitious disorder?

By considering the patient's suicidal ideation, and any history of previous attempts.

Application

What resources can be helpful for mental health professional treating patients with factitious disorder?

Consulting with specialists in factitious disorders, attending workshops on the topic, and collaborating with other mental health professionals who have experience with this complex condition.

How can a healthcare team work collaboratively to manage a patient with factitious disorder?

Through regular communication, shared treatment goals, and a unified approach that prioritizes the patient's safety and well-being while minimizing unnecessary tests and procedures.

Ethical

Be mindful of ethical and legal issues. Refer the Chapter-4

****

Healing Hearts: Finding Hope through Connection

A patient in mental health care frequently expresses warm feelings towards their mental health care professional, describing them as wise, caring, and helpful. During a session, the patient talks extensively about these positive feelings. What is the most appropriate response from the mental health care professional?

a) Tell the patient their feelings aren't real and are due to transference.
b) Inform the patient the mental health care professional can't reciprocate the positive feelings.
c) Dismiss the feelings as unhelpful for mental health care.
d) Suggest there are hidden negative feelings beneath the positive ones.
e) Encourage the patient to explore these feelings and any related emotions.

Explanation: The most appropriate approach is **Ask the patient to explore related feelings he has about the topic**. While some psychoanalytic theories might view these positive feelings as solely transference (projecting past experiences onto the mental health care professional), most modern mental health care professionals acknowledge the mental health care professional's role in fostering a positive therapeutic relationship. Exploring these feelings can provide valuable insights. Why the other options are less ideal: Discrediting Feelings: This can damage trust and discourage openness; Setting Boundaries: While boundaries are important, mental health care professionals can acknowledge positive feelings without reciprocating them romantically; Dismissing Feelings: All emotions have value in mental health care, even positive ones; Assuming Underlying Negativity: This can be discouraging and inaccurate

Additional Questions and Answers:

Knowledge

What is the difference between transference and therapeutic alliance?

Transference is the unconscious projection of feelings from past relationships onto the mental health care professional. Therapeutic alliance is the collaborative bond of trust and respect between mental health care professional and client. Both are important, but the alliance is a more conscious and collaborative concept.

Cognition

How can a mental health care professional differentiate between genuine positive feelings towards the mental health care professional and transference?

Considering the timing of the feelings, the patient's history, and the overall therapeutic relationship can help make this distinction.

How can mental health care professionals differentiate between countertransference and a genuine concern for a patient's well-being?

Consulting with colleagues, considering the patient's objective needs, and reflecting on their own emotional state.

Attitude

How can a mental health care professional maintain a positive therapeutic relationship while setting professional boundaries?

By fostering empathy and understanding, communicating clearly, and respecting the patient's autonomy while maintaining appropriate professional distance.

Application

Can negative transference be a positive force in mental health care?

While challenging, exploring negative transference can help patients understand their emotional patterns and develop healthier coping mechanisms.

How can a mental health care professional use positive transference to benefit the therapeutic process?

Positive feelings can create a sense of safety and trust, which can facilitate exploration of difficult topics and promote healing.

****

From Withdrawn to Wonderful: Reconnecting with Son

The parents of a 20-year-old son diagnosed with schizophrenia are struggling to cope with his declining mental state. Once a social and engaged student, their son now spends most of his time isolated in his room, muttering to himself or watching the street with binoculars. What family therapy approach would likely be most beneficial in this situation?

a) Train the parents to manage their emotional responses while interacting with their son.
b) Uncover hidden family dynamics and free the son from the "identified patient" role.
c) Encourage the parents to express their disappointment and grief directly to their son.
d) Analyse how the son's behaviour benefits him in some way (secondary gains).
e) Discuss the impact of the son's illness on the parents' marital relationship.

Explanation: The most helpful approach in this situation is **teaching the parents about reducing expressed emotions in the family's interactions**. Research shows that managing high emotional reactivity within families can significantly benefit patients with schizophrenia and reduce the risk of relapse. Why the other options are less suitable: Unmasking Family Dynamics: While family dynamics can be relevant, focusing solely on this might not directly address the son's current needs; Direct Expression of Emotions: This could overwhelm the son and escalate tension; Analysing Secondary Gains: While worth considering, it's not the initial priority; Discussing Marital Problems: This could burden the son and create additional stress.

Additional Questions and Answers:

Cognition

How can a mental health care professional assess the emotional climate within a family with a member diagnosed with schizophrenia?

Through family therapy sessions, observing interactions, and using assessment tools designed to measure expressed emotions.

How can mental health care professional differentiate between healthy emotional expression and unhelpful expressed emotions in a family session?

Considering the context of communication, the intent behind the words, and the impact on the person with schizophrenia.

Knowledge

What are some examples of expressed emotions that can negatively impact someone with schizophrenia?

Criticism, hostility, and emotional over-involvement.

What are some of the benefits of family therapy for schizophrenia?

Reduced risk of relapse, improved family communication, and decreased burden on caregivers.

Attitude

How can mental health care professional create a safe and supportive environment for open communication within family therapy sessions?

By establishing clear ground rules, emphasizing confidentiality, and validating the emotions of all family members.

How can family members develop healthier communication patterns to support someone with schizophrenia?

By focusing on "I" statements, practicing active listening, and expressing concern with respect. “I" statements shift the focus from blame to one’s own feelings and needs. Instead of: "You never take your medication!" (accusatory) try "I worry when you miss your medication because I care about your health." (Focused on your concern) "I" statements allow for a more productive conversation where the focus is on solutions rather than assigning fault.

Application

What are some resources available to families coping with schizophrenia?

Support groups, educational workshops, online resources from reputable mental health organizations, and individual therapy for family members.

How can family therapy be used to help families cope with the stress of having a member with schizophrenia?

By providing psychoeducation about the illness, teaching coping skills, and fostering emotional support for all family members.

****

Commotion in the ER: Calming the Chaotic with the Right Route

A 24-year-old male patient arrives in the Emergency Department (ED) brought in by police. Officers found him running erratically into traffic while yelling and screaming. In the ED, he is uncooperative with attempts to take a medical history, perform a physical examination, or insert an intravenous (IV) line. He exhibits significant agitation and has tried to assault staff members on multiple occasions, verbally referring to them as "interlopers" and "agents of destruction”. To manage effectively, which route of administration is most appropriate for initial antipsychotic medication in this scenario?

a) Oral
b) Dissolvable oral
c) Intravenous (IV)
d) Intramuscular (IM)
e) Intramuscular depot (IM)

Explanation: The most suitable route for administering initial antipsychotic medication in this case is **Intramuscular (IM)**. Why the other options are less suitable: Oral and B. Dissolvable oral: Due to the patient's extreme agitation, there's a high chance he wouldn't swallow oral medication or might spit it out, rendering these routes ineffective; Intravenous (IV): Given the patient's resistance to procedures, establishing an IV line would likely be difficult or impossible; Intramuscular depot (IM): Depot injections are long-acting formulations intended for maintenance therapy after a medication has been proven effective. They are not suitable for initial administration in an agitated patient. Therefore, IM injection is the most practical and effective route for delivering initial antipsychotic medication in this situation.

Pertinent Questions for Ward Rounds/OSCE:

Cognition

What are the different routes of administration for antipsychotic medications, and what are the advantages and disadvantages of each route?

Antipsychotic medications can be administered orally, intramuscularly (IM), intravenously (IV), and in some cases, via intramuscular depot injection (long-acting). Oral: Advantages - Easy to administer, non-invasive. Disadvantages - Slow onset of action, potential for non-compliance; IM: Advantages - Faster onset of action than oral, good option for agitated patients. Disadvantages - More invasive than oral, potential for injection site pain; IV: Advantages - Fastest onset of action, precise dosing. Disadvantages - Most invasive route, requires establishing IV access which can be difficult in agitated patients; IM Depot: Advantages - Long-acting, reduces need for frequent injections. Disadvantages - Not suitable for initial administration, slow onset of action, difficult to reverse if needed.

What factors influence the choice of route for administering antipsychotic medications in an agitated patient?

Factors influencing route choice for antipsychotics in agitated patients include: Patient cooperation: If oral medication is an option, it's preferable due to ease of administration, but cooperation is necessary; Speed of action: IM injections offer a faster onset compared to oral medications, crucial in calming an agitated patient; Safety considerations: Establishing an IV line in an agitated patient may be difficult and pose safety risks for both patient and staff.

What are some potential side effects of IM antipsychotic medications, and how can these be monitored and managed?

Potential side effects of IM antipsychotic medications include: Drowsiness: A common effect, monitor for impaired coordination or alertness; Extrapyramidal symptoms (EPS): Abnormal movements like tremors or rigidity, requiring medication adjustments; Hypotension (low blood pressure): Monitor vital signs regularly, especially after administration.

What other considerations might influence the choice/dosage of specific antipsychotic medication in this scenario

Choosing the specific antipsychotic medication may consider factors like:

- Patient's medical history: Existing medical conditions may influence medication selection.
- Potential substance abuse: Certain antipsychotics may interact with addictive substances
- Previous medication responses: Prior experience with antipsychotics can guide selection

What ongoing monitoring is necessary after administering antipsychotic medication to an agitated patient?

- Ongoing monitoring after administering antipsychotic medication includes:
- Monitoring vital signs: Watch for changes in blood pressure, heart rate, and respiration.
- Monitoring for side effects: Look for signs of EPS, dizziness, or allergic reactions.
- Assessing response to treatment: Evaluate if the patient's agitation has subsided.

Attitude

How would you ensure the safety of yourself and other staff members while approaching and treating an agitated patient?

Ensuring safety involves several steps: Maintain a calm and professional demeanour; Approach the patient with a team and ensure adequate staffing; verbally de-escalate the situation by speaking calmly and explaining procedures; Have a plan for physical restraint as a last resort if de-escalation fails. Have an informed written consent for this.

What de-escalation techniques could be employed to calm the patient before administering medication?

De-escalation techniques include:

- Active listening: Pay attention to the patient's concerns and validate their feelings
- Non-threatening body language: Maintain eye contact but avoid appearing aggressive
- Speak in a calm, reassuring tone: Avoid shouting or arguing
- Offer choices where possible: For example, offer a choice of arm for the injection
- Provide clear and concise explanations of procedures

Application

What documentation is essential after administering IM antipsychotic medication to an agitated patient?

- Essential documentation after administering IM antipsychotic medication to an agitated patient includes:
- Medication name, dose, route, and time of administration.
- Details of the patient's condition and behaviour before and after medication.
- Any de-escalation techniques used.
- Vital signs and any observed side effects.

How would you assess the effectiveness of the medication and determine the need for further interventions?

Evaluating medication effectiveness involves:

- Observing changes in the patient's behaviour: Are they less agitated or more cooperative?
- To rule out organic causes

****

From Erratic to Critical: A Race against Time

A 24-year-old male patient was brought to the Emergency Department (ED) by police due to violent and abusive behaviour in the road. He received an intramuscular (IM) antipsychotic medication to manage his agitation. Following admission to the psychiatric unit, he continued to exhibit agitation and required further antipsychotic doses. The patient's family arrived, reporting they had been searching for him and that he had never experienced a similar episode. Several hours later, the patient's condition deteriorated in the ward. He became confused, developed muscle rigidity, and febrile. His vital signs included an elevated heart rate (HR 122), high blood pressure (BP 172/140), and rapid respiration (RR 20). In this scenario, which intervention is NOT recommended?

a) Admit to the medical ICU
b) Withdraw all antipsychotics
c) Administer dantrolene
d) Continue treating in psychiatric ward
e) Aggressive cooling procedures

Explanation: The patient's symptoms strongly suggest Neuroleptic Malignant Syndrome (NMS), a potentially life-threatening complication to antipsychotic medications. Here's why all options are correct except being treated at psychiatric ward as it is a medical emergency; **Admit to the medical ICU:** Close monitoring and advanced life support may be necessary in NMS due to potential complications; **Withdraw all antipsychotics:** Stopping the offending antipsychotic medication is essential in NMS treatment; **Administer dantrolene:** Dantrolene is a peripherally acting skeletal muscle relaxant by inhibiting the release of calcium ions from sarcoplasmic reticulum stores by antagonizing ryanodine receptors. Aggressive physical cooling measures are preferred; Rapidly lowering body temperature is crucial in NMS management.

Questions with Answers:

Cognition:

What are the classic symptoms of Neuroleptic Malignant Syndrome (NMS)?

NMS is characterized by a triad of symptoms: fever, muscle rigidity, and altered mental status (confusion, agitation, or coma).

What factors increase a patient's risk of developing NMS?

Risk factors include high-potency antipsychotics, rapid dose escalation, dehydration, and concurrent use of certain medications.

What are some potential complications of NMS if left untreated?

Untreated NMS can lead to kidney failure, respiratory failure, sepsis, and even death.

How does the mechanism of action of dantrolene help manage NMS symptoms?

Dantrolene relaxes skeletal muscles by interfering with calcium release within muscle cells, alleviating rigidity.

Attitude

How would you approach a patient experiencing NMS while maintaining safety for yourself and others?

Maintain a calm demeanour, prioritize de-escalation techniques, and ensure adequate staffing for potential physical restraint if needed.

How would you communicate effectively with the patient's family about NMS and its treatment plan?

Use clear and empathetic language, explain the condition and treatment plan in detail, and address their concerns with compassion.

What ongoing monitoring is crucial after initiating treatment for NMS?

Monitor vital signs, muscle rigidity, mental status, and laboratory tests to assess response to treatment and identify potential complications.

When would you consider restarting antipsychotic medication after a patient recovers from NMS?

Re-initiation would be determined by a mental health professional after a thorough evaluation, considering alternative medications or lower doses to minimize NMS risk.

Application

Describe the steps involved in initiating aggressive cooling measures for NMS.

Measures may include removing excess clothing, applying ice packs to specific areas, and using cooling blankets or evaporation techniques.

Outline the essential components of documenting the management of NMS in a patient's medical record.

Document the patient's presenting symptoms, vital signs, medications used, cooling measures implemented, and response to treatment.

Ethical and Legal issues: Report to pharmacovigilance and enter in case record accordingly.

****

Fresh Start, Feverish Fight: Man's New Life Takes a Scary Turn

A 33-year-old male arrives at Emergency Department complaining of a sore throat and fever. He emphasizes the severity, stating it's "the worst he's ever felt." Vital signs reveal an elevated heart rate (HR 104), low blood pressure (BP 90/60), normal respiratory rate (RR 16), and fever (temperature 101.7°F). Laboratory tests show a critically low absolute neutrophil count (ANC) of 0.4 x 10^9/L. Further questioning reveals he recently moved across the country a month ago to "start fresh after a mental block". Based on the presentation, what medication is most likely responsible for the patient's condition?

a) Haloperidol
b) Chlorpromazine
c) Clozapine
d) Olanzapine
e) Aripiprazole

Explanation: The patient's symptoms and critically low ANC point towards agranulocytosis, a potentially life-threatening side effect of certain medications. Why **clozapine (choice C)** is the most likely culprit: **Agranulocytosis presentation:** Symptoms often include sore throat, fever, and chills, aligning with the patient's complaints. **Lab findings:** A low white blood cell count (WBC) despite infection is a hallmark of agranulocytosis, reflected by the low ANC. **Recent move:** His recent relocation might have disrupted his established care, potentially leading to a lack of close monitoring for clozapine side effects. **Medications:** While the other listed options (haloperidol, chlorpromazine, olanzapine, aripiprazole) can have side effects, agranulocytosis is not a complication of these medications.

Questions and Answers

Cognition

What is agranulocytosis, and how does it affect the body?

Agranulocytosis is a severe reduction in neutrophils, a type of white blood cell crucial for fighting infections. This leaves the body highly susceptible to infections.

What is CLIA?

It is Clozopine induced agranulocyctosis – a idiosyncratic reaction and is still unclear.

What are the long-term considerations for a patient who experiences agranulocytosis from clozapine?

The possibility of restarting clozapine with close monitoring or exploring alternative medications needs to be discussed with a hematologist and psychiatrist.

Attitude

How would you approach a patient with suspected agranulocytosis while maintaining empathy and effective communication?

Actively listen to their concerns, explain the potential cause and next steps clearly, and express reassurance while acknowledging the seriousness of the situation.

What ethical considerations arise when managing a patient who might be non-compliant with medication monitoring due to a recent move?

Respect the patient's autonomy while emphasizing the importance of monitoring for their safety. Offer options for facilitating continuity of care, such as connecting them with local mental health services.

Application

Describe the initial steps in managing a patient with suspected agranulocytosis.

Immediate steps include isolation to prevent infection, discontinuing the suspected medication (clozapine in this case), and administering broad-spectrum antibiotics to combat potential infections.

Outline the essential components of documenting the patient's presentation and initial management plan for agranulocytosis.

Document the patient's symptoms, vital signs, laboratory findings, suspected cause (clozapine), and details of the implemented treatment plan.

What ongoing monitoring is necessary after a patient recovers from agranulocytosis?

Regular blood tests to monitor white blood cell count and ensure recovery. Close follow-up with a healthcare professional is essential.

What preventative measures can be implemented to minimize the risk of agranulocytosis in patients taking clozapine?

Frequent blood monitoring, especially during the initial treatment period, and patient education on recognizing signs and symptoms of infection.

Psychiatrist Practice Pearls:

- Hiding mental illness and seeking medicines is very common
- Never encourage patient getting medicines without prescription from a **competent psychiatrist**.
- Never encourage self-medication or self-titration of drugs

****

Exploring Sleep Paralysis and Cataplexy

During morning rounds, Dr. Krishnan meets with a 30-year-old woman who describes experiencing vivid dreams as she drifts off to sleep (hypnogogic hallucinations). Additionally, she has temporary loss of muscle tone and falls down. These episodes are concerning, and Dr. Krishnan delves deeper to explore the possibility of narcolepsy, a sleep disorder with serious safety implications**.** Dr. Krishnan asks the patient some additional questions. Which question is LEAST likely relevant to diagnosing narcolepsy?

a) Do you ever experience sudden muscle weakness triggered by strong emotions like laughter or anger? (Cataplexy is a symptom of narcolepsy)
b) Have you ever fallen asleep unexpectedly during activities like watching television or eating? (Excessive daytime sleepiness is a symptom of narcolepsy)
c) Do you feel refreshed after a full night's sleep, or do you still feel tired during the day? (Excessive daytime sleepiness is a symptom of narcolepsy)
d) Do you experience vivid dreams or nightmares frequently? (hypnogogic and hypnopompic hallucinations)

Explanation: While vivid dreams can be present in narcolepsy, they are not a core diagnostic symptom. Dr. Krishnan's other questions target the cardinal features of narcolepsy: cataplexy (muscle weakness with emotions), excessive daytime sleepiness, and sleep paralysis.

Pertinent Questions and Answers for Ward Rounds

Knowledge

- **What are the tetrad of narcolepsy?** (Excessive daytime sleepiness, cataplexy, hypnagogic/hypnopompic hallucinations, sleep paralysis)
- **How can narcolepsy cause safety concerns for individuals?** (Excessive daytime sleepiness can lead to falling asleep during activities, and cataplexy can cause sudden muscle weakness)
- **What are the treatment options available for narcolepsy?** (Stimulant medications, sodium oxybate, scheduled naps)

Attitude

- **Why is it important to take a detailed sleep history when evaluating a patient for a sleep disorder?** (Specific sleep patterns and experiences can point towards different diagnoses)
- **How can doctors balance patient privacy with the need to report potentially dangerous situations like falling asleep while driving?** (Explore options for managing narcolepsy to prevent future incidents, while maintaining confidentiality)

Application

- **What additional tests might Dr. Krishnan recommend to confirm a diagnosis of narcolepsy?** (Sleep study with multiple sleep latency test (MSLT), hypocretin levels in CSF)
- **How might Dr. Krishnan explain the risks of narcolepsy to the patient in a way that is clear and encourages her to seek treatment?** (Explain the safety concerns, emphasize the availability of treatment to improve her quality of life)

Communication Skills

- **What is a good follow-up question after Dr. Krishnan asks about the patient's sleep paralysis?** ("How long do these episodes of paralysis typically last?")
- **How can Dr. Krishnan explain cataplexy to the patient in a way that is easy to understand?** (Use simple language, quote popular movies for better connect and understanding)

Cultural Sensitivity

- **How might Dr. Krishnan adapt his communication if the patient comes from a culture with specific beliefs about dreams or sleep disturbances?** (Acknowledge cultural beliefs, explore if the patient has consulted traditional healers, explain narcolepsy from a medical perspective while respecting cultural interpretations of sleep experiences)

****

Lost in the Hospital

An 81-year-old woman is admitted to the hospital for IV antibiotics to treat a UTI. During her second night, she wakes up at 2:30 am disoriented and tries to get out of bed. In the process, she pulls out her IV and keeps repeating, "I'm going home." When you talk to her, she remembers her name but not where she is or why she's in the hospital. What's the best course of action?

a. Restrain the patient
b. Initiate an immediate work-up for causes of delirium
c. Administer antipsychotic medications
d. Arrange for a sitter
e. Increase the dose of antibiotics

Explanation: The most appropriate approach is arranging for a sitter while working up for delirium. This patient exhibits signs of delirium, a sudden change in mental state that requires immediate attention. Restrain the patient: Restraint should be a last resort due to potential physical and psychological harm. Initiate immediate workup for delirium causes: While this is generally crucial, a UTI is a common cause of delirium in older adults. Administer antipsychotic medications: While these can shorten delirium duration, a sitter may offer immediate calming reassurance. Increase antibiotic dose: Antibiotics treat the infection, not the delirium.

Additional Considerations

Knowledge

- Delirium: Causes, symptoms, management strategies.
- De-escalation techniques for agitated patients.
- Importance of patient safety and fall prevention, especially in geriatric patients

Skills

- Assessing mental status and delirium severity.
- Communicating effectively with a delirious patient is challenging – Develop the skill
- De-escalation techniques to calm an agitated patient.

Application

- Using de-escalation skills to prevent self-harm or injury.
- Collaborating with nurses and other healthcare professionals to create a safe environment and treatment plan.

Communication

- With patient: Use simple, calm language. Explain procedures gently and offer reassurance.
- With caregivers: Explain the patient's condition, treatment plan, and safety measures.
- Make sure they are present 24 X 7

Further Questions

- Does the patient have a history of delirium or dementia?
- Are there any other potential causes of her confusion (e.g., dehydration, medication side effects)?
- What steps can be taken to prevent future episodes of delirium (e.g., improving sleep hygiene, optimizing medications, prevent infections)?

Furthermore: The patient calms down somewhat and agrees to return to bed. However, when the nurse tries to replace the IV, she becomes agitated again, yelling, "I don't want it! I don't want it!" What's the best course of action now?

a. Perform a capacity evaluation
b. Attempt to find a surrogate decision maker
c. Consult psychiatry
d. Consult ethics
e. Restrain the patient and place the IV

Explanation: The most appropriate step is **attempt to find a surrogate decision maker**. This patient seems to lack the capacity to make informed decisions due to her confusion. **Perform a capacity evaluation:** While this might be done later, identifying a surrogate is more pressing for immediate treatment. **Consult psychiatry:** Useful in borderline capacity cases, but here, lack of capacity is clear. **Consult ethics:** Ethics might be involved later if a surrogate can't be found, but focus on finding one first. **Restrain the patient and place the IV:** Restraint is a last resort, and if the infection likely isn't life-threatening, allowing time for finding a surrogate.

Additional Considerations

- **Knowledge: -** Decision-making capacity: Criteria for assessing capacity to consent to treatment; Surrogate decision-makers: Roles and legal considerations.
- **Skills:-** Assessing decision-making capacity in a confused patient; Identifying potential surrogate decision-makers (family, healthcare proxy); Communicating effectively with agitated patients and their families.
- **Application:** Applying knowledge of capacity assessment to determine the patient's current state; Using communication skills to explain the situation and importance of the IV to the patient (even if she doesn't fully understand); Initiating the process of identifying a surrogate decision-maker.
- **Communication:- With patient:** Speak calmly, explain the procedure simply, and offer reassurance; **With family:** Explain the patient's condition, lack of capacity, and need for a surrogate decision-maker. Seek their help in identifying a suitable person.

Further Questions

- Does the patient have a healthcare proxy named in her medical records?
- Can you reach any family members who can provide information and potentially act as a surrogate?
- What alternative treatment options might be considered if an IV proves impossible (e.g., oral antibiotics)?

****

Love's Heavy Burden: Can We Help Her Carry It?

A 72-year-old, otherwise healthy woman visits her physician for the first time in over ten years. She reveals that her husband of over 52 years suffered a stroke two months ago, leaving him severely incapacitated. Her sons and daughter are leading their life abroad. She is the only caregiver for her husband. She feels constantly exhausted and depressed due to the burden of caring for him. While she acknowledges the guilt of wishing for his passing, she denies suicidal thoughts. Her appetite and concentration remain normal. What's the most appropriate next step?

a) Refer for therapy
b) Reassure the patient that her symptoms are normal
c) Discuss risks and benefits of medications
d) Provide referrals to social resources such as caregiver support
e) All of the above

Explanation: The best course of action is **All of the above**. The patient likely experiences adjustment disorder due to the recent life stress of her husband's stroke and resulting emotional toll. **Refer for therapy:** Supportive therapy can equip her with coping mechanisms to manage stress and emotional strain. **Reassure the patient that**

her symptoms are normal: Acknowledge the situation's difficulty and validate her feelings. Let her know it's common to experience emotional distress in such circumstances. **Discuss risks and benefits of medications:** Briefly discuss medications as an option, but prioritize non-pharmacological interventions like psychotherapy first given her relatively mild symptoms. **Provide referrals to social resources such as caregiver support:** Connect her with social services or support groups specifically for caregivers facing similar challenges. This can offer practical help and emotional connection.

Additional Considerations

- Knowledge: Awareness of prevalent caregiver support resources (government programs, NGOs, community support groups); Understanding of cultural and familial expectations around elder care in India.
- **Skills:** Conducting a culturally sensitive mental health assessment; Identifying appropriate support groups or community resources considering the patient's background and location.
- **Application:** Adapting communication style and therapeutic approach to resonate with the patient's cultural values and preferences; utilizing available resources within the Indian healthcare system to provide comprehensive support.
- **Communication: With patient:** Speak empathetically, acknowledging the cultural significance of marital bonds and filial duties; **With family (if appropriate):** Explore possibilities of involving family members in caregiving to alleviate some burden

Further Questions

- Does the patient have any existing support system (family, friends, and neighbours)?
- Would the patient be open to exploring alternative care arrangements for her husband (in-home care, assisted living facility)?
- Are there any financial constraints that might limit access to recommended resources?

****

Forgotten Love: 21-Year-Old's Memory Maze

A 21-year-old man arrives at the emergency department with his worried parents. Two days ago, during a phone call, he seemed to have forgotten who they were. Parent went to his hostel in a metropolis and brought to home. They brought him to the hospital in for evaluation. The patient acknowledges memory loss, stating, "I've lost my memory" and is confused. He denies feeling depressed and insists he feels fine despite everyone's concern. But parent narrates a recent breakup with his long-time girlfriend. A physical and neurological exam reveals no abnormalities. He can recall 5 words presented to him by the psychiatrist 10 minutes earlier. What best describes the memory problem he's experiencing?

a) Anterograde amnesia
b) Retrograde amnesia
c) Global amnesia
d) Memory errors of commission
e) Dissociative Amnesia

Explanation: The most likely explanation is **Dissociative amnesia**.

Additional Considerations

- **Knowledge**
  - Different types of amnesia (retrograde, anterograde, and global) and their causes.
  - Potential causes of sudden memory loss in young adults (e.g., head injury, substance use, neurological conditions like TEA).
- **Skills**

  - Conducting a focused mental status examination to assess memory function.
  - Differentiating between different types of amnesia based on patient history and presentation.
- **Application**
  - Applying knowledge of amnesia to interpret the patient's memory difficulties.
  - Determining the need for further investigations based on the patient's history and presentation (e.g., brain imaging, blood tests).
- **Communication**
  - **With patient:** Speak calmly and patiently. Explain the memory assessment and its purpose. Validate his concerns and offer reassurance.
  - **With caregivers:** Explain the type of amnesia and potential causes. Discuss the next steps in evaluation and treatment.
- **Further Questions**
  - Did the patient experience any recent head injury, drug use, or significant stress?
  - Are there any other symptoms like headaches, dizziness, or confusion?
  - Does the patient have a history of mental health disorders or learning disabilities?

Further more, The patient's parents reveal he was diagnosed with ADHD as a child but supposedly "outgrew" it. During the interview, the father cries, "He can't remember who we are! Will he ever know us again?" What's the best response for the father?

a. Absolutely! There's no doubt he'll remember everything.
b. There's a very good chance he'll recover his memories. Try not to worry.
c. It's too early to tell for sure. There's a possibility he might, but it's also possible he might not
d. While regaining the lost memories might be unlikely, we'll be here to support all of you through this process.
e. I understand this is difficult, but it's possible those memories might not come back

Explanation: The most empathetic and accurate response is there's a very good chance he'll recover his memories. Try not to worry. (Supportive and hopeful) - While we can't guarantee memory return, dissociative amnesia often resolves with good support. Absolute certainty of memory return is misleading; A 50/50 chance adds unnecessary worry. While true, it doesn't address the father's immediate emotional state. Though honest, it can be discouraging at this stage. What the choices reflect is given in brackets: Absolutely! There's no doubt he'll remember everything. (Overly optimistic); There's a very good chance he'll recover his memories. Try not to worry. (Supportive and hopeful); It's too early to tell for sure. There's a possibility he might, but it's also possible he might not. (Uncertain and neutral); While regaining the lost memories might be unlikely, we'll be here to support all of you through this process. (Honest but reassuring); I understand this is difficult, but it's possible those memories might not come back. (Direct but empathetic)

Additional Considerations

Knowledge:

- Dissociative amnesia: Characteristics, causes, and prognosis.
- Importance of providing emotional support to families experiencing memory loss in loved ones.

Skills:

- Conducting a mental health assessment that considers past diagnoses and current stressors.
- Communicating effectively with patients and families experiencing emotional distress.

Application:

- Applying knowledge of dissociative amnesia to offer a hopeful prognosis while acknowledging uncertainty.

- Identifying potential triggers for the memory loss based on the patient's history.

Communication:

- **With patient:** Speak patiently and validate his confusion. Reassure him that you're working to understand what's happening.
- **With caregivers:** Acknowledge their emotional pain and offer support resources. Explain the amnesia type and its typical course, emphasizing the likelihood of memory return.

Further Questions

- Has the patient experienced any recent stressful events or reminders of his past trauma?
- Are there any cultural beliefs or practices that might influence the family's understanding of memory loss?

****

Focus on the Future: Understanding ADHD Treatment

A 9-year-old boy arrives at the psychiatry department with his mother after a difficult parent-teacher meeting. The teacher had earlier reported that the boy struggles to sit still in class, frequently cuts in line, and is failing his classes. The mother confirms similar behaviour at home for several years. She expresses concerns about medication, particularly prescription stimulants, believing them to be "no different than street drugs." How would you explain the key characteristic that distinguishes prescription stimulants from recreational stimulants, making them a safer and more controlled treatment option?

a) Long half-life
b) Involvement of serotonin
c) Once-daily dosing
d) Weaker ability to release monoamines (brain chemicals)
e) Antagonism of neurotransmitter receptors (blocking brain chemicals)

Explanation: The most significant difference between prescription stimulants and recreational stimulants lies in their **weaker ability to release monoamines**. Prescription stimulants like methylphenidate are specifically formulated to gradually release these brain chemicals, primarily dopamine and norepinephrine, over a controlled period. This controlled release helps manage symptoms of Attention Deficit Hyperactivity Disorder (ADHD) such as inattentiveness, impulsivity, and hyperactivity. In contrast, recreational stimulants like methamphetamine have a much higher potency and release a large amount of monoamines very quickly. This rapid and excessive release leads to the intense but short-lived "high" associated with drug abuse; the other answer choices, while potentially true for some prescription stimulants, are not the key factor differentiating them from recreational drugs. Choice-**A has Long half-life:** While some prescription stimulants may have a longer half-life than others, it's not the defining factor compared to recreational drugs; Choice-B shows **Involvement of serotonin:** Some stimulants can also affect serotonin, but this is not the primary mechanism for treating ADHD; Choice -C **Once-daily dosing:** Dosing frequency depends on the specific medication, not a key differentiator; Choice -E**. Antagonism of neurotransmitter receptors:** Prescription stimulants typically increase the availability of neurotransmitters, not block them.

Pertinent Questions for Ward Rounds/OSCE

Cognition

- **What are the core symptoms of Attention Deficit Hyperactivity Disorder (ADHD)?** Inattentiveness, impulsivity, hyperactivity.
- **How do prescription stimulants work to manage ADHD symptoms?** They increase the availability of dopamine and norepinephrine in the brain, promoting focus and regulating behaviour.

- **What are some potential side effects of prescription stimulants?** Decreased appetite, difficulty sleeping, irritability, headaches, and anxiety.

Attitude

- **How would you approach a parent hesitant about medication for their child's ADHD?** Listen to their concerns, provide education about ADHD and medication benefits, and emphasize the importance of a comprehensive treatment plan.
- **What ethical considerations are important when discussing medication for children with ADHD?** Informed consent, shared decision-making, considering non-medication approaches, and ensuring access to appropriate resources.

Application of the Concept

- **What other treatment options are available for managing ADHD in children?** Behavioural therapy, educational support, parent training programs.
- **How would you monitor the effectiveness and potential side effects of prescription stimulants?** Track symptoms, assess academic performance, monitor for side effects through regular check-ins with parents and teachers.
- **When might it be appropriate to discontinue or adjust the dosage of prescription stimulants?** If symptoms are well-controlled, side effects are problematic, or the child reaches adulthood and no longer requires medication.
- **What community resources can help families of children with ADHD?** Support groups, ADHD advocacy organizations, and mental health professionals specializing in ADHD.
- **How can we combat the stigma associated with ADHD and its treatment?** Education campaigns, promoting awareness of ADHD as a medical condition, and sharing success stories of effective treatment.

****

8. Tech Allies & e-Mental Health Tools

(Including Mobile, Internet, Artificial Intelligence, Internet of Medical Thing tools for e-mental health programs)

Finding Joy after Retirement: Mr. Kumaran's Journey to Rediscover Purpose

Mr. Kumaran, a 65-year-old retired clerk, pays a visit to his family physician for a routine check-up. During their conversation, Mr. Kumaran shares that he has observed changes in his appetite and sleep patterns since retiring nearly a year ago. Additionally, he expresses a sense of purposelessness in his day-to-day life and occasionally lacks the motivation to engage with others or leave his house. Given Mr. Kumaran's overall good physical health, the physician delves into a discussion about his mental well-being and mood. Together, they explore strategies to address his low mood, boost his activity levels, and alleviate mild depressive symptoms.

The physician's recommendations include maintaining a daily mood and sleep pattern log and allocating time for hobbies or enjoyable activities. Furthermore, the physician suggests mobile mood-tracking apps as an alternative to manual recording. Although initially indifferent to the idea of a mood diary, Mr. Kumaran agrees to give it a try, and the physician offers to review the diary logs during their next appointment to assess progress and determine if additional support is necessary.

Are e-mental health apps an appropriate option for someone like Mr. Kumaran? Yes, e-mental health apps can be a suitable option for Mr. Kumaran. These apps offer convenient tools for monitoring mood, tracking emotional patterns, and managing mental well-being. Given that Mr. Kumaran is in good physical health, using an app to address his mild depressive symptoms and low mood could be beneficial. However, it's essential to recognize that these apps are not a substitute for professional face-to-face care but can complement therapy or serve as a convenient starting point for healthier habits.

What are some reasons Mr. Kumaran might initially hesitate to use an app to monitor his mood?
Mr. Kumaran might have several reservations:

- Technological unfamiliarity: As a 65-year-old retired individual, he may not be accustomed to using smartphone apps.
- Privacy concerns: App usage involves sharing personal data, which some people find uncomfortable.
- Resistance to change: Adjusting to new routines or technologies can be challenging, especially after retirement.
- Perceived complexity: Mr. Kumaran might worry that using an app requires technical skills or effort.
- Skepticism about effectiveness: He may question whether an app can genuinely improve his mood or well-being.

What assumptions do clinicians sometimes make about patients when recommending e-mental health apps?
Clinicians may unintentionally assume:

- Universal smartphone access: That everyone has a smartphone and is comfortable using it. However, this overlooks potential barriers (e.g., lack of familiarity, affordability, or physical limitations).
- Digital literacy: Assuming patients are tech-savvy enough to navigate app interfaces and features.
- Homogeneity: Treating all patients as if they have similar preferences, needs, and lifestyles.
- Consistent internet connectivity: Not considering variations in network availability or data plans.

- Motivation: Assuming that patients will consistently engage with the app without considering individual motivation levels.

What did the clinician do to increase the likelihood that Mr. Kumaran would use the app after the appointment?

The clinician took specific steps:

- Personalized recommendation: Recognizing Mr. Kumaran's preference for using an app over manual recording, the clinician suggested mood-tracking apps.
- Offering alternatives: By proposing mobile mood-tracking apps, the clinician accommodated Mr. Kumaran's preference while addressing his reluctance to maintain a mood diary.
- Follow-up commitment: The clinician offered to review the diary logs during their next appointment. This commitment encouraged Mr. Kumaran to give the app a try, knowing that his progress would be monitored.

How can Mr. Kumaran incorporate the mood-tracking app into his daily routine effectively?

Mr. Kumaran should set a specific time each day to log his mood & sleep patterns using app. Consistency is key.

What features should Mr. Kumaran look for when choosing a mood-tracking app?

Mr. Kumaran should prioritize user-friendly interfaces, privacy settings, customizable reminders, and data visualization.

Are there any potential drawbacks or risks associated with relying solely on an app for mental health monitoring?

Yes, potential risks include overreliance on technology, lack of human interaction, and inaccurate self-assessment.

How can Mr. Kumaran stay motivated to consistently use the app over time?

Setting reminders, tracking progress, and involving a friend or family member can help maintain motivation.

What other lifestyle changes/activities might complement the app-based approach to managing his mood?

Regular exercise, social interactions, hobbies, and mindfulness practices can enhance mood management.

What role can social support play in improving Mr. Kumaran's mental well-being?

Social connections provide emotional support, reduce isolation, and positively impact mental health.

How can Mr. Kumaran address any privacy concerns he may have about using the app?

Choosing reputable apps with strong privacy policies and being mindful of data sharing can mitigate concerns.

What strategies can Mr. Kumaran employ to find purpose and engagement in his day-to-day life post-retirement?

Exploring new interests, volunteering, interacting with grand-children, participating in more domestic chores or joining clubs can add meaning and structure to his days.

Are there any community resources/ support groups that Mr. Kumaran can explore alongside using app?

Yes, local senior centres, hobby groups, and mental health organizations can offer valuable support.

How can Mr. Kumaran track progress and recognize positive changes in his mood using the app?

Regularly reviewing his mood logs and noting improvements or patterns will help him track progress.

In the case described above, the physician recently engaged with a representative to discuss the use of mobile mental health apps in primary care. During this interaction, participants evaluated several depression-focused apps using a rating checklist. The physician identified **three evidence-informed apps** suitable for adults dealing with mild to moderate anxiety or depression.

When Mr. Kumaran visited the physician, the latter emphasized some unique features of these apps. One of them was designed like a game, complete with achievement badges that users could unlock after completing specific activities. Mr. Kumaran was particularly intrigued by this game-based aspect and expressed his intention to download the app once he returned home. Recognizing the potential benefit, the physician proposed a follow-up appointment to assess Mr. Kumaran's progress. They agreed to review the mood diary logs together during that next visit.

What training or support would a clinician need to begin using apps as part of patient care?
Clinician would benefit from the following training and support:

- **App selection training**: Understanding how to evaluate and choose evidence-based mental health apps.
- **Privacy and security awareness**: Learning about data protection, encryption, and user privacy.
- **Clinical integration guidance**: Knowing how to incorporate app usage seamlessly into patient interactions.
- **Monitoring and follow-up protocols**: Establishing procedures for tracking app effectiveness and patient progress.

Are there any risks or limitations to using the app to monitor and address low mood that the physician should have addressed with Mr. Kumaran?
Yes, the physician should consider the following risks and limitations:

- **Accuracy and reliability**: Apps may not always provide accurate mood assessments or reliable data.
- **User engagement**: Ensuring Mr. Kumaran consistently uses the app over time.
- **Privacy concerns**: Discussing data security and assuring Mr. Kumaran of confidentiality.
- **Appropriate support**: Recognizing that apps are a complement, not a replacement, for professional care.
- **Emergency situations**: Clarifying how to handle crises or urgent needs through the app.

Additionally, the physician should have addressed the potential limitations of app-based monitoring, such as:

- **Lack of context**: Apps may not capture the full context of Mr. Kumaran's emotions or life events.
- **User bias**: Self-reporting can be influenced by mood fluctuations or subjective perceptions.
- **Technological barriers**: Mr. Kumaran's comfort level with using apps and potential technical challenges.
- **App reliability**: Ensuring the app chosen is evidence-based and regularly updated.
- **Follow-up plan**: Discussing how the physician will review the mood logs and adjust treatment if needed

What considerations should the physician keep in mind when recommending specific mental health apps to patients? The physician should consider:

- **Evidence base**: Choosing apps with demonstrated effectiveness through research or clinical trials.
- **User population**: Selecting apps appropriate for the patient's age, mental health condition, and preferences.
- **Features**: Assessing whether the app aligns with the patient's needs (e.g., mood tracking, coping strategies).
- **Usability**: Prioritizing user-friendly interfaces and intuitive navigation.
- **Privacy and security**: Ensuring the app protects user data and complies with privacy regulations.

How can the physician address potential resistance from patients who are hesitant to use mental health apps? The physician can:

- o **Educate**: Explain the benefits of app usage, emphasizing convenience, self-awareness, and tracking.
- o **Normalize**: Share that many individuals find apps helpful and that they complement traditional care.
- o **Offer alternatives**: Propose manual mood diaries or other non-app options if preferred.
- o **Empower choice**: Allow patients to explore and choose apps that resonate with them.

What role can caregivers or family members play in supporting app usage for patients like Mr. Kumaran? Caregivers can:

- o **Assist with setup**: Help patients download and navigate the app.
- o **Encourage consistency**: Remind patients to use the app regularly.
- o **Monitor progress**: Collaborate with the patient and discuss insights from the app data.
- o **Provide emotional support**: Acknowledge the effort and progress made using the app.

How can the physician address any misconceptions patients may have about app-based mental health support? The physician can:

- o **Clarify expectations**: Explain that apps are tools, not a replacement for professional care.
- o **Highlight benefits**: Emphasize how apps enhance self-awareness, coping, and communication.
- o **Address concerns**: Discuss privacy, data security, and the app's role within the overall treatment plan.

What strategies can the physician use to track patient engagement and adherence to app usage? The physician can:

- o **Set follow-up appointments**: Regularly review app data during visits.
- o **Ask directly**: Inquire about app usage, challenges, and benefits.
- o **Monitor progress**: Assess changes in mood, sleep patterns, and overall well-being.
- o **Adjust recommendations**: Modify app suggestions based on patient feedback and outcomes.

****

From Being Persistently Anxious to Joyfully Thriving: A Student's Journey to Better Mental Health

Ms. Kalki, a 24-year-old student, recently joined a master's program, which is usually considered as a very intense and stressful one. In her second semester, she sought help from her student mentor and in-house counsellor due to feelings of anxiety. Following university policy, she completed an online form that assessed her mood, daily functioning, symptom severity, suicide risk, and readiness for psychotherapy.

During her initial assessment, the staff discussed Ms. Kalki's stressors. She felt pressure to perform well in college and experienced loneliness after moving away from home. When asked about coping strategies, support networks, and her desire to improve, she mentioned her family's support and motivation to feel better. Overall, the mentor staff found her self-awareness and mental health literacy impressive.

Based on their discussion, the student mentor and counsellor ranked Ms. Kalki's anxiety symptoms as "mild to moderate" and her self-harm risk as "low." They suggested a low-intensity behavioural treatment plan, including online self-help resources using evidence-based cognitive behavioural therapy techniques. Additionally, they shared their social events calendar and encouraged her to meet new people and make friends. The counsellor provided Ms. Kalki with a copy of the treatment plan, including her current steps, chosen online options, and contact information. The plan is flexible, and Ms. Kalki can request a follow-up session if she notices changes in her mental health or needs further support, if the online program does not seem to be beneficial.

Six months later, Ms. Kalki returned to see her counsellor with her student mentor. She explained that her anxiety had gotten worse due to her mother's recent cancer diagnosis. The counsellor asked Ms. Kalki to complete the same online assessment they had done before. This helped them compare how her symptoms had changed over time. After reviewing the results, the counsellor found that Ms. Kalki's anxiety was now **"moderate to severe."**

The counsellor then asked Ms. Kalki about her preferences for more intensive treatment. Ms. Kalki liked using online resources but felt that talking to someone might be helpful. Although she was a bit uncomfortable with face-to-face counseling, she agreed to try short video sessions. The counsellor proposed a **seven-week online program** with **15-minute video conferencing** sessions.

Once Ms. Kalki agreed, the counsellor connected her with an online coordinator to schedule her first coaching session and provide access to the program's resources. They planned to meet again in about **two months** to review the treatment plan and decide on the next steps.

What are the aspects should be explored before proposing e-mental health solutions:

- **Personal History**: Understanding a client's personal history is crucial. One should inquire about their upbringing, family dynamics, past traumas, and significant life events. This helps contextualize their current mental health challenges.
- **Readiness to Change**: Assessing a patient/client's motivation and willingness to engage in e-mental health solutions is essential. Exploration of their openness to technology, previous experiences with online resources, and any barriers patient/subject perceive should be worked on.
- **Therapeutic Alliance**: Building trust and rapport is vital. Staff-mentor or counsellor should discuss their preferences for communication (e.g., text, video), their expectations from therapy, and their comfort level with virtual interactions.

What is the ideal e-mental health resources that can be prescribed for individuals like Ms. Kalki:

- **Mobile Apps**: Recommend mental health apps for self-monitoring, mood tracking, and relaxation techniques.
- **Online Cognitive Behavioural Therapy (CBT)**: Suggest evidence-based platforms that offer structured CBT programs.
- **Telecounseling**: Propose video-based counselling sessions for personalized support.

Flexibility in e-mental health treatment plans:

- **Regular Review**: Regularly assess the client's progress and adjust the plan as needed. E-mental health plans should be dynamic, allowing modifications based on changing symptoms or life circumstances.
- **Open Communication**: Encourage clients to share any changes in their mental health. If their needs evolve, team can adapt the treatment plan accordingly.

Exploring strengths for self-management:

- **Strength-Based Approach**: Identify the client's existing coping skills, resilience, and social support networks. Leverage these strengths to empower them in managing their mental health.
- **Goal Setting**: Collaborate with the client to set achievable goals using e-mental health tools. Celebrate small victories to boost confidence.

What can be the additional support persons for young people using e-mental health services:

- **Peers**: Peer support groups or forums can provide empathy, shared experiences, and encouragement.

- **Caregivers**: Involve parents, siblings, or close friends who can reinforce positive behaviours and monitor progress.
- **Graduate Program Coordinators**: Academic advisors can offer guidance and refer students to relevant resources.
- **Indigenous Elders**: Culturally sensitive support for Indigenous youth, respecting traditional healing practices.

How can e-mental health solutions address specific populations?

- **Youth**: tailor e-mental health resources to resonate with young people. Engage them through interactive apps, relatable content, and peer support.
- **Seniors**: simplify user interfaces and provide clear instructions for older adults. Consider telehealth options for those less familiar with technology.

How should be the act of balancing privacy and accessibility in e-mental health:

- **Privacy**: explain data security measures to clients. Assure them that their information is confidential.
- **Accessibility**: ensure user-friendly platforms that accommodate diverse needs (e.g., screen readers, language options).

What points to consider when considering e-mental health applications and cultural sensitivity:

- **Cultural competence**: understand cultural nuances. Avoid assumptions and stereotypes. Offer resources in multiple languages.
- **Inclusivity**: collaborate with community leaders and organizations to promote culturally relevant e-mental health services.

How to monitor progress and adjusting e-mental health plans:

- **Regular check-ins**: schedule follow-up sessions to assess progress and adapt the plan. Use self-report tools or app data.
- **Client empowerment**: encourage clients to self-monitor and communicate changes. Empower them to request adjustments.

How to involve and collaboration with other health-care providers, if required.

- **Primary care physicians**: coordinate care by sharing insights from e-mental health interventions.
- **School counsellors**: collaborate to support students' mental health using online resources.
- **Community health workers**: extend reach by involving local health workers in promoting e-mental health.

How did the e-mental health option Ms. Kalki selected support her unique needs and preferences?

The e-mental health option Ms. Kalki chose aligned with her preferences. She appreciated the convenience of online resources but also recognized the value of talking to someone. By opting for 15-minute video sessions, she found a balance that suited her. This approach acknowledged her comfort level and need for personalized support.

Would this stepped e-mental health approach work outside the university setting? Why or why not?

The stepped e-mental health approach could work beyond universities, but some considerations apply:

- **Access:** Availability of technology and internet access varies. In non-academic settings, ensuring equal access becomes crucial.
- **Privacy:** Privacy concerns exist outside universities too. Clear policies and secure platforms are essential.

- **Resource Availability:** Community-based services may have different resources. Collaboration with local health centers is vital. Telemanas in India might be an option.

How might Ms. Kalki's 15-minute sessions (instead of the typical 60-minute sessions) affect a health-care provider's workflow?

- **Time Efficiency**: Shorter sessions (15 minutes) allow more flexibility. Providers can accommodate multiple clients in a day.
- **Scheduling**: Easier scheduling for both providers and clients. However, maintaining continuity and rapport within shorter sessions requires skill.
- **Documentation**: Less time spent on session notes, but concise documentation becomes critical.
- **Adaptation**: Providers must adjust their communication style and therapeutic techniques to maximize the shorter timeframe.

****

Beyond Appointments: How Electronic Instant Communication Saved a Patient (and Updated Clinic Policy)

Dr. Murugan, a junior doctor, has been part of a collaborative mental health team, working alongside psychiatrists, physicians, psychologists, nurses, social workers, and an office manager. Embracing technology, he began using various tools to connect with adult clients between counselling sessions, sending appointment reminders, words of encouragement, and links to additional support. The results were very encouraging and appreciated by the team.

As Dr. Murugan prepared for a week-long overseas conference, he informed his clients about his absence. While at the overseas conference, a colleague requested to use Dr. Murugan's phone, revealing notifications of texts and emails from clients. Among them was an email from a distressed client detailing challenging interactions with her teenage daughter, including mental health history and attached screenshots of social media activity.

Concerned and facing time differences and communication challenges, Dr. Murugan sought help from clinic staff to connect the parent with appropriate resources. After the conference, he raised the issue in a clinic team meeting. A nurse argued against using email and technology for client communication, while a community outreach worker defended their value, suggesting improved guidelines rather than a ban. The lack of clarity on electronic communication policies led to a decision to revisit and update the outdated technology policy.

Collaborating with the hospital team, Dr. Murugan and the team discovered the outdated policy focused on an old telehealth system. Recognizing the need for a comprehensive update, they developed a new electronic communication policy following health practice guidelines. Over the next six months, all staff members were trained on the new policy, ensuring a standardized approach. The policy is scheduled for review every two years to adapt to evolving needs and technology.

What privacy and security concerns did Dr. Murugan encounter or potentially create by his actions?

Dr. Murugan encountered several privacy and security concerns through electronic communication. Sharing sensitive client information, including mental health history and screenshots of social media activity, via email raised the risk of unauthorized access. Additionally, the lack of secure videoconferencing and the use of personal devices for professional communication posed potential breaches of confidentiality.

What laws, privacy policies or guidelines have you read about electronic communication with clients?
The scenario doesn't explicitly mention specific provincial or federal privacy policies. However, best practices would involve adherence to laws like India's Information Technology Act and Health Information Privacy laws. Compliance with international standards such as HIPAA (Health Insurance Portability and Accountability Act) for data security in healthcare may also be relevant.

How would you build consensus among people who support and people who don't support the use of e-mental health in clinical practice?
To build consensus, fostering open communication and understanding is crucial. Holding regular meetings where both supporters and sceptics, like the nurse and community care providers can voice their concerns, experiences, and expectations would be beneficial. Conducting training sessions to address apprehensions and showcase success stories of e-mental health implementation can help bridge the gap.

How does the 24*7 nature of technology change client and provider expectations about contact and communication?
The 24/7 nature of technology alters expectations for both clients and providers. Establishing clear communication boundaries and response time expectations in the electronic communication policy can help manage these expectations and prevent burnout among healthcare providers.

How might management support clinic staff members to embrace the changes and not slip back into former habits?
Management can support staff by providing comprehensive training on the new policy, addressing concerns, and actively soliciting feedback. Regular check-ins, acknowledging successful implementations, and fostering a culture of adaptability can prevent a regression to former habits.

How could Dr. Murugan communicate the new policy to clients and families? What positive things might come out of a conversation about privacy and security concerns?
Dr. Murugan could communicate the new policy to clients and families through multiple channels, such as emails, newsletters, and informational sessions. Highlighting the positive aspects, like increased security measures, streamlined communication, and standardized expectations, can help reassure clients about the importance of the changes.
Discussing privacy concerns openly can lead to increased awareness and understanding among staff, fostering a culture of responsibility. It may also encourage the development of innovative solutions to address these concerns, ultimately enhancing the overall security and privacy of client information.

What ways could a clinic like this review compliance and accountability in terms of the new policy
Regular audits, internal assessments, and feedback mechanisms can be implemented to review compliance with the new policy. Designating a compliance officer and conducting periodic training sessions can reinforce the importance of accountability among clinic staff. Incentives for compliance and addressing non-compliance constructively can further enhance adherence to the policy.

How might the use of electronic communication impact the therapeutic relationship between Dr. Murugan and his clients?
Electronic communication can enhance accessibility and support between sessions, but it also introduces challenges such as ensuring privacy, setting boundaries, and managing expectations. The potential benefits

include increased client engagement and convenience, while risks involve the potential for breaches of confidentiality and miscommunication.

What considerations should Dr. Murugan take into account when selecting and implementing new technologies for client communication in a mental health setting?
Dr. Murugan should prioritize technologies with robust security features, ensuring encryption of sensitive data. Additionally, he should consider user-friendliness, accessibility, and compatibility with existing systems. Regularly updating software and conducting risk assessments can help mitigate potential privacy and security risks.

In what ways can the clinic involve clients and their families in the development and revision of electronic communication policies to ensure their perspectives are considered?
The clinic can conduct surveys, focus groups, or feedback sessions with clients and families to gather their input on electronic communication policies. This collaborative approach can help identify concerns, preferences, and expectations, fostering a sense of inclusivity and shared responsibility.

What steps can be taken to address the nurse's concerns about the appropriateness of electronic communication in client interactions during team meetings?
Organizing training sessions to educate staff about the benefits and risks of electronic communication, as well as providing evidence-based examples of successful implementations, can address concerns. Establishing clear guidelines within the clinic's policy and offering ongoing support and communication channels can also alleviate apprehensions.

How can the clinic balance the need for standardized policies with the individualized nature of mental health care in a diverse community?
The clinic can develop a flexible policy framework that allows for customization based on individual client needs while maintaining a core set of standardized guidelines. Regular communication and training can ensure that staff understands how to adapt policies to meet diverse cultural, linguistic, and clinical requirements.

What strategies can Dr. Murugan employ to ensure the confidentiality and security of client information when communicating through electronic means, especially during his absence at the conference?
Dr. Murugan should use secure communication channels, password protection, and encryption for client information. Clearly communicating privacy guidelines to colleagues and reminding them of the sensitivity of the information is essential. Implementing remote access controls and regular cybersecurity training for staff can also enhance data security.

How can the clinic establish a feedback loop to continuously improve electronic communication policies based on evolving technologies and changing client needs?
The clinic can institute regular reviews and updates to the policy, incorporating feedback from staff, clients, and technology experts. Establishing a technology committee responsible for monitoring advancements, conducting risk assessments, and recommending policy revisions can ensure that the clinic remains responsive to emerging challenges and opportunities.

****

Bridging the Valley: Remote Care Heals Ex-Army Man

In a remote village in the ravines of Chambal valley in Central India, there was a retired-military Havildhar named Mr. Shankar, aged 63, who's been feeling down and having memories from his military days. The nearest city with a specialist for mental health is a four-hour drive away. Mr. Shankar's family doctor suggested meeting a psychiatrist through video conference using a system from their capital city.

Although Mr. Shankar wasn't familiar with video technology, the doctor explained how it worked and assured him that the psychiatrist had experience helping veterans like him through video calls. Despite feeling a bit "old-fashioned," Mr. Shankar agreed to try the video conference. To make him more comfortable, the doctor offered to be present during the first session. The doctor also considered Mr. Shankar's preferences, such as language (he speaks two languages) and submitted a referral for the virtual care.

Soon after, a virtual care coordinator contacted Mr. Shankar to set a date and time. When he and his wife reached the designated centre, a staff member welcomed them and guided them to a private video-conferencing room in a travelling mobile van. The online psychiatrist introduced himself, explained the session, and ensured Mr. Shankar was comfortable with the technology. To address Mr. Shankar's privacy concerns, the psychiatrist showed him around his office with the camera and reassured him that the session wouldn't be recorded or shared online. The psychiatrist also reviewed the clinic's privacy standards. With everyone comfortable, the session began with the doctor supporting Mr. Shankar and his wife, who could provide additional information or translate if needed.

The psychiatrist conducted a structured interview to assess Mr. Shankar's mental health and discussed the results. At the end, the psychiatrist reviewed medications, sending a new prescription securely. Mr. Shankar left feeling positive, and he and his doctor continue follow-up appointments with the psychiatrist through video conferences.

Is tele-mental health Mr. Shankar's best option, considering what you know about him? How might telehealth for seniors differ from (or be similar to) its use with other age groups?

Given Mr. Shankar's rural location and the distance to the nearest mental health specialist, tele-mental health seems a practical option for him. Telehealth for seniors may differ in terms of familiarity with technology, potential physical limitations, and unique mental health concerns related to aging. However, like other age groups, seniors can benefit from the accessibility and convenience of telehealth.

Does Mr. Shankar believe his limited experience with technology will take away from the benefits he receives from the session?

Initially, Mr. Shankar expressed concerns about his limited experience with technology. However, with proper support and assurance from the healthcare provider, he agreed to try the tele-mental health session. Ongoing encouragement and guidance can help him adapt and maximize the benefits.

What could psychiatrists do to build their telehealth communication and rapport-building skills?

Psychiatrists can undergo specialized training in telehealth communication, including non-verbal cues through video, active listening, and fostering a connection. Role-playing scenarios and seeking feedback from patients can enhance their skills in building rapport remotely.

Does Mr. Shankar have access to the necessary equipment and facilities (camera, microphone, video screen, internet connection, private room, etc.)? If not, where and how can he obtain access?

The scenario doesn't provide specific information about Mr. Shankar's access to equipment. Usually, the Primary Health Centre or designated centres or mobile vans with facility would be available. NIMHANS Telemanas project may be contacted for details. If patient lacks necessary resources, the healthcare provider or virtual care coordinator could explore options such as providing equipment, facilitating community resources, or guiding him on accessing affordable devices and internet services.

In what situations might a health-care provider favour tele-mental-health over face-to-face services? What situations might not be suitable for delivering mental health services at a distance?
Tele-mental health is favoured in situations involving distance, accessibility challenges, or for individuals with mobility issues. It may not be suitable in emergencies, cases requiring physical examinations, or situations where a lack of privacy compromises confidentiality.

How could a health-care provider introduce tele-mental health to a client with privacy and confidentiality concerns?
Providers should initiate an open discussion about the client's concerns, emphasizing the security measures in place, such as encrypted communication and privacy standards. Offering a demonstration of the telehealth platform and addressing specific privacy features can help alleviate concerns.

What is a provider's most important skills or competencies when connecting with clients via video conferencing? Are these different from the ones required for successful face-to-face interactions?
Key skills for tele-health include effective communication through video, active listening, adaptability to technology, and maintaining a therapeutic presence remotely. While some skills overlap with face-to-face interactions, tele-health requires additional proficiency in managing technology and building rapport without physical proximity.

How can the healthcare provider ensure cultural sensitivity and competence when offering tele-mental health services to diverse populations, considering Mr. Shankar's bilingualism?
The provider should inquire about cultural preferences, offer language options, and be aware of cultural nuances during tele-mental health sessions. Ensuring that language interpretation services are available when needed is essential for providing culturally competent care. For example, the NIMHANS's Telemanas has facility in 20 Indian Languages.

What measures can the healthcare provider take to address potential challenges in Mr. Shankar's rural community, such as limited internet connectivity or technological resources?
The provider can explore community resources, collaborate with local organizations to improve internet access, or provide guidance on affordable technology options. Developing contingency plans for technical issues and communicating them clearly to patients is crucial.

Considering the sensitive nature of mental health discussions, how can the healthcare provider establish a sense of trust and confidentiality in a virtual setting?
The provider can explicitly discuss privacy measures, reassure clients about the secure nature of the platform, and explain confidentiality standards. Offering information about encryption, secure connections, and the clinic's commitment to privacy can help build trust.

In what ways can the clinic encourage family involvement in the tele-mental health process, as seen with Mr. Shankar's wife attending the session?

The clinic can educate clients on the benefits of family involvement, address concerns, and actively seek the family's participation. Offering flexible scheduling to accommodate family members, providing resources for their understanding, and involving them based on the client's preferences contribute to a supportive environment.

How can the healthcare provider tailor the tele-mental health experience to suit the preferences of elderly patients, considering potential challenges like hearing or vision impairments?
The provider can offer accessible platforms with user-friendly interfaces, provide options for closed-captioning or subtitles, and ensure good lighting and clear visuals during sessions. Offering additional support or involving caregivers, if necessary, can enhance the overall experience for elderly patients.

What strategies can the clinic implement to address potential disparities in access to tele-mental health services, especially in rural areas?
The clinic can collaborate with local authorities, leverage community resources, and explore partnerships to improve access. Providing financial assistance for technology, organizing informational sessions in the community, and developing outreach programs can help bridge the gap in access to tele-mental health services.

****

From Rejections to Rejuvenation: A Young Patient's Journey for Feeling Better

Ms. Mekala, a young woman from Lucknow in her early twenties, had been applying for jobs in her field for a while but hadn't found anything yet. After a few months, the constant rejections started affecting her mood. Her mother first noticed a change in Ms. Mekala's behaviour. She became easily annoyed by little things, argued more often with those around her, withdrew from social interactions, and avoided activities she used to enjoy. Concerned, her mother encouraged Ms. Mekala to visit their family doctor and discuss her low mood. During the interaction, the doctor spoke with Ms. Mekala about the recent changes in her behaviour and emotional state. Ms. Mekala confided that it was difficult to talk to her family because she felt they wouldn't understand. Considering this, the doctor suggested a combination of online support and a therapy approach called "cognitive behavioural therapy" (CBT) to help Ms. Mekala manage her mood.

The idea of online support resonated with Ms. Mekala, who was active on social media and familiar with online groups. The doctor helped her find a peer support tool with an interactive digital platform and emotional well-being services. This platform offered self-help programs for mild to moderate depression or anxiety, providing 24/7 support through an online community. Here, people could share their experiences and express themselves through text or even images.

Two features particularly appealed to Ms. Mekala - anonymity and the presence of moderators on open forums. The doctor advised her to carefully review the platform's privacy and security policies before joining, and to learn how to report any issues that might arise.

He also recommended regular participation in the online group, so they could track her progress together at her next appointment. Additionally, he referred Ms. Mekala to a local mental health clinic for weekly CBT sessions. The doctor reminded Ms. Mekala that while online support groups can be helpful in managing anxiety and depression symptoms, they are not a replacement for more intensive evidence-based therapy. However, the online peer support could provide valuable comfort and connection while she waited for her in-person CBT sessions to begin.

As a health-care provider, what would you look for in an online peer support group in order to recommend it to patients as safe and reliable?

- Professionally organized and responsibility declared.
- Qualified Moderation: Look for groups with moderators trained in mental health and online safety. They should be able to monitor conversations, remove harmful content, and intervene in conflicts.
- Clear Guidelines: The platform should have clear rules of conduct and expectations for respectful interaction.
- Privacy and Security: The platform should have strong data security measures to protect user privacy. This includes ensuring all communication is encrypted.
- Credibility: Look for groups affiliated with reputable mental health organizations or hospitals.
- Anonymity: The option for anonymous participation can encourage more open and honest sharing

What are the benefits of online peer support groups, versus an educational website or face-to-face group? What are the drawbacks?

Online Peer Support Groups

- Benefits: Accessibility (24/7, location-independent), anonymity, sense of community and belonging, sharing experiences with others who understand, reduced stigma, potentially lower cost compared to in-person therapy.
- Drawbacks: Lack of professional guidance, potential for misinformation, risk of encountering negativity or triggering content, limited ability to build deep connections.

Educational Websites

- Benefits: Provide information and resources on mental health topics, self-help strategies.
- Drawbacks: Lacks the interactive and supportive element of peer support, information may not be tailored to individual needs.

Face-to-Face Groups

- Benefits: Offers more opportunities for deep connection and support, professional guidance from a therapist, personalized feedback and interaction.
- Drawbacks: Accessibility (limited by location and schedule), cost, potential stigma associated with attending a support group.

What are the biggest barriers for clinicians when recommending online peer support

- Lack of Awareness: Clinicians might not be familiar with available online resources or their features.
- Concerns about Safety and Quality: Concerns about the potential for misinformation or lack of moderation in online groups.
- Focus on Traditional Methods: Clinicians may be more comfortable with traditional in-person approaches.

What is a health-care provider's responsibility when recommending online peer support to patients as a treatment option?

- Evaluation: Assess the patient's needs and suitability for online support (e.g., comfort with technology, internet access).
- Selection: Choose a safe and reliable platform based on the criteria mentioned earlier.
- Guidance: Educate the patient on how to use the platform safely and effectively.
- Monitoring: Discuss the importance of informing the clinician of any negative experiences or concerns encountered online.

Where do you see the biggest opportunity for online peer support to complement face-to-face clinical practice?

- Enhanced Support: Online groups can provide additional support between therapy sessions.

- Reduced Stigma: Exposure to a supportive online community can normalize experiences and reduce feelings of isolation.
- Increased Access: Online groups can help reach patients in remote areas or with limited mobility.
- Sharing Resources: Patients can share helpful resources or coping strategies discovered online with their therapist.

What questions would you ask Ms. Mekala at a follow-up appointment to assess the impact and value of the online peer support in helping to manage her low mood?

- Have you participated in the online peer support group?
- What did you find most helpful about the group?
- Did you encounter any negative experiences or concerns while using the group?
- Has participating in the online group helped you feel more connected to others and less alone?
- Do you feel the online support has been helpful in managing your low mood? (Explore how - feeling less isolated, sharing experiences, learning coping strategies)
- How comfortable are you using online forums and social media platforms? (This helps the doctor understand Ms. Mekala's general comfort level with navigating online communities)
- Have you ever encountered any negativity or trolling experiences online in the past? (This helps assess if Ms. Mekala might be more vulnerable to negativity within the online support group)
- For Understanding Ms. Mekala's Experience with the Specific Platform
    - Can you describe the atmosphere of the online support group? Was it welcoming and supportive? (This gauges if the chosen platform aligns with Ms. Mekala's needs for a positive and safe space)
    - Did you find the moderators helpful and present when needed? (This assesses if the platform's moderation met Ms. Mekala's expectations for safety and respectful interaction)
    - Did you primarily use the text-based communication or did you explore features like image sharing? (Understanding Ms. Mekala's preferred mode of communication helps determine if the platform effectively facilitates her self-expression)
- Gauging the Impact on Ms. Mekala's Mental Wellbeing:
    - Did participating in the online group help you feel less alone in your struggles? (This explores if the online community addressed Ms. Mekala's need for belonging and reduced social isolation)
    - Have you learned any new coping strategies or techniques for managing your low mood through the online interactions? (This assesses if the online support group fostered knowledge sharing and self-management skills for Ms. Mekala)
    - Do you feel comfortable discussing any specific examples of positive interactions or support you received online? (Encouraging Ms. Mekala to share positive experiences reinforces the value of the online support group)
- Future Use of Online Support:
    - Would you be interested in continuing to participate in the online support group alongside your CBT sessions? (This explores Ms. Mekala's openness to using the online support as a complementary tool for her ongoing treatment)
    - Do you feel the online support group could be a helpful resource for you even after your CBT sessions end? (This assesses the potential for the online group to provide long-term support for Ms. Mekala's mental well-being)

****

From Exam Fear to Finding Hope: A Teenager's Journey with Anxiety

Ms. Janet, a sixteen-year-old, has been under the care of a psychiatrist for anxiety over the past six months. She openly shared with the psychiatrist that her fear of failure significantly exacerbates her anxiety, particularly during exam periods. Additionally, Ms. Janet has a family history of completed suicides. Her anxiety occasionally becomes so overwhelming that she avoids school for days.

As the end of the school year approaches, Ms. Janet contemplates how to prepare for her final exams. During a clinical session, she confides in her psychiatrist about occasional suicidal thoughts. Although these thoughts tend to dissipate after a few days, she has engaged in self-harm during particularly distressing moments. Ms. Janet assures the psychiatrist that her parents and family physician are aware of these thoughts and feelings, and she has never been hospitalized for a suicide attempt before.

The psychiatrist conducted a standardized risk assessment, determining that Ms. Janet's suicide risk is low. The psychiatrist educated her parents about the situation. However, as a precaution, the family doctor referred Ms. Janet to another psychiatrist for a second opinion and additional treatment and support. Meanwhile, the current psychiatrist initiated a transitional treatment plan to help Ms. Janet manage her anxiety related to school exams.

In their discussions, Ms. Janet expressed interest in using a mobile app to track her anxious symptoms and reinforce the coping skills she has learned in therapy. She sought advice from the psychiatrist on which app would best assist her in practicing relaxation techniques, monitoring mood and behaviour, and reframing her anxious and negative thoughts.

What aspects of the treatment plan you expect the app to support?

- **Mood tracking**: The app allowed her to monitor her mood and behaviour.
- **Relaxation practice**: It provided relaxation techniques to manage anxiety.
- **Cognitive reframing**: The app helped her challenge anxious and negative thoughts.

How would you evaluate a mobile app for quality, effectiveness, and relevance? What criteria would you use to determine if an app is worth recommending?

To evaluate an app, one need to ensure

- **Evidence base**: Check if the app is backed by research or clinical trials.
- **Usability**: Assess user-friendliness, navigation, and design.
- **Functionality**: Ensure it meets specific needs (e.g., mood tracking, coping strategies).
- **Privacy and security**: Verify data protection measures.
- **User feedback**: Consider ratings, reviews, and real-world experiences.

To be effective, do you think it's necessary to design e-mental health tools specifically for young people? Would an adult-focused app meet Ms. Janet's needs?

Designing youth-specific tools is crucial. Young people have unique needs, preferences, and technological literacy. An adult-focused app may not fully address their concerns. Tailoring content, language, and features to youth enhances engagement and relevance.

From your clinical experience, what do you think of using e-mental health tools for anxiety and self-harm behaviour? What kind of safety follow-up would you incorporate?

E-mental health tools can be valuable for anxiety and self-harm. Safety follow-up includes:

- **Risk assessment**: Regularly assess suicidal ideation and self-harm risk.
- **Emergency contacts**: Ensure users have access to crisis helplines; Triggers message to pre-entered emergency contacts, if there are reliable indicators of excessive anxiety or exaggerated response in assessment of self-harm behaviour.

- **Monitoring:** Review app data during follow-up appointments.
- **Education:** Teach coping strategies and alternatives to self-harm.
- **Referral:** Refer to professional help if needed

What strategies can clinicians use to encourage consistent app usage among patients? Clinicians can:

- **Set reminders**: Encourage patients to set app reminders for daily use.
- **Discuss benefits**: Highlight how consistent usage contributes to better self-awareness and progress tracking.
- **Review progress**: Regularly assess app data during follow-up appointments.
- **Normalize setbacks**: Remind patients that occasional lapses in usage are normal and not a failure.

How can mental health apps address cultural diversity and sensitivity? Apps should:

- **Avoid assumptions**: Not assume universal experiences or cultural norms.
- **Provide customizable content**: Allow users to tailor the app to their cultural context.
- **Include diverse representation**: Feature images, stories, and examples from various cultural backgrounds.
- **Offer multilingual support**: Provide content in different languages.

What role can peer support play in app-based mental health interventions? Peer support can:

- **Enhance engagement**: Users may feel more comfortable sharing experiences with peers.
- **Provide empathy**: Peers understand similar struggles and can offer emotional support.
- **Share coping strategies**: Peer-led discussions can exchange practical tips.
- **Reduce stigma**: Peer involvement normalizes seeking help.

How can clinicians address concerns about data privacy and security when recommending mental health apps? Clinicians should:

- **Educate**: Explain how data is stored, encrypted, and protected.
- **Recommend reputable apps**: Choose apps with strong privacy policies.
- **Discuss risks**: Acknowledge potential data breaches and reassure patients about safeguards.
- **Empower choice**: Allow patients to decide how much data they share.

What are the ethical considerations when integrating e-mental health tools into clinical practice? Clinicians must:

- **Informed consent**: Ensure patients understand app usage implications.
- **Beneficence**: Prioritize patient well-being over app adoption.
- **Non-maleficence**: Avoid harm related to app usage.
- **Transparency**: Disclose any financial interests in app recommendations.
- **Continual assessment**: Regularly evaluate app effectiveness and adjust recommendations.

****

Using an Internet of Medical Things (IoMT) Device for Early Intervention in Depression

Mr. Patel, a 56-year-old accountant, has been battling depression for several years. He experiences symptoms like fatigue, loss of interest in activities he once enjoyed, and difficulty concentrating. While he manages his depression with medication and therapy, there are times when his symptoms worsen without him realizing it. In the post-COVID19 situation, any moderate stressor would trigger a barrage of negative thought patterns, rumination and catastrophizing. These, if not promptly addressed, they contribute to Mr. Patel's feelings of hopelessness and helplessness. To escape the overwhelming feelings of stress, Mr. Patel often resort to wilful avoidance behaviours worsening his mood and make it harder to cope with daily life. Mr. Patel's psychiatrist, at the request of Mr. Patel's USA returned engineer son, recently recommended a new IoMT device to monitor his physiological signs of stress. This device, worn like a wristwatch, tracks heart rate variability, sleep patterns, and skin conductance, which can all indicate early changes in stress levels. The changes are communicated digitally in real time to Mr. Patel's son and the consultant, once the stress level spike. They would institute appropriate remedial measures.

How the IoMT device can help Mr. Patel and his doctor:

- **Early Detection of Worsening Depression:** The IoMT device can pick up subtle changes in Mr. Patel's physiological data before he even notices a shift in his mood. This allows for earlier intervention from his doctor.
- **Data-Driven Treatment Adjustments:** By analyzing the data collected by the IoMT device, Mr. Patel's doctor can gain valuable insights into the effectiveness of his current treatment plan. This data can help them identify triggers for his depression and adjust medication or therapy as needed.
- **Improved Patient Engagement:** Wearing the IoMT device can empower Mr. Patel to take a more active role in managing his depression. By tracking his own data, he can see how his daily activities and behaviors impact his stress levels.

Can the IoMT device diagnose depression? No, the IoMT device cannot diagnose depression. However, it can provide valuable data points that can support a doctor's diagnosis and treatment plan.

What happens if the IoMT device detects a significant change in Mr. Patel's stress levels? If the device detects a significant change, it could send an alert to Mr. Patel's psychiatrist and son, prompting them to reach out and assess his well-being. This allows for early intervention and potentially prevents a depressive episode.

Are there any privacy concerns with using an IoMT device? Yes, it's crucial to ensure the data collected by the IoMT device is secure and only accessible to authorized personnel. Mr. Patel should discuss data privacy with his doctor before using the device.

How accurate are IoMT devices in detecting changes related to depression? The accuracy of IoMT devices in detecting depression is still under investigation. More research is needed to validate their effectiveness and establish clear thresholds for triggering alerts.

Are IoMT devices a cost-effective addition to depression treatment? The cost-effectiveness of IoMT devices depends on factors like device cost, data analysis fees, and potential cost savings from early intervention. More studies are needed to determine their long-term financial impact.

How can IoMT data be best integrated with existing depression treatment plans (medication, therapy)? Clear guidelines are needed for how healthcare professionals can incorporate IoMT data into treatment decisions. This could involve training on interpreting the data and using it to personalize treatment approaches.

How can healthcare professionals educate patients on using IoMT devices effectively for depression management? Patients need clear instructions on using the device, interpreting data, and understanding its limitations. This can empower them to engage actively with their treatment.

Could wearing an IoMT device create anxiety for patients worried about constant monitoring? The potential psychological impact of IoMT devices needs to be considered. Some patients might find constant monitoring stressful. Open communication and patient education are key to address potential anxieties.

9. Practice Questions

1. A 23-year-old with no prior psychiatric history starts experiencing auditory hallucinations, agitation, and paranoia after being prescribed XXXXXX for osteoarthritis-knee. The hallucinations are distressing and involve hearing threatening voices. The agitation is severe, leading to physical restlessness and difficulty sitting still. The paranoia causes the patient to suspect that others are plotting against them, leading to social withdrawal and isolation. The psychiatrist suspects that the medication may be responsible for inducing psychotic symptoms, necessitating further evaluation and a potential change in treatment. What could be the drug XXXXXX?
2. A 29-year-old experiences confusion, memory impairment, and hallucinations after taking an overdose of XXXXXX, an antihistamine. The patient presents to the emergency room with altered mental status, exhibiting disorientation to time and place. They have difficulty recalling recent events and exhibit impaired attention and concentration. Additionally, they report visual hallucinations, seeing things that are not present. The psychiatrist recognizes the potential for anticholinergic toxicity, which can lead to central nervous system disturbances, and recommends appropriate management and monitoring. What could be the drug XXXXXX?
3. A 48-year-old with no history of mental illness develops symptoms of anxiety, restlessness, and insomnia after being prescribed XXXXXX for a chronic pain condition. The patient reports feeling on edge and unable to relax, with excessive worrying about upcoming events. The restlessness leads them to pace and fidget. The insomnia causes difficulty falling asleep and maintaining sleep throughout the night. The psychiatrist suspects that the medication may be causing these anxiety-like symptoms and considers alternative pain management strategies. What could be the drug XXXXXX?
4. A 27-year-old with no psychiatric history starts experiencing depression, social withdrawal, and suicidal thoughts after being prescribed XXXXXX for a skin condition. The patient feels persistently sad, with a loss of interest in previously enjoyable activities. They isolate themselves from friends and family, preferring to be alone. The suicidal thoughts are intrusive and distressing. The psychiatrist identifies the potential for medication-induced depressive symptoms and recommends a thorough assessment and possible discontinuation of the drug. What could be the drug XXXXXX?
5. A 50-year-old with a history of anxiety experiences worsening symptoms, including panic attacks and agitation, after taking high doses of XXXXXX for chronic pain management. The patient experiences sudden-onset panic attacks, characterized by intense fear and physical symptoms, such as palpitations and shortness of breath. The agitation is severe, leading to restlessness and irritability. The psychiatrist recognizes the potential for medication-induced panic attacks and agitation, and advises a dosage adjustment or change in pain management strategy. What could be the drug XXXXXX?
6. A 32-year-old with no prior mental health issues develops symptoms of psychosis, including delusions and disorganized thinking, after using XXXXXX recreationally. The patient exhibits fixed false beliefs, such as believing they are being followed or targeted. Their thoughts are disorganized, making it difficult to maintain coherent conversations. The psychiatrist suspects that the recreational drug use may have triggered a drug-induced psychosis and recommends substance use evaluation and appropriate interventions. What could be the drug XXXXXX?
7. A 42-year-old experiences memory problems, confusion, and cognitive impairment after starting a new medication, XXXXXX, for hypertension. The patient struggles with forgetfulness and has difficulty learning

and retaining new information. The cognitive impairment affects their daily functioning, leading to difficulties in work and social activities. The psychiatrist suspects that the medication may be causing cognitive side effects, necessitating a review of the treatment plan and consideration of alternative antihypertensive medications. What could be the drug XXXXXX?

8. A 36-year-old, with BMI of 31, experiences exacerbation of mood swings, irritability, and impulsivity after being prescribed XXXXXX for obesity. The patient's mood fluctuates rapidly, showing manic states. The irritability leads to conflicts with others, and the impulsivity results in risky behaviours. The psychiatrist recognizes the potential for medication-induced mood disturbance and advises a careful re-evaluation of the treatment plan. What could be the drug XXXXXX?

9. A 31-year-old with a history of depression develops symptoms of agitation and low mood after starting treatment with XXXXXX, an anti-smoking medication. The anxiety causes difficulty relaxing and concentrating. The psychiatrist recognizes the potential for medication-induced depression-like symptoms and considers adjusting the treatment plan. What could be the drug XXXXXX?

10. A 46-year-old with no history of mental illness develops symptoms of depression, loss of interest, and social withdrawal after being prescribed XXXXXX for a cardiovascular condition. The patient feels persistently sad, with a lack of motivation and interest in activities they once enjoyed. The social withdrawal leads to isolation and avoidance of social interactions. The psychiatrist suspects that the medication may be contributing to the depressive symptoms and recommends a thorough assessment and possible discontinuation of the drug. What could be the drug XXXXXX?

11. A 51-year-old with no psychiatric history starts experiencing symptoms of depression and lethargy after being prescribed XXXXXX for a neurological condition. The patient feels persistently down, with a notable lack of energy and motivation. The psychiatrist recognizes the potential for medication-induced depressive symptoms and recommends a thorough assessment and possible discontinuation of the drug. What could be the drug XXXXXX?

12. A 29-year-old with no history of mental illness develops symptoms of anxiety, panic attacks, and restlessness after taking XXXXXX, a decongestant, for a cold. The patient experiences sudden-onset panic attacks, characterized by intense fear and physical symptoms, such as palpitations and shortness of breath. The restlessness leads them to pace and fidget. The psychiatrist suspects that the decongestant may be causing these anxiety-like symptoms and recommends alternative treatments for cold relief. What could be the drug XXXXXX?

13. A 26-year-old with no psychiatric history starts experiencing mood swings, impulsivity, and suicidal thoughts after using XXXXXX recreationally. The patient's mood fluctuates rapidly, alternating between depressive and manic states. The impulsivity leads to risky behaviours, including suicidal ideation. The psychiatrist suspects that the recreational drug use may have triggered a mood disorder and recommends substance use evaluation and appropriate interventions. What could be the drug XXXXXX?

14. A 45-year-old with no prior mental health issues develops symptoms of psychosis, including delusions and hallucinations, after taking XXXXXX for a gastrointestinal condition. The patient exhibits fixed false beliefs, such as believing they are being followed or targeted. Their thoughts are disorganized, making it difficult to maintain coherent conversations. The psychiatrist suspects that the medication may be inducing psychotic symptoms and advises a careful review of the treatment plan. What could be the drug XXXXXX?

ANSWERS

1. The drug XXXXXX prescribed for the chronic medical condition could be a corticosteroid. Corticosteroids can rarely induce psychiatric symptoms, such as auditory hallucinations, agitation, and paranoia.
2. The drug XXXXXX (antihistamine) overdose could be Promethazine. Antihistamines in high doses can cause confusion, memory impairment, and hallucinations. An alternate drug that could cause similar symptoms is cyproheptadine.
3. The drug XXXXXX prescribed for chronic pain could be gabapentin. Gabapentin can induce symptoms of anxiety, restlessness, and insomnia.
4. The drug XXXXXX prescribed for the skin condition could be isotretinoin. Isotretinoin has been associated with symptoms of depression, social withdrawal, and suicidal thoughts.
5. The drug XXXXXX prescribed for chronic pain could be tramadol. Tramadol can worsen symptoms of anxiety, panic attacks, and agitation in susceptible individuals. An alternative drug that could cause similar symptoms is tapentadol.
6. The recreational drug XXXXXX causing psychosis could be methamphetamine. Methamphetamine use can induce delusions and disorganized thinking. An alternative drug that could cause similar symptoms is phencyclidine (PCP).
7. The drug XXXXXX prescribed for hypertension could be atenolol. Beta-blockers like atenolol may lead to memory problems, confusion, and cognitive impairment. Beta-blockers is a reversible cause of memory impairment
8. The drug XXXXXX prescribed for the obesity could be Sibutramine.
9. The drug XXXXXX prescribed for smoking cessation could be varenicline. Varenicline has been associated with symptoms of anxiety, restlessness, and irritability.
10. The drug XXXXXX prescribed for the cardiovascular condition- Hypertension could be beta-blockers (e.g., propranolol). Beta-blockers can lead to symptoms of depression, loss of interest, and social withdrawal. An alternative drug that could cause similar symptoms is clonidine.
11. The drug XXXXXX prescribed for the neurological condition could be Levetiracetum.
12. The drug XXXXXX (decongestant) could be pseudoephedrine. Pseudoephedrine can cause symptoms of anxiety, panic attacks, and restlessness. An alternative drug that could cause similar symptoms is phenylephrine.
13. The recreational drug XXXXXX causing mood swings and impulsivity could be MDMA (ecstasy). MDMA use can trigger mood swings and impulsive behaviour. An alternative drug that could cause similar symptoms is LSD.
14. The drug XXXXXX prescribed for gastrointestinal issues could be metoclopramide. Metoclopramide can induce symptoms of psychosis, including delusions and hallucinations. This drug can cause supersensitivity psychosis.

****

1. A 28-year-old presents with depressed mood, loss of interest in activities, and feelings of hopelessness. A thorough evaluation and tests, reveals decreased levels of a neurotransmitter associated with mood regulation. The patient exhibits symptoms consistent with a major depressive disorder. Identify the neurotransmitter involved.

2. A 35-year-old experiences sudden episodes of intense fear and panic attacks. Extensive tests reveal elevated levels of a neurotransmitter related to the fight-or-flight response. The patient's symptoms are consistent with a diagnosis of panic disorder. Identify the neurotransmitter involved.

3. A 22-year-old presents with memory and language problems. Extensive tests show decreased levels of a neurotransmitter essential for memory and cognition. The patient's symptoms are consistent with cognitive impairments seen in Alzheimer's disease. Identify the neurotransmitter involved.

4. A 45-year-old exhibits symptoms align with schizophrenia, including hallucinations and disorganized thinking. Tests reveal elevated levels of a neurotransmitter associated with psychosis. Identify the neurotransmitter involved.

5. A 31-year-old experiences persistent feelings of worry and apprehension. Tests show decreased levels of a neurotransmitter that regulates anxiety. The patient's symptoms are consistent with generalized anxiety disorder (GAD). Identify the neurotransmitter involved.

6. A 50-year-old presents with motor symptoms such as tremors, rigidity, and bradykinesia. Tests reveal decreased levels of a neurotransmitter involved in movement control. The patient's symptoms are consistent with Parkinson's disease. Identify the neurotransmitter involved.

7. A 33-year-old presents with inability to remember and recall. Academic pressure leads to excessive worry about memory lapses. The patient's symptoms are consistent with generalized anxiety disorder (GAD). Identify the neurotransmitter involved.

8. A 36-year-old presents with mood swings, impulsivity, and self-harming behaviours. Tests show abnormal levels of a neurotransmitter associated with emotional regulation. The patient's symptoms are consistent with borderline personality disorder. Identify the neurotransmitter involved.

9. A 42-year-old experiences a persistent and exaggerated negative belief about oneself, others, and the world, ideas of reference. Tests reveal decreased levels of a neurotransmitter that regulates mood and cognition. The patient's symptoms are consistent with a depressive disorder with paranoid features. Identify the neurotransmitter involved.

10. A 31-year-old presents with an intense and irrational fear of social situations. Tests show abnormal levels of a neurotransmitter involved in anxiety regulation. The patient's symptoms are consistent with social anxiety disorder. Identify the neurotransmitter involved.

11. A 36-year-old experiences episodes of elevated mood, increased energy, and impulsive behaviour. Tests reveal abnormal levels of a neurotransmitter involved in mood regulation. The patient's symptoms are consistent with bipolar disorder. Identify the neurotransmitter involved.

12. A 26-year-old experiences recurrent and distressing memories, nightmares, and hypervigilance. Tests show abnormal levels of a neurotransmitter involved in the stress response. The patient's symptoms are consistent with post-traumatic stress disorder (PTSD). Identify the neurotransmitter involved.

13. A 34-year-old presents with decreased motivation, low energy, and loss of interest in activities. Tests show decreased levels of a neurotransmitter associated with mood regulation. The patient's symptoms are consistent with a major depressive disorder. Identify the neurotransmitter involved.

14. A 32-year-old presents with recurrent and intrusive thoughts, as well as repetitive behaviours. Tests show abnormal levels of a neurotransmitter involved in anxiety regulation. The patient's symptoms are consistent with obsessive-compulsive disorder (OCD). Identify the neurotransmitter involved.

ANSWERS

1. The neurotransmitter involved is serotonin. Decreased levels of serotonin are associated with mood disorders such as major depressive disorder. Serotonin is a neurotransmitter that plays a crucial role in regulating mood and emotional stability. Low levels of serotonin are often linked to symptoms of depression, including persistent sadness, loss of interest in previously enjoyable activities, and feelings of hopelessness. Serotonin reuptake inhibitors (SSRIs) are commonly prescribed to treat depression by increasing serotonin levels in the brain.

2. The neurotransmitter involved is noradrenalin. Elevated levels of norepinephrine are associated with panic disorder. Noradrenalin is a neurotransmitter and hormone that plays a central role in the body's stress response. Excess noradrenalin can lead to heightened anxiety, panic attacks, and an overactive fight-or-flight response. Medications that block the effects of noradrenalin, such as beta-blockers, are sometimes used to manage symptoms of panic disorder.

3. The neurotransmitter involved is acetylcholine. Decreased levels of acetylcholine are associated with cognitive impairments and may be seen in conditions such as Alzheimer's disease. Acetylcholine is a neurotransmitter that plays a critical role in memory and cognitive function. In conditions like Alzheimer's disease, there is a progressive decline in acetylcholine-producing neurons, leading to memory problems, language problems, and difficulty in decision-making. Cholinesterase inhibitors are a class of drugs used to slow down the breakdown of acetylcholine and are prescribed to manage cognitive symptoms in Alzheimer's disease.

4. The neurotransmitter involved is dopamine. Elevated levels of dopamine are associated with psychotic disorders such as schizophrenia. Dopamine is a neurotransmitter that plays a crucial role in reward, motivation, and cognition. An imbalance in dopamine levels, specifically increased dopamine activity in certain brain regions – mesolimbic pathway, has been linked to the development of psychotic symptoms such as hallucinations and delusions. Antipsychotic medications, which block dopamine receptors, are used to manage symptoms of schizophrenia.

5. The neurotransmitter involved is gamma-aminobutyric acid (GABA). Decreased levels of GABA are associated with anxiety disorders. GABA is an inhibitory neurotransmitter that helps regulate anxiety and stress responses in the brain. Reduced GABA activity can lead to an imbalance in neural excitability, contributing to the persistent feelings of worry and apprehension seen in GAD. Medications that enhance GABAergic transmission, such as benzodiazepines, are sometimes prescribed to alleviate anxiety symptoms.

6. The neurotransmitter involved is dopamine. Decreased levels of dopamine are associated with movement disorders such as Parkinson's disease. Dopamine is critical for smooth motor function, and its deficiency can lead to the characteristic motor symptoms seen in Parkinson's disease. Parkinson's is a neurodegenerative disorder characterized by the loss of dopamine-producing neurons in the brain's substantia nigra (Niagro-Striatal pathway). Treatment for Parkinson's disease often includes medications that increase dopamine levels

or mimic its effects to improve motor symptoms. In psychiatry, drug induced Parkinson is due to Dopamine receptor antagonism by anti-psychotics.

7. The neurotransmitter involved is glutamate. Abnormal levels of glutamate are associated with anxiety disorders. Glutamate is the brain's primary excitatory neurotransmitter, responsible for enhancing neuronal activity. In anxiety disorders, there may be dysregulation in glutamate levels, contributing to excessive worrying and difficulty in memory consolidation. Medications that modulate glutamate receptors, such as NMDA receptor antagonists, are being explored as potential treatments for anxiety disorders.

8. The neurotransmitter involved is serotonin. Serotonergic dysfunction is associated with affective lability and borderline personality disorder. Serotonin is a neurotransmitter involved in regulating mood and emotions. In individuals with borderline personality disorder, there may be abnormalities in serotonin levels, leading to emotional instability, impulsivity, and self-destructive behaviours. Treatment for borderline personality disorder often includes psychotherapy, and in some cases, medications that modulate serotonin levels may be used to manage specific symptoms.

9. The neurotransmitter involved is serotonin. Decreased levels of serotonin are associated with depressive disorders with paranoid features. Serotonin is a neurotransmitter that plays a crucial role in regulating mood and emotional stability. In depressive disorders with paranoid features, there may be abnormalities in serotonin levels, contributing to the development of negative beliefs about oneself, others, and the world, sensitive ideas of reference. Treatment for this condition often involves a combination of psychotherapy and antidepressant medications that increase serotonin levels.

10. The neurotransmitter involved is serotonin. Abnormal levels of serotonin are associated with social anxiety disorder. Serotonin plays a role in anxiety regulation, and an imbalance in serotonin levels can lead to increased anxiety, particularly in social situations. Selective serotonin reuptake inhibitors (SSRIs), which increase serotonin availability in the brain, are commonly prescribed to manage symptoms of social anxiety disorder.

11. The neurotransmitter involved is dopamine. Abnormal levels of dopamine are associated with bipolar disorder. Dopamine plays a role in regulating mood, and its dysregulation is implicated in bipolar disorder. In the manic phase of bipolar disorder, there is an excess of dopamine activity, leading to elevated mood, increased energy, and impulsivity. In the depressive phase, dopamine activity is reduced.

12. The neurotransmitter involved is norepinephrine. Abnormal levels of norepinephrine are associated with post-traumatic stress disorder (PTSD). Norepinephrine is a neurotransmitter and stress hormone that plays a key role in the body's fight-or-flight response. In individuals with PTSD, there may be dysregulation of norepinephrine, leading to hyperarousal, recurrent distressing memories, and nightmares related to the traumatic event. Medications that target norepinephrine activity may be used to manage symptoms of PTSD.

13. The neurotransmitter involved is dopamine. Decreased levels of dopamine are associated with mood disorders such as major depressive disorder. Dopamine is a neurotransmitter that plays a crucial role in motivation, reward, and pleasure. In major depressive disorder, there may be abnormalities in dopamine levels, contributing to the characteristic symptoms of decreased motivation, low energy, and loss of interest in activities. Treatment for major depressive disorder often includes medications that increase dopamine levels or enhance dopamine receptor sensitivity.

14. The neurotransmitter involved is serotonin. Abnormal levels of serotonin are associated with obsessive-compulsive disorder (OCD). Serotonin is a neurotransmitter that plays a role in anxiety regulation. Abnormal

serotonin levels have been implicated in the development of OCD symptoms, which include recurrent and intrusive thoughts (obsessions) and repetitive behaviours (compulsions). Selective serotonin reuptake inhibitors (SSRIs) are commonly used to manage symptoms of OCD by increasing serotonin availability in the brain.

****

1 A 60-year-old presents with slurred speech, and weakness on one side of the body. Imaging reveals a localized hypodense brain lesion. In the following days, the patient is also experiencing emotional lability and depressive symptoms. Identify the neuro-psychiatric abnormality involved.

2 A 45-year-old presents with recurrent seizures, and personality changes. MRI reveals hippocampal sclerosis in the brain. EEG reveals temporal lobe discharges. The patient is also exhibiting excess speech, stickiness and hyper-religious. Identify the neuro-psychiatric abnormality involved.

3 A 35-year-old presents with involuntary movements of the limbs, facial grimacing, and difficulty walking. Imaging reveals atrophy in the caudate nucleus and putamen of the brain. The patient is also exhibiting behavioural changes, including aggression and irritability. Identify the neuro-psychiatric abnormality involved.

4 A 50-year-old presents with brief periods of sudden loss of consciousness, urinary incontinence and involuntary movements of limbs. Imaging shows a scar in the brain tissue. The patient also reports experiencing memory gaps and feelings of confusion after the episodes. Identify the neuro-psychiatric abnormality involved.

5 A 60-year-old presents with progressive muscle weakness, difficulty swallowing, and slurred speech. Imaging shows degeneration of the motor neurons in the brain and spinal cord. The patient is also experiencing emotional lability and episodes of uncontrollable laughter. Identify the neuro-psychiatric abnormality involved.

6 A 28-year-old presents with fever, severe headache, neck stiffness, and sensitivity to light. Lumbar puncture reveals elevated white blood cells (neutrophils) in the cerebrospinal fluid. The patient is also experiencing confusion and altered mental status. Identify the neuro-psychiatric abnormality involved.

7 A 55-year-old presents with a history of recurrent headaches, along with episodes of visual disturbances such as flashes of light and blind spots. MRI shows a circular area of signal change in the occipital lobe with peri-ventricular white matter hyper intensities in T2 weighted images. The patient is also experiencing mood swings and irritability. Identify the neuro-psychiatric abnormality involved.

8 A 32-year-old presents with tremors, muscle rigidity, and bradykinesia. Imaging shows a decrease in dopamine-producing neurons in the substantia nigra of the brain. The patient is also experiencing depression and anxiety. Identify the neuro-psychiatric abnormality involved.

9 A 38-year-old presents with brief episodes of lip smacking with impairment of consciousness lasting for few seconds to minutes. EEG recordings show abnormal electrical discharges in the brain. The patient is also experiencing memory lapses and feelings of confusion after the episodes. Identify the neuro-psychiatric abnormality involved.

10 A 60-year-old presents with a gradual decline in cognitive function, including forgetfulness and difficulty with problem-solving. Imaging shows widespread brain atrophy, particularly in the temporal lobes. The

patient is also experiencing changes in personality and social withdrawal. Identify the neuro-psychiatric abnormality involved.

11 A 25-year-old presents with sudden-onset severe headache (thunderclaps), nausea, vomiting, and confusion. CSF reveals xanthochromia. The patient is also experiencing sensitivity to light and neck stiffness. Identify the neuro-psychiatric abnormality involved.

12 A 30-year-old presents with progressive visual loss in one eye, along with episodes of double vision and lack of coordination and resolves after few days. Imaging shows multiple white matter lesions in the brain and spinal cord. The patient is also experiencing feelings of anxiety and panic attacks. Identify the neuro-psychiatric abnormality involved.

13 A 70-year-old presents with a gradual decline in cognitive function, including memory loss and difficulty with problem-solving, incontinence and gait disturbance. Imaging shows an enlarged ventricles and reduced brain volume. The patient is also experiencing feelings of depression and worthlessness. Identify the neuro-psychiatric abnormality involved.

14 A 30-year-old presents with progressive visual and hearing loss, along with difficulty with balance and coordination. Imaging shows bilateral acoustic neuromas. The patient is also experiencing symptoms of depression and social withdrawal. Identify the neuro-psychiatric abnormality involved.

15 A 65-year-old presents with a gradual decline in cognitive function, including memory loss and difficulty with language. Imaging shows atrophy in the frontal and temporal lobes of the brain. The patient is also experiencing changes in behaviour, including aggression and agitation. Identify the neuro-psychiatric abnormality involved.

16 A 45-year-old presents with sudden-onset weakness and numbness in one side of the body, along with difficulty speaking and understanding speech. Imaging shows a hypodense area in the right middle cerebral artery territory. The patient is also experiencing symptoms of depression and social withdrawal. Identify the neuro-psychiatric abnormality involved.

17 A 50-year-old presents with progressive weakness and spasticity in the legs, along with loss of proprioception and vibration sensation. Imaging shows degeneration of the dorsal columns in the spinal cord. The patient is also experiencing symptoms of depression and apathy. Identify the neuro-psychiatric abnormality involved.

ANSWERS

1 The neuro-psychiatric abnormality involved is a cerebrovascular accident - stroke, specifically a cerebral infarction in the brain. The slurred speech, and weakness on one side of the body are classic signs of a stroke, indicating the disruption of blood flow to a specific area of the brain. The emotional lability and depressive symptoms are common psychological manifestations after a stroke due to the brain damage and disruption of neural connections or it could be an involuntary emotional expression disorder – IEED, pathological laughing and crying (PLC)

2 The neuro-psychiatric abnormality involved is a Geschwind Personality. The presence of recurrent, seizures, personality changes, and EEG showing temporal lobe discharges pointing to temporal lobe epilepsy (TLE). Stickiness circumstantiality are part of personality.

3 The neuro-psychiatric abnormality involved is Huntington's disease. The involuntary movements of the limbs, facial grimacing, and difficulty walking, along with imaging findings of atrophy in the caudate nucleus and putamen, are classic features of Huntington's disease. The behavioural changes, including aggression and irritability, are common psychiatric manifestations of the disease and can occur at any stage.

4 The neuro-psychiatric abnormality involved is a history of seizures. The episodes of sudden loss of consciousness and convulsions, along with imaging findings of a scar in the brain tissue suggest a history of seizures. The memory gaps and feelings of confusion after the episodes are common postictal symptoms that may occur following a seizure.

5 The neuro-psychiatric abnormality involved is amyotrophic lateral sclerosis (ALS), also known as Lou Gehrig's disease. The progressive muscle weakness, difficulty swallowing, slurred speech, and imaging findings of motor neuron degeneration in the brain and spinal cord are characteristic of ALS. The emotional lability and episodes of uncontrollable laughter are features of pseudobulbar affect (PBA), a condition that can occur in individuals with ALS.

6 The neuro-psychiatric abnormality involved is meningitis, specifically bacterial meningitis. The sudden-onset severe headache, neck stiffness, sensitivity to light, elevated white blood cells in the cerebrospinal fluid (indicating inflammation), and altered mental status are consistent with bacterial meningitis. This condition is a medical emergency requiring prompt treatment with antibiotics.

7 The neuro-psychiatric abnormality involved is a migraine with aura. The recurrent headaches, episodes of visual disturbances, and imaging findings of a circular area of signal change in the occipital lobe are suggestive of a migraine with aura. The mood swings and irritability may be associated with the neuro-psychiatric changes that occur during migraine episodes.

8 The neuro-psychiatric abnormality involved is Parkinson's disease. The tremors, muscle rigidity, and bradykinesia, along with imaging findings of a decrease in dopamine-producing neurons in the substantia nigra, are characteristic features of Parkinson's disease. The depression and anxiety may be associated with the emotional impact of the disease or a non-motor manifestation of Parkinson’s disease.

9 The neuro-psychiatric abnormality involved is seizure, specifically complex partial seizures. The recurrent episodes of impairmenet of consciousness, lip smacking, and EEG findings of abnormal electrical discharges in the brain are indicative of epilepsy. The memory lapses and feelings of confusion after the episodes are common postictal symptoms that may occur following a seizure.

10 The neuro-psychiatric abnormality involved is Alzheimer's disease. The gradual decline in cognitive function, memory loss, difficulty with problem-solving, and imaging findings of widespread brain atrophy predominantly in the temporal lobes are characteristic features of Alzheimer's disease. The changes in personality and social withdrawal are common psychiatric manifestations of the disease as it progresses, called as BPSD- Behavioural and psychological symptoms of dementia.

11 The neuro-psychiatric abnormality involved is a subarachnoid hemorrhage. The sudden-onset severe headache, nausea, vomiting, confusion, imaging findings of blood in the cerebrospinal fluid, and sensitivity to light and neck stiffness are indicative of a subarachnoid haemorrhage. This condition is a medical emergency requiring immediate attention and intervention.

12 The neuro-psychiatric abnormality involved is multiple sclerosis (MS). The progressive visual loss in one eye, episodes of double vision, lack of coordination, imaging findings of multiple white matter lesions in the brain and spinal cord, feelings of anxiety, and panic attacks are characteristic features of MS. MS is an autoimmune

demyelinating disease that affects the central nervous system, leading to a wide range of neuro-psychiatric and psychological symptoms, which can mimick conversion disorder.

13 The neuro-psychiatric abnormality involved is normal pressure hydrocephalus. The gradual decline in cognitive function, memory loss, difficulty with problem-solving, imaging findings of enlarged ventricles and reduced brain volume, and feelings of depression and worthlessness are suggestive of normal pressure hydrocephalus. Normal pressure hydrocephalus is a condition characterized by an increase in cerebrospinal fluid in the brain's ventricles, leading to cognitive and neuro-psychiatric symptoms characterized by a traid of dementia, urinary incontinence and gait disturbances.

14 The neuro-psychiatric abnormality involved is neurofibromatosis type II (NF2). The progressive visual and hearing loss, difficulty with balance and coordination, imaging findings of bilateral acoustic neuromas, and symptoms of depression and social withdrawal are characteristic features of NF2. NF2 is a genetic disorder that causes the growth of noncancerous tumors on the nerves, including the auditory nerves (acoustic neuromas).

15 The neuro-psychiatric abnormality involved is frontotemporal dementia. The gradual decline in cognitive function, memory loss, difficulty with language, imaging findings of atrophy in the frontal and temporal lobes of the brain, and changes in behaviour, including aggression and agitation, are characteristic features of frontotemporal dementia. Frontotemporal dementia is a group of disorders that primarily affect the frontal and temporal lobes of the brain, leading to cognitive and behavioural changes.

16 The neuro-psychiatric abnormality involved is an acute ischemic stroke in the right middle cerebral artery territory. The sudden-onset weakness and numbness in one side of the body, difficulty speaking, imaging findings of a hypodense area in the right middle cerebral artery territory, and symptoms of depression and social withdrawal are indicative of an acute ischemic stroke. The hypodense area on imaging may represent an area of decreased blood flow or infarction.

17 The neuro-psychiatric abnormality involved is subacute combined degeneration of the spinal cord. The progressive weakness and spasticity in the legs, loss of proprioception and vibration sensation, imaging findings of degeneration of the dorsal columns in the spinal cord, and symptoms of depression and apathy are characteristic features of subacute combined degeneration of the spinal cord. This condition is often caused by vitamin B12 deficiency and affects the sensory and motor pathways in the spinal cord.

10. Inspired From….

To read more on the subject, consider reading the books/manuscripts

- Babu, A. (2024). Family Acceptance and Mental Health in LGBTQIA+ Individuals: An Urgent Call for Culturally Sensitive Research in the Indian Context. *Indian Journal of Psychological Medicine*, *46*(2), 182–183. https://doi.org/10.1177/02537176231207983
- Benbassat, J. (2024). Teaching Professional Attitudes and Basic Clinical Skills to Medical Students: A practical guide. Springer International PU.
- Brown, T., & Eagles, J. (2011). Teaching psychiatry to undergraduates. Royal College of Psychiatrists.
- Chatterjee, S., & Kar, S. K. (2023). Undergraduate Research Elective under Competency- Based Medical Education (CBME) in India: Challenges and Directions. *Indian Journal of Psychological Medicine*, *45*(5), 548–551. https://doi.org/10.1177/02537176231165219
- Coll, X. (Ed.). (2012). Communication skills in mental health care: An introduction. Radcliffe Pub.
- Duong, T., Tamas, R. L., & Ureste, P. (2021). Psychiatry morning report: Beyond the Pearls. Elsevier.
- Fadem, B. (2013). High-yield behavioral science (4th ed). Wolters Kluwer/Lippincott Williams & Wilkins Health.
- Gomez, J. (2019). Liaison psychiatry: Mental health problems in the general hospital. Routledge.
- Green, B. (2009). Problem based psychiatry (2nd ed). Radcliffe.
- Guerrero, A., & Piasecki, M. (Eds.). (2008). Problem-based behavioral science and psychiatry. Springer.
- Heldt, J. P. (2017). Memorable psychopharmacology (First edition). CreateSpace Independent Publishing Platform.
- Heldt, J. P. (2018). Memorable psychiatry: An evidence-based approach to psychiatric diagnosis.
- Hughes, P. E., & Martin, J. L. (Eds.). (2023). Teaching psychiatry to undergraduates (Second edition). Cambridge University Press.
- Huline-Dickens, S., & Casey, P. (Eds.). (2022). Clinical Topics in Teaching Psychiatry: A Guide for Clinicians (1st ed.). Cambridge University Press. https://doi.org/10.1017/9781009053938
- Kadiyala, P. K. (2020). Mnemonics for diagnostic criteria of DSM V mental disorders: A scoping review. General Psychiatry, 33(3), e100109. https://doi.org/10.1136/gpsych-2019-100109
- Kishor M. (2024). Psychiatry Training in Competency-Based Medical Education: What to Teach? How to Teach? *Indian Journal of Psychological Medicine*, *46*(2), 101–102. https://doi.org/10.1177/02537176241237962
- Klamen, D. L., & Pan, P. (2009). PreTest psychiatry: PreTest self-assessment and review (12th ed.). McGraw-Hill Medical.
- O'Dwyer, A.-M., & Campion, M. (2022). Practical psychiatry for students and trainees (1st ed.). Oxford University Press.
- Parija, S. C., & Adkoli, B. V. (Eds.). (2020). Effective Medical Communication: The A, B,C, D, E of it. Springer Singapore. https://doi.org/10.1007/978-981-15-3409-6
- Patra, S. (2023). Is There a Need for an Entrustable Professional Activity-Based Psychiatry Curriculum for Medical Interns? *Indian Journal of Psychological Medicine*, *45*(5), 547–548. https://doi.org/10.1177/02537176231166783
- Privitera, M. R., Lyness, J. M., & Lyness, J. M. (2009). Psychiatry mentor: Your clerkship & shelf exam companion (2nd ed). F.A. Davis.

- Salazar, L. J., Chari, U., Sharma, P., & Sreedaran, P. (2022). Facilitators and Barriers to Student Learning and Impact of an Undergraduate Clinical Posting in Psychiatry: A Thematic Analysis. *Indian Journal of Psychological Medicine*, *44*(4), 392–398. https://doi.org/10.1177/02537176211056366
- Stern, T. A. (2008). Mnemonics in a mnutshell: 32 aids to psychiatric diagnosis. Current psychiatry, 7(10), 27-33.
- Thomasson, R., Guthrie, E., & House, A. (Eds.). (2023). Seminars in Consultation-Liaison Psychiatry (3rd ed.). Cambridge University Press. https://doi.org/10.1017/9781911623533
- Woods, D. (2004). Communication for doctors: How to improve patient care and minimize legal risks. Radcliffe Pub.
- Wright, B., Dave, S., & Dogra, N. (2017). 100 cases in psychiatry (2nd edition). CRC Press/Taylor & Francis Group.

www.ingramcontent.com/pod-product-compliance
Lightning Source LLC
LaVergne TN
LVHW070422170826
845679LV00035BA/1865
9798893631722